A THOUSAND PLACES LEFT BEHIND

A THOUSAND PLACES LEFT BEHIND

One Soldier's Account of Jungle Warfare in WWII Burma

Peter K. Lutken, Jr.   Edited by E. R. Lutken

University Press of Mississippi / Jackson

The University Press of Mississippi is the scholarly publishing agency of
the Mississippi Institutions of Higher Learning: Alcorn State University,
Delta State University, Jackson State University, Mississippi State University,
Mississippi University for Women, Mississippi Valley State University,
University of Mississippi, and University of Southern Mississippi.

www.upress.state.ms.us

The University Press of Mississippi is a member
of the Association of University Presses.

Maps by Mapping Specialists, Ltd, Fitchburg, Wisconsin

Unless otherwise stated in the text, photos come from
the personal scrapbook of P. K. Lutken, Jr.
Many were taken by him, others given to him by wartime friends.
Names and dates are those found in the scrapbook, recorded by P. K. Lutken, Jr.

First printing 2023

∞

Library of Congress Cataloging-in-Publication Data

Names: Lutken, Peter K. (Peter Koch), author. | Lutken, E. R., editor.
Title: A thousand places left behind : one soldier's account of jungle
warfare in WWII Burma / Peter K. Lutken, Jr. ; edited by E. R. Lutken.
Description: Jackson : University Press of Mississippi, [2023]
Identifiers: LCCN 2022058172 (print) | LCCN 2022058173 (ebook) | ISBN
9781496845146 (hardback) | ISBN 9781496845153 (epub) | ISBN
9781496845160 (epub) | ISBN 9781496845177 (pdf) | ISBN 9781496845184 (pdf)
Subjects: LCSH: Lutken, Peter K. (Peter Koch) | United States.
Army—Biography. | World War, 1939–1945—Campaigns—Burma. | World War,
1939–1945—Personal narratives, American. | Kachin (Asian
people)—Social life and customs. | Naga (South Asian people)—Social life and customs.
Classification: LCC D767.6 .L87 2023 (print) | LCC D767.6 (ebook) | DDC
940.54/4209591—dc23/eng/20230113
LC record available at https://lccn.loc.gov/2022058172
LC ebook record available at https://lccn.loc.gov/2022058173

British Library Cataloging-in-Publication Data available

dedicated to the Kachins

The day's lay-out—the mornin' sun
Beneath your 'at-brim as you sight;
The dinner-'ush from noon till one,
An' the full roar that lasts till night;
An' the pore dead that look so old
An' was so young an hour ago,
An' legs tied down before they're cold—
These are the things which make you know.

Also Time runnin' into years—
A thousand Places left be'ind—
An' Men from both two 'emispheres
Discussin' things of every kind;
So much more near than I 'ad known,
So much more great than I 'ad guessed—

—from the poem "The Return" by Rudyard Kipling

CONTENTS

INTRODUCTION

On the second anniversary of Pete Lutken's death, a woman traveled from what is now called Myanmar to visit his grave, bringing flowers and the DVD of a ceremony that had been held there in his honor. She was the manager of Project Old Soldier, a crop exchange program that Pete and other veterans of OSS Detachment 101 had organized to help the Kachins, an ethnic group, many of whom were their comrades-in-arms during World War II. Pete and his friends from halfway across the world never forgot each other.

Often folks don't like to talk about their wartime experiences, but Pete did, and not because he wanted to brag. Many of his stories were of his own mistakes and misjudgments. But the war, in spite of its horrors, was a defining part of his life, where he made many of his closest friends, and he wanted to remember. Our family assumed that, after his retirement, he would write a book. Instead, he put his efforts into Project Old Soldier, working from home and taking trips to Myanmar from the 1990s through the mid-2000s. My brother David bought a tape recorder in 2007, got out some maps, and cornered Pete for a few weeks, just for us to have a record of his experiences, so my father traced his journey and recalled adventures. He frequently digressed when one thing reminded him of another, but eventually got around to most of the stories that my brothers and I remembered and some we had never heard. For several years after the tapes had been transcribed, Pete worked sporadically with a typist, changing the form into an unbroken narrative and fine tuning the chronology, but still spent most of his time with his beloved project for his Kachin friends.

By the time I retired, Pete was slowing down, so he and I were able to do some serious work on the book. We eliminated repetitions, removed all but a couple of secondhand stories, and rephrased confusing sections. We also reviewed the text for accuracy as best we could. If he was not sure of particular names or dates, he stated so in the text or didn't use them. Of course, remembrance of war is the subject of many a serious and ponderous text and is bound to be

imperfect when separated from the occurrence by almost seventy years. But
having told the stories over and over, even at age ninety-three, it was as if he
played a recording in his mind as he spoke. The stories seemed to evolve into
a series of well-contained vignettes, like pearls covered by the nacre of repeti-
tion, but with rough authenticity still within.

Surprisingly, however, the written version seemed somewhat different from
my brothers' and my memories. We were small when we first heard Pete's "Burma
stories" around the fire on campouts or listening in the dark from our bunk
beds at home, a crack in the door providing the only light. My father would
squat flat-footed and rock slightly, like a Kachin *myrhtoi*, as he spoke. Those
stories had a fairy tale quality, the jungle a character in itself that swallowed
lost airmen and hid huge battalions of the enemy. There were tales where silver
rupees showered down from air drops, where the full moon shone on terrified
rafters who slipped downriver past the enemy at night, where little boys led
troops of big men through the trackless jungle to battle. The events recounted
in the book are unquestioningly the same, but the tone a bit different.

Several factors may have contributed to this aside from the magic that
childhood lends to memory. First was my father's desire for accuracy. Since the
book was to bear scrutiny, he refrained from exaggerations he might have used
when weaving a tale for us, no "eyes as big as saucers" in this text. Second, oral
histories are inherently unique, received by different senses, just as songs are
not simply lyrics, or plays manuscripts. I remember Pete's voice varying from a
whisper when describing the stillness before an ambush to the sharp rendition
of staccato machine gun fire in the thick of it. He would sometimes burst into
laughter when relating an embarrassing mishap, spread his arms wide to show
the size of a huge tree trunk, bow his head when describing those who passed
on. So, when reading this account of a man's wartime adventures, I hope you
will picture a tall, lanky fellow with a deep rolling voice, squatting by a fire,
surrounded by listeners rapt in attention, as he brings those memories to life.

For a history of World War II in Burma, there are other narratives that list
with great precision the movements of troops and statistics of battles gleaned
from various reports and records. But for an individual account of a young
soldier wandering the jungle half a world away from home, forgetting his socks
on a long march, battling daily with leeches and mosquitos, rafting along raging rivers, a young man learning a foreign language and a different way of life,
amazed at the friendship and violence, the beauty and terror confronting him
at every turn, this is the book.

—E. R. Lutken, September 2020

A THOUSAND PLACES LEFT BEHIND

PART I

JOURNEY TO WAR

May 1941–September 1942

In the Army Now

In the spring of 1941, I graduated from Mississippi State College and was anxious to join the army. My classmates in ROTC all received commissions as second lieutenants right away, but I was younger and had to wait until I turned twenty-one. So I took a job on a survey crew with the Union Producing Company up in Yazoo County, where they had just discovered a big oil field. On my birthday, September 5, 1941, I went straight for my army physical. At the time, I'd been scrambling around the woods in the Delta and had a bad case of eczema, or maybe poison ivy, and the doctor said he couldn't pass me. He must have noticed my disappointment because he said he'd just tear up the record, and I could try again later. I did, and by November the 20th, I was commissioned as a second lieutenant in the Coast Artillery. Then of course, after December the 7th, everything speeded up.

I left home in Jackson, Mississippi, the day after Christmas to report for duty at Fort Monroe in Virginia, an old stone fort at a place called Hampton Roads. I stayed there about two months. It was a stark introduction to war. The Germans had really good hunting right outside of that fort. U-boats blew up ships within sound and sight of us. One time a huge column of smoke filled the sky, and pretty soon we saw them towing in the back part of a ship that had been blown in half.

From Fort Monroe, two of us were assigned to Fort Sheridan north of Chicago. I don't think I'd ever been that far north before. The other fellow had a car, so he and I drove through snow to Illinois. I was only there about two weeks, but I remember antiaircraft machine gun practice on a bluff overlooking Lake Michigan. That was the coldest place I'd ever been in my whole life. The wind blew off of the lake, and it cut you to the bone. We'd be out there all day long shooting those dang machine guns. And we didn't use any ear protectors. Nobody ever even thought about it. I'm sure that's where my hearing began to decline. Some of the bravest pilots I ever saw were there, flying light planes, towing the banner targets that we shot at. The ropes were not very long, and we were not very good marksmen. The airfield would telephone in complaints, "You got two bullet holes in the tail of the plane. You guys have got to do better than that."

From there, I was shipped to Fort Bliss in Texas, where I became a platoon leader. It was a heck of a lot warmer there, and we had a grand time in the short while we spent in El Paso. I've got a bunch of pictures of some of the gatherings we had. I was in the 703rd Automatic Weapons Antiaircraft Battery, I think they called it. There were about two hundred in our outfit, four platoons, and all the bits and pieces. A platoon didn't consist of but twenty-one men, so the outfit was mostly tail instead of dog, lots of supply folks and clerks. We were only there for a few weeks when we were ordered to go overseas. It was supposed to be a secret move. We all had to take out insurance right quick and sign mimeographed wills. The 702nd, the 703rd, 704th, 705th, and 706th all boarded the train right there in Fort Bliss that night. In spite of the fact that it was "secret" and at 2:00 a.m., half the town of El Paso was there to see us off. Of course, we had no idea where we were going; not even Captain Pidgeon, our commanding officer, knew. All we knew was that we were headed east, and we were going to war.

Just outside of Longview, Texas, I was sleeping in an upper bunk, when all of a sudden, my head jammed into the partition between bunks, as the train came grinding to a stop. In spite of my throbbing head, I piled out along with everyone else, all still in our pajamas. Our train had run into a truck loaded with telegraph poles. The locomotive hit it dead center, and the truck crumpled up like a tin can around the front end of that solid-iron steam engine. There were telegraph poles scattered all over, like matchsticks.

We were not far from Longview, so pretty quick, here came another locomotive with a cable and chains. They put the engines nose to nose, and the one from Longview commenced backing up, pulling the truck off the front of our locomotive. In the process, it began to tear the truck driver's body to pieces. He was hung up in there, dead. A medical major who was on our train jumped up and said, "Hold up, hold up just a minute." He climbed up on the locomotive, took out his pocketknife and cut the dead fellow's arm off. Then they got a whole bunch of us who were all standing around to push the truck, and between the engine pulling and us pushing, we rolled the truck down into the ditch, driver and all. That cleared the track. Then the locomotive from Longview backed away, we all got on our train, and off we went.

We passed through Jackson, Mississippi, later that same day. I leaned out the window and saluted my hometown as we went by. My family, friends, and all my old haunts jumped fresh into my mind. I didn't have any idea when or even if I'd ever see them again. The train kept on, and a day later, we arrived at Sullivan's Island, Charleston, South Carolina. We got physical examinations there and waited for a ship to take us to parts unknown. The day we were to depart, we boarded a bus at about 6:00 a.m. On the drive, we passed a freighter that had been hit by a torpedo, with a hole in the hull as big as a two-story house. I thought about what I'd seen at Fort Monroe. We all knew we were going out where boats got holes punched in them.

Finally, we got to the ship. Ours was the SS *Santa Paula*, and there was another, the *Mariposa*. The *Santa Paula* was a British liner that used to work between North and South America. The *Mariposa* had been in the Hawaiian trade. Both of them were painted gray and rigged up as troop ships. The ship we were to board carried about three thousand men. The *Mariposa* was much bigger. It must have carried eight or ten thousand.

All day long, while other troops were boarding, we just sat on the dock. There were some air corps replacements, some Black troops who were engineers (the army was pretty much segregated at the time), some other artillery outfits boarding, and some RAF maintenance men already on board. We waited all day for somebody to tell us where to go. We just sat there, no food, no instructions. Captain Pidgeon finally got so mad that he said, "We're going on board the ship," and he sent some scouts to find a place for us to stay. They came back and said, "Captain, we found a place, looks like it's a dining room. There are temporary tables in it, but we can get them out of there. We found a whole bunch of extra bunks, unassembled, down in the hold of the ship." So we boarded without anyone's say so and went straight up to the dining room, got some tools from somewhere, and set to work. We took the tables out and threw them on the deck. Then we brought in the bunks and screwed them to the ceiling and the floor. We had enough room in there for the whole outfit. Furthermore, we were right next to what turned out to be the PX, where they'd sell you a candy bar if you had any money. But nobody had any money. They had given everybody five dollars advance pay when we got on the ship. And that's all I had was the five dollars, and a twenty-dollar gold piece that had been given to me by a friend of my father, but that was not for spending.

The Brig

During all the ruckus, Captain Pidgeon sent me to find the purser. He said, "The purser is supposed to be in room number 9 on such-and-such a deck. Go down there and tell him that we need some more tools." I was mad, just like he was, that this was all such a scramble. I was convinced we were going to lose the war, as screwed up as everything was. Nobody knew what they were doing; nobody knew where to go. And here we were taking over a part of the ship without permission from anybody.

When I found room number 9, it was probably around 2:00 a.m. I was in a bad mood, so I pounded on the door. At first there was no answer. Finally, I could see the knob turn, and the door open just a crack. This woman, with her hair all in curlers, stuck her head out the door timidly. She said, "Yes?" And I said, "Lady, I beg your pardon. I was informed that this was the purser's state room." About that time, a voice behind me screamed, "What the hell are you doing here?" I turned around and found myself face to face with a colonel and two burly MPs. It was obvious that the colonel had been drinking heavily. I could smell the alcohol from six feet away. The lady hastily shut the door. That was the last I saw of her.

There I was face to face with this man. He cussed me up and down, saying he was going to court martial me and then commanded the MPs to take me to his office. They grabbed me by the arms and marched me down the hall. My feet were hardly hitting the floor. When they let me loose, the colonel gave me a vicious shove. I turned around. I don't know whether I doubled up my fist or not, but I pushed him, and he fell flat on his back. He got up and glared. From then on, I was in the real doghouse. I had assaulted an officer, a colonel, no less. He had wings on! The MPs took me into the office, where the colonel railed at me some more. I asked several times to be allowed to contact my commanding officer, but he didn't listen. Then the MPs took me down into the bilges of the ship. That's where the pokey was, with bars on it. There were two soldiers already in there, and it was a small area, hardly room enough for three. I don't remember why they were there, but we commiserated. There were no lights, no nothing, down in the bottom of the ship. We could hear the engine start up. The ship was finally going out to sea, and there we were, locked up. We sat for several hours. I don't know exactly how long. There was no way to tell whether it was daylight or dark. Finally, two MPs came down, unlocked the pokey, and took me out. They didn't grab a hold of me or anything. They just said, "Come with us."

I followed them back to the colonel's office. Captain Pidgeon was there. It was obvious that Pidgeon had figured out the colonel had been drunk, and at a very crucial time in his command. I reckon Pidgeon threatened him with court martial for dereliction of duty or whatever because the colonel was very subdued. In fact, he apologized to me, kind of mumbling, but he did apologize. Then Pidgeon said, "Come with me," and we went back to our dining-room quarters. I don't remember exactly what happened to the two other fellows in the brig, but I know they got out alright.

Sailing into the Unknown

The battleship *Texas* and two British corvettes were our escorts, and a Dutch freighter was along for the ride. Our outfit was assigned the duty of manning some of the guns on the ship since we were familiar with large firearms. There was a five-inch gun on the back of the ship, two three-inch guns on the bow, and about ten or twelve Lewis guns for antiaircraft protection, thirty-caliber machine guns, air cooled. Navy men with earphones took orders from the bridge on the big guns. We were on the machine guns, and we had to stand watch all the way across, just like the sailors. Actually, it was good for us to have something to do because we were on that ship for fifty-eight days.

Early on about the second or third morning of the voyage, an alarm sounded, and everybody was ordered on deck. The corvettes and the *Texas* were dropping depth charges. In the cold, gray light, we could see several lifeboats, a life raft or two, and debris and oil all over the water. We got word that a German submarine had sunk a freighter right near us. The battleship shot an airplane from a catapult, and the plane circled all around, trying to find any signs of the submarine. While all this was going on, our ships circled and zigzagged. After a while, they decided that there were no submarines still in the vicinity. The plane landed in the ocean, taxied over near the battleship, and a big crane hooked it, picked it up, put it back on the catapult.

There were some survivors from the freighter. The corvettes got them and just left the lifeboats floating empty. We were not far from Bermuda, so we changed course and put the survivors ashore there. I was on duty as we anchored in the harbor at Hamilton. The water was deep, but you could look down the anchor chain and see all the way to the bottom. It was beautiful, and the beach was spectacular, but nobody went ashore except the survivors. If those folks got stuck in Bermuda for the rest of the war, they were lucky.

We cast off from Hamilton and headed roughly southeast for many days. One thing that saved us from extreme boredom during the voyage was that group of British RAF men on board. They had been on the ship since it came from Australia and were a great source of entertainment. They put on skits and sang songs all the time. My favorite was an adaption of the old tune "The Quartermaster Store." They concocted verses like "There was beer, beer, but none of it was here, in the store, in the store. There was beer, beer, but none of it was here, in the Santa Paula store . . ." Another verse I remember was "There were eggs, eggs, walking around on legs, in the store . . ." Without those fellows, we might have lost our minds.

As I mentioned earlier, everybody had gotten five dollars when we started out. Almost immediately, crap games and poker games broke out all over the ship. At first, everybody was in there playing. But the number of people diminished over time until finally there was only one big crap game and one big poker game on the back end of the ship with the white soldiers and one big crap game and poker game up on the front end with the Black soldiers. All the money in the whole damn ship was concentrated in those games. You've never seen such piles of money, worn, crumpled bills constantly changing hands. One man from our outfit, a sergeant by the name of Rosenberg, I think, was a winner. He really cleaned up. He was also a medic. While on the voyage, Captain Pidgeon would try to keep everybody busy, so he organized first aid courses. Rosenberg lectured several times, and every lecture he delivered began with, "The main thing is not to get excited. If you see somebody with a leg gone or whatever, you're no help if you're in a panic." That goes for poker as well, I guess.

We finally put in at Freetown, Sierra Leone. There was a beautiful harbor there, too, but the water was not so clear. We stayed for about a week, just sitting in the harbor. While there, a bunch of soldiers were smitten with ptomaine or something. Out of three thousand men on the ship, about eight hundred got so sick that some of them lost consciousness. And it happened all at once. Those of us who didn't get sick had to go up and down the decks, checking people. That harbor is on the equator and hot as the hinges of hell, and this was late May or June. Most slept on deck that night, and our orders were to check them all. If they looked bad, we were to bring them down to the infirmary. Well, I'm telling you, that was the biggest mess you ever saw. There was a swimming pool on the back of the ship which they had converted into a latrine, with a whole row of seats over it. And that thing was full. I don't want to be too gruesome, but everybody was going from both ends. There was vomit and excrement all over the deck. Anybody who could get there would try to drop it over the rail, but a lot of people couldn't make it. The crew had to get fire hoses out to wash the deck off.

Mostly, everything we ate was boiled because they had plenty of steam. We ate lots of ham, hard boiled eggs, and parsnips, I think they were Australian parsnips, great big things, looked like carrots, but white and tasted kind of like a radish. And we usually ate two meals a day, but on that day, after everyone got sick, no one ate anything else. So Captain Pidgeon sent a crowd out foraging for food. They broke into the stores down in the bottom of the ship and came up with these extra fancy Danish hams and other canned stuff. We just stole it. When I think back, I cannot believe how chaotic it was.

The navy fellows and the Merchant Marines on board the ship had a big coffee urn going all the time. They considered us part of the crew, since we had to stand watch, so we got in on the coffee. But we didn't get the same food they got. They ate pretty well, in a separate place. Our grub was awful. And some of it had gone bad, obviously. Or maybe that particular episode happened because the ships discarded their waste right into the water. As long as we were out at sea, it didn't make any difference. But sitting in one place for a week, it was terrible. I think they washed all the dishes in saltwater, so it just came back and messed everything up.

Ships kept pouring into Freetown while we were there. They assembled a convoy. There were forty-one ships when we left, most of them British, and one battleship, the *Rodney*, whose claim to fame was that it had participated in the battle during which the *Bismarck* was sunk in 1941. The *Rodney* was a huge, ungainly looking thing, more than seven hundred feet long. We also had two destroyers with us and what they called an armed merchantman, a merchant ship which they had fitted with guns.

Our convoy left Freetown and sailed towards the Cape of Good Hope. We got into a violent storm off of the Cape, and lots of folks got seasick. The men on the *Mariposa* laughed at us. We were a small ship, maybe ten thousand tons. The *Mariposa* was about twenty thousand tons. When we were rolling from side to side, one fellow from the *Mariposa* told us later, "You were rolling so far over, we could look down your funnels." Their ship didn't have near that much trouble.

Stopover at Durban

When we put into the harbor at Durban, the convoy broke up. A bunch of the ships kept on going, I'm not sure where. We stayed a couple of days, and Captain Pidgeon decided to take us ashore. He found out about a place called Marine Parade up on the beach, so he marched us out there, and we carried our guns. I don't think we were supposed to have them, but by this time Pidgeon was going to do what he damn well pleased. Somehow, he also got us a little extra cash to spend, five more dollars. Pidgeon was a West Point man, a good man, and a good commanding officer.

We knew fancy drills, so when we got to the spot, Pidgeon found a policeman and said, "We'd like to put on a little show for the people here." It was a big square, and there were a lot of folks. At this particular moment, June of 1942, the South African Army was bottled up at Tobruk in North Africa, and Rommel was pounding them to pieces. I think that's part of the reason we received such a great welcome in Durban. Maybe they thought we were going on to rescue their sons and husbands and fathers. Everybody in South Africa was feeling pretty grim about the war and needed some cheering up. The policeman said, "I'll clear folks out, and you can do whatever you want." So we did our little doozie, marching up and down.

When we got through with our show, the crowd cheered and hollered. A man named Mr. Ross came out and said, "I want to feed all you men. We'll clear this restaurant out, and you can order anything you want. It's on me." And we were almost two hundred people! So everybody moved out. People were leaving with their plates in their hands. They came out on the sidewalk and sat down on the curb to finish their meals. And I'll tell you, I remember steak and fresh eggs. That seemed to be the thing that everybody wanted, so I had a steak with a big fried egg on top of it right along with the rest of them. Then Pidgeon turned us loose and said, "You've got to be back on the ship by such-and-such a time, and don't you forget it. Otherwise, we're going to leave you."

I had imagined Africa as a country of villages with thatched roofs, but Durban was sophisticated, with big buildings and traffic. Oley Olson, whose real name was Creighton B. Olson, was another platoon leader, a first lieutenant. He and I found our way to a nice beach and ran across two good-looking girls in the company of some Polish officers. The officers didn't speak any English, so we were able to walk off with the girls. They invited us to dinner at their home. We all went there on the streetcar. I think the district was called Greenway Park.

I remember the houses had red tile roofs, and there wasn't a chimney on any of them. Of course, the climate there is mild. It was June, winter for them, and still very pleasant. We got to the end of the streetcar line and walked to Betty Bashforth's house. Beryl Easton was the other girl's name; she was Betty's cousin. When Mr. Bashforth saw us, he let out, "A couple of bloody Yanks!" But all were very hospitable. They served a big rare roast beef. After the main course, Mrs. Bashforth says to me, "Sweets, Peter?" I didn't know what she was talking about. I said, "I beg your pardon?" She repeated herself, and I finally figured out she meant dessert. We had trifle, which was delicious, and stayed around to visit a while; then we had to get back to the ship.

There was a blackout because the Japanese had control of the Indian Ocean. They were bombing Ceylon, so everyone was pretty skittish. There was not a light anywhere, it was a challenge just to find our way back. The streetcars were running, everything was running, just without lights. When we did get near the ship, a big crowd was all gathered around some soldier, drunk as a hoot owl, lying on the ground. A group of mostly British sailors was trying to help him out. He was cussing them all, but they finally got him on his feet.

The next day, we went to a picture show with the girls. We gave them our parents' addresses. Since we couldn't say anything to relatives about where we were, I asked Betty, "Please, write a letter to my mother and tell her I've been here, and that I'm okay." That started a correspondence between Betty and my mother and later myself, that has lasted to this good day. My wife and I still get letters from Betty and her husband, Colin.

We left Durban that night and set sail out into the Indian Ocean, this time only the *Santa Paula*, the *Mariposa*, and the armed merchant vessel. Two or three days out of Durban, an emergency call sounded, and we all ran up on deck with our life preservers on. In the distance was a warship. The merchantman was madly laying down a smoke screen with some device in the boilers that puts out tons of smoke. It was going at top speed, trying to get between us and the warship with that screen. The merchantman would get ahead for a little while, and then here again the warship would come past the screen. Finally, the other ship began to signal with a light. Turns out it was a British ship, so the merchantman quit putting out the smoke, and we turned back around and went where we were supposed to go. But there was a scramble for a while trying to get away from the supposed enemy.

India

We finally put into the harbor in Karachi on July 20, 1942. When we first got there, I was asked to go into town to send Sergeant Rosenberg's money home to his mother, also to draw some money from the consul so Captain Pidgeon could pay the purser back for the extra money he had borrowed for us to spend at Durban. A principal means of transportation in Karachi was by carriage, "gary" they called it, a regular carriage with doors, drawn by one horse, like you see in the cowboy movies except a little clumsier looking. I caught a gary to the Imperial Bank.

I had read a whole lot of Kipling, so I figured I knew a little bit about India, but I was unprepared. On the way, clipclop, clipclop in the horse-drawn gary, we passed a street corner. Standing on that corner were a man and a woman with wild hair standing out in all directions. They were completely covered with white ashes and were both buckbald naked, didn't have a stitch on, just standing, waiting to cross the street. They were what the Indians called fakir, holy people, who do nothing but contemplate. I thought to myself, well, I'm in the real India now. And the streets were crowded with folks; people pulling carts you'd think would be hard for a team of oxen to pull, people calmly walking with huge loads balanced on their heads. There were snake charmers tweedling on pipes with cobras waving their caped heads around. It was amazing.

I finally got to the Imperial Bank, a building with columns so big, it would take about three or four people to reach around them. I understand that bank is still there, and I wouldn't be surprised if it were there a thousand years from now. The ceiling was about fifty feet high with fans hanging down. And all the bank business was done by hand with these accountants all over the bank floor with green eyeshades, doing their figuring.

When I made my way back to the ship, right next to where we were docked, some workers were unloading a coal barge. A series of very narrow planks led from down in the barge up and over the bank to railroad cars where they dumped the coal. The men down in the bottom of the barge shoveled the coal into the baskets, which were so heavy, they had to pick them up and put them on the women's heads. Then the women bounced along on the planks, without touching the baskets, on up to the railroad. From our deck, it looked just like a conveyor belt. All the workers were covered in coal dust, jet black, clothes and all. A huge crowd of soldiers gathered at the rail of the ship to watch. The Americans had never seen people being worked like that. There in the hot sun in Karachi, in July, the soldiers began to get mad and started heckling the boss. Some officers had to clear the rail.

After a couple of days, they finally let us off the ship and took us out to North Malir cantonment, an army base. It was a dreary-looking place, no trees, just barracks and desert. We stayed there until late September. I was lucky enough to be sent to town every now and then. Once, Captain Pidgeon sent me to see if I could find some music. I found a hand-cranked Victrola. They didn't have but one record of American origin; on one side was "St. Louis Blues," and the other side was "L'Amour, Toujours L'Amour." I took that thing back to camp, and folks played that record constantly every day, every night. I knew "St. Louis Blues," of course, and it stood up to being played over and over, but the other was awful.

We had some free time while we were at North Malir, and I noticed a lot of doves around. They looked a lot like the doves back home. Oley had never been hunting but was interested. On a trip to town, I found a gun store, and got the proprietor to explain the rules. If you wanted to hunt with a muzzleloader, you could get a license for about 10 rupees, the equivalent of maybe 3 dollars. But if you wanted to hunt with a breach loader, you had to pay 150 rupees, more like 50 dollars. So I said, "What kind of muzzleloaders have you got?" He showed me a double 12 gauge. By this time, I'd earned some money, so I bought it and a supply of shot, powder, and caps for 20 rupees. It was a pretty good gun. The barrel was imitation Damascus. Oley got a single barrel, which didn't cost him but 12 rupees. We also managed to buy licenses from the office of a local magistrate. I've still got mine somewhere. It's a book with a ribbon hanging out of it with a big royal seal in wax.

When we took the guns to Malir, some of the enlisted men began joshing us. They especially kept egging Oley, "That gun won't even go off. It looks fake." Oley got irritated. The latrine was right out in the middle of everything with a ring of barracks all around it. It had screened windows to keep the flies out, the only place in the whole barracks with screens. It just so happened at that point it was fully occupied. So, when the men kept joshing Oley about his gun, he loaded it up, and before I could stop him, he pointed it right at the latrine. And all these men were sitting there looking out, facing him. They realized what was going to happen, so they all ducked down below the boards. He hauled off and, "blam," he blasted the latrine. Everybody came running out of there with their pants half hanging down, afraid he was going to shoot again. But he didn't have but one shot. That night, I'm telling you, he got the worst chewing out I ever heard Captain Pidgeon give anybody. "It shows a complete lack of judgment. You're an officer. You've got to learn to behave yourself!"

Crocodile Hunt

Not far from camp, we found a man-made pond, what they'd call a tank in Texas. When we got through with our day's activities, we would hike out into the desert and sit around that pond in the late afternoon. Oley, it turned out, was a pretty good shot, and we got lots of doves. We got the cook to fix them for us and fed everybody in the outfit that wanted one. Most of the men had never eaten a dove before. I found out then, and I guess it's still the case, that they don't hunt doves up north in the US.

Late one afternoon, we decided to sneak up over the tank dam to surprise the doves. As we walked toward the dam, right in front of us, this crocodile jumped up. Until then, we had no idea that there were any crocodiles out there. I figured they were in India, but I didn't expect to find one out in the middle of the desert. But here was this crocodile; he was big, and he ran just like a lizard, I mean quick, up the backside of the dam, over and into the water.

On our hunting trips, we had become acquainted with an Indian goat herder who watered his goats at that pond. We didn't know the language worth a hoot but managed to ask the goat herder about the crocodile. He said to the effect, "He's a big problem. He eats my goats. Can you kill this crocodile?" The crocodile would get one of his goats fairly often, so he was anxious for us to dispatch it. We talked about it, and finally decided, yeah, why don't we see if we can't help this fellow out. The pond was not all that big. I would guess it was about fifty yards long and maybe thirty-five yards wide, and by the height of the dam, it didn't seem all that deep. When I told the herdsman we'd try, he was pretty happy.

Next visit to town, I got some heavy buckshot and some single balls as big as jawbreakers for my shotgun. One afternoon I managed to get time off, so I asked the men in my platoon if they would help. At least a dozen fellows agreed. I brought the shotgun and a Thompson submachine gun in case things got out of control. It had a drum about as big around as a hubcap with what must've been a hundred rounds in it, the same kind of gun Al Capone's crowd carried. Me and my platoon marched out there. Oley didn't go for some reason, in retrospect, a wise decision.

When we got there, I instructed everyone to find sticks and line up on the dam. My idea was for them to wade from the deep end toward the shallow end, hitting the surface and splashing as they went. Hopefully, the crocodile would swim away from the big ruckus, and when he came up, I would shoot him. So I got in place and got my double-barrel loaded. The men took their positions and started into the water. It was deeper than I thought. They got down off the dam, and right away found themselves up to their necks. They were obviously frightened. But I urged them on, "Come on, fellas. Come on. It's going to get shallower. It can't help but get shallower." So, standing as tall as they could, they began violently beating the water. They didn't know what was out there. They'd read stories about crocodiles, but none of them had ever even seen one.

When they got about a quarter of the way along, the water dropped to about waist high, and they regained a little courage. While they were thrashing away, this crocodile's head silently came out of the water in front of them. He was big, with two big eyes—they stick up, you know—and all these teeth. I tried to draw a bead on him, but before I could get a shot off, he went back underwater. The men saw him and hesitated. I hollered at them, "Come on, fellas. You've got him going now. Keep hitting the water. Get him to come up again and keep him up there."

So they kept going. The water got shallower, about hip deep, when this dadgum thing came up again, but he went back down even quicker. I still prodded them on. When they were a little more than knee deep, all of a sudden, two heads came up out of the water. There were at least two crocodiles in that pond. This really shook my crowd, and they began to falter. I called to them to keep going, and they did, but they were losing heart. Then the final insult. Somebody turned his head around and screamed, "My God, they're behind us!" The water was so muddy, they just couldn't see, and the crocodiles had gone underwater, in between the men, and come up behind them. At that point, the whole crowd broke and ran for their lives. None of my urging was going to get them to do anything. Those crocodiles had gone between their legs! I never got off a shot, and suddenly realized I had put my men in danger of being eaten alive.

Our goat herder, who had been standing by while all this was going on, was one disappointed man. The whole thing was a colossal failure. Although no one was hurt, I'd been outwitted by two crocodiles and was the laughingstock of the whole outfit. "The Great Crocodile Hunt" taught me my first lesson east of the Suez—foolish mistakes thereabouts could lead to unexpected and dangerous consequences.

Keeping Busy

While we were out messing around, the Japanese were taking Burma and bombing Assam on the other side of India. That fact galled us. Of course, our main task at the time was not to chase crocodiles, but to dig gun pits around the Karachi airport. Each platoon had four guns, .50 caliber air-cooled machine guns with extra exchangeable barrels. They were designed to defend against low-flying, strafing planes. We spent the days trying to dig those gun pits in solid rock. Since we were unable to make much progress, we went to town, got some dynamite, and finally managed to get below the surface of the ground by blowing holes out and digging around them. At least we got some experience with explosives that way. While trying to dig one hole, we encountered a huge boulder. We couldn't move it, couldn't break it, couldn't even get a hole in it to blast it. As we struggled, this wizened Indian man watched us.

Indians were hanging around watching us all the time. We must have been amusing to them. This man reminded me of a picture of Mahatma Gandhi. He was just a bundle of sticks, probably didn't weigh much over a hundred pounds, a little rag tied around his waist. He stood there and watched us struggle with the rock. We had a bunch of big, burly farmers from Nebraska down in there, sweating and swinging picks. The Indian came up to me and indicated he'd like a try. I said, "Go ahead; have at it." So this small fellow climbed down in there with the pick. He scratched around and brushed the top off of the rock with some straw, found a spot he liked, then backed off, and, man, he came down on that rock and busted into it with one lick. Now, it didn't fall apart immediately, because it was big, but he got a crack in it. Then he worked on that crack and got that dang thing into two pieces. While we were standing there watching him, why, he did the same thing several times, broke pieces into smaller ones with powerful blows. He finally beckoned to us to come down there and help him. By then the pieces were small enough that with some pry poles, we got them. I had learned a valuable word in Urdu, *shabash*, which means "well done." I told him "*Shabash!*" and he broke into a big grin. We got along all right with the Indians. But we felt like we were spinning our wheels waiting to go to war.

Captain Pidgeon decided to stage a maneuver to keep us active, a mock attack on a hill we could see from our camp. My platoon was on the left flank and Stanley Smith, we called him "Smitty," and his platoon were on the right. Fulford and his platoon were to hold the hill. The hill stuck up like a cone and looked to be several hundred feet high, but we didn't have any map to tell how far away it was. So I took my platoon, and we walked and walked and walked. That day I had done something I'd never done before. I didn't have any clean socks, so I went with just my shoes on.

We started out early in the morning and marched as hard as we could go. And it was hot as blazes. The temperature at times got to 120 out there on that desert. We finally got to the hill about 2:00 or 3:00 in the afternoon. We spread out, sent scouts ahead, and marched up the hill. The scouts came back and said, "Lieutenant, there's nobody up there." The whole rest of the 703rd had more sense than I did. When they found out it was so far away, they had gotten ahold of Captain Pidgeon and said, "We've been marching all morning, and we're not even close, maybe we'd just better try this another time." But the word didn't get to me. I think they sent somebody out, but he couldn't catch up. So we went the whole round trip of twenty or twenty-five miles that day for nothing.

Coming back, we ran out of water, and we didn't have any food since we didn't figure it was going to take that long. When I got back to camp, my feet were all blistered to heck and back. And my men's feet were blistered, too, whether they had socks on or not. I got a chewing out by Captain Pidgeon. I had obeyed orders, but he said, "You've got to use a little judgment." He admitted he had made a mistake, too. He said, "I had no idea that hill was so far away. I could see it like it was right there. Marching in that kind of sun, it's a wonder you didn't have somebody drop dead from heat stroke." Another episode in my education east of Suez.

Geography and War

Seemed like all the news of the war was bad. Even in India, Gandhi was stirring up trouble. They had put him under house arrest because he was speaking against India's support of Britain, trying to prevent the British from recruiting Indians. Fortunately for us, many volunteered anyway. In fact, the

British Indian Army was the biggest volunteer army the world has ever seen. And they fought all the way through the war and did a great job. But Gandhi was trying hard to prevent their involvement, so I didn't think very much of him at the time. His group would sometimes lie down on railroad tracks to interfere. They weren't shooting at anybody, but they would occasionally blow things up. Once we passed a train that had been derailed. We went very slowly over the track, which was in the process of being repaired. We just crept along at about five miles an hour. They told us Gandhi's group had done that, not the Japanese.

In the meantime, the Japanese were beating up on the British and Commonwealth forces in Burma. In December of 1941 and early January 1942, the Japanese had come up the Malaysian Peninsula into Thailand and straight across into Burma. The Chinese went in to try to help the allies, but they were too late to do any good, and they were ill-equipped, so the Japanese mopped up on them. In the latter part of the summer of '42, the first Burma Campaign had resulted in the disastrous defeat of the Allied Forces.

What followed was a giant tragedy; people, both civilian and military, fled from the Japanese, and many died in the attempt to escape, mainly because of formidable geographic barriers. There are huge mountains on three sides of Burma, and the ocean on the fourth. The highest mountains are in the north, Hkakabo Razi is almost twenty thousand feet, but there are also significant mountain ranges to the east and the west that come down to the sea. From those mountain ranges flow many large rivers, with the Irrawaddy running right down the middle. In the rainy season, those rivers became deathtraps. Civilians died in countless numbers, trapped by mountains and by swollen, impassable rivers. I saw the aftermath of those losses, but not until much later.

The Japanese aim in taking Burma was mainly to cut China off from the outside world. They already held the whole coast of China, so access to and from the sea was out of the question. There was a railroad running from Rangoon to Lashio, and at the beginning of 1937, the British, with the help of coolies, had managed to hack out a road from there up into China, the "Burma Road." That was the last land route for China to get supplies from the allies. After the Japanese came in, the only way left was by air; the Hump Route. From airfields in Assam in northeastern India, the allies were madly flying supplies over the Himalayas into China. There were more than a million Japanese tied down in China. If the Chinese dropped out of the war, that would have meant another million Japanese we'd have had to contend with. So, in September of '42, the British and Americans were working hard to build up airfields in Assam. While we were stationed in Karachi, they began moving artillery batteries to protect those airfields from Japanese attacks.

On P. K. Lutken's way from Ft. Sheridan to Ft. Bliss. (left to right) Brothers Wesley, Donald, Peter, and their mother in Jackson, Mississippi. Spring 1942.

(left to right) Captain DeCoursey, Captain John J. Pidgeon, Lieutenant Stanley Smith at practice firing session north of Malir near Karachi. August 1942.

House of a Naga *gampura* (headman) at a village in the Naga Hills. Spring 1943.

Chinese 112th Regiment moving out of Tagap Ga. October 1943.

Bill Cummings (left) and others at pistol practice in Assam. 1943.

C47 airdrop, Tagap Ga. Spring 1943.

Captain Hector Meston (left) and Captain J. R. Wilson at Hkalak Ga. Fall 1942. Wilson later became Lieutenant Colonel and V Force commanding officer at Tagap Ga. 1943–44.

Nagas at airdrop pickup, overseen by quartermaster soldier (second from right) at Tagap Ga. On the ground are rice hulls used in packing to break impact. Spring 1943.

Engineers logging to make way for the Ledo Road. Late 1943 or early 1944.

Young Nagas at construction site on Ledo Road. They are carrying knives and a crossbow. Late 1943 or early 1944.

Colonel Seagrave (far right) and
his hospital staff and nurses
around the table at Tagap Ga.
Spring 1943.

Hello 'Big foot
love
Little foot.

Than Shwe, nurse with Seagrave's
hospital, Ramgarh. 1942.

Lieutenant Johnny Colling (in foreground) leaving a Naga village. Several women porters and other villagers are in the background. Spring 1943.

Sergeant Martin C. Thrailkill, who served in KC8, V Force, and OSS Detachment 101, seen here (on right) with soldiers preparing to distribute opium to informants as payment. Spring 1943.

Quartermaster soldiers and a group of Nagas throwing dice. The women have beautiful cylinders of amber in their pierced earlobes. Tagap Ga. Spring 1943.

Lieutenant Pete Lutken cleaning carbine. Picture in Ledo, Assam prior to entering Burma. Early 1943.

Pete after several months in the Patkai Hills and Hukawng Valley. Tagap Ga. Summer 1943.

Mahka La joined Pete's group in the V Force at Hkatyaw in summer of 1943. He stayed with Pete in OSS Detachment 101 and became *subedar* major of the 7th Battalion, American Jinghpaw Rangers. Picture from Hungwe. January or February 1945.

Doctor Abdul Halim Banday from the Indian Army Medical Corps in the V Force with Pete in 1943. Picture taken summer 1944.

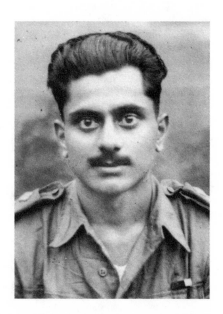

V force personnel crossing the Tabyi Hka, including Mihelich (2nd from right) and Pete (far right). February 1944.

Elephant train on the trail between Hwehka and Nadawng. Maung Tu lead driver. July 1944.

Ting Bawm (OSS alias Ring Ting) commander of I&R Platoon, served fourteen months with Pete in OSS Detachment 101. Picture taken at Longtawk. February 1945.

Pete (center) receiving Bronze Star. Medal presented in Nazira by Major Joseph Alderdice.
Bill Cummings second from right. September 1944.

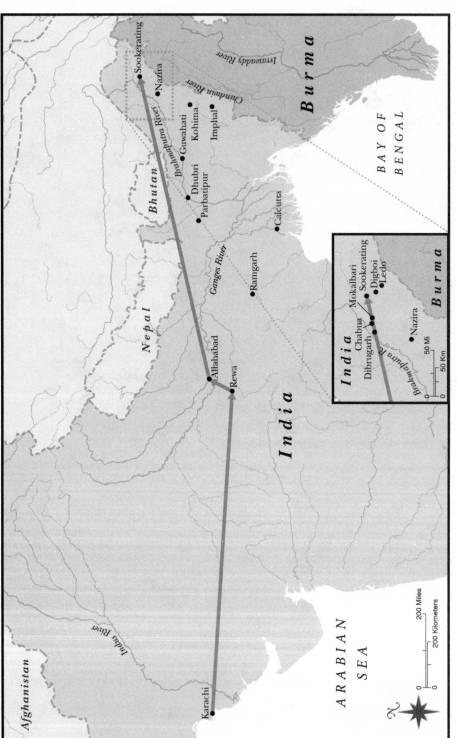

Map 1: India (with inset map of a portion of Assam) and Burma. Arrows show the path of the C-47 aircraft taking Pete Lutken's Coast Artillery platoon from Karachi to Assam. Also on this map, Ramgarh and the places along Pete's journey from Ramgarh to Ledo with the 112th Chinese Regiment.

PART II

INTO THE JUNGLE

September 1942–March 1943

Upper Assam by Air

We'd been hanging around the desert twiddling our thumbs since July. Our trip to Assam took place in late September of '42. There were initially five antiaircraft batteries at Karachi; the 702nd, 703rd, 704th, 705th, and 706th. They had already moved two before they got around to us. We received notice one afternoon that we were to board airplanes for Assam the next morning, without anything except guns and ammunition. There were twenty-one men in my group, barely enough to operate the guns that we had. We took off at 2:00 a.m., nine planes heading up to Assam to defend the airfields. It's almost two thousand miles from Karachi to Assam, and we were flying in the back of a C-47. Those planes were just bare bones on the inside. We sat on the floor and on metal bucket seats that flapped down from the sides. The air crew had parachutes, but not us. We flew in the dark over the heart of India and were droning along as the sun came up, when somehow our plane got separated from the rest. There was only one other plane in sight.

The door opened to the front of our plane. The engineer came out and said, "Lieutenant, the pilot would like to talk to you." When I got there, the pilot turned around and said, "We're lost. I've got no idea where we are. We were riding a radio beam, and all of a sudden, it just shut off." He admitted he hadn't been watching the ground or the map or anything else; he was just going along on the beam knowing that it would take us to Allahabad, where we were supposed to stop and refuel. The pilot said, "The only radio contact we've got is with that one airplane over there; nobody else." Below us there were trees and small patches of farmland as far as we could see.

I asked if he had a map. "I've got one of these silk maps, but it doesn't have much detail. All I know is that we're somewhere between Karachi and Alla-habad." I said, "When I got my pilot's license, the instructor always told me, 'If you get in trouble, look for a railroad.'" So we got to looking, and sure enough, we spotted a railroad track and then station. Our intent was to go down and see if we could read the sign from the air. The other plane waited upstairs, while we dropped down to treetop level. It turned out the sign was in Hindi. Of course, none of us could read that. Underneath, the name was in English, but in small print. We made two passes but couldn't get low enough to read it. The pilot piped up, "I spotted what looked like a pretty-good-sized field off to the left. Let's land and ask somebody where the hell we are." I went back and told my men, "Get your belt fastened if you have one, otherwise hold on because we're fixing to go down for a rough landing."

The spot he picked was a polo field with stands on either side. The British were great polo players—lucky for us. As we began to descend, the pilot gritted his teeth and said, "Lord, help us, this field is awful short." But he was a good pilot, and it was a grassy, smooth surface. He set that plane down, stood on the brakes, and managed to get it stopped before we hit the trees at the other end.

Buzzing the station had stirred up the whole town. When we landed, people swarmed out of the woods. I'm sure most had never seen an airplane close up before. A C-47 is pretty high above the ground, so we let out a ladder. A huge mob gathered around us as we climbed down. We had to post men around the plane to keep people from climbing up, while we searched for somebody who could speak English. This plane, by the way, had a door that you could close. Later on, they took the doors off the C-47s and just left them off since they were used mainly to drop supplies and didn't need the extra weight.

A policeman finally showed up who could speak a fair amount of English. He told us we were at Rewa, a town not too far from Allahabad. We were able to locate it on the old silk map. With that information, we got back on the plane. Two of us stayed on the ground to crank up the engines by hand. Each crank handle was about six or seven feet long and fit into a socket under the engine cell cover. It turned a big, heavy flywheel, which the pilot connected to the engine with a clutch. After several attempts, we got both engines started up with a big racket. We tried to get people to leave and asked the policeman to clear off the field. The pilot taxied as far as he could to the end of the field, turned us around, and faced against the wind. He set the brakes and revved up the engines. The field was still full of people, literally hundreds just milling around, when he suddenly released the brakes. The plane leapt forward, and we charged right toward them. They ran in every direction, but we just kept going. I don't think we hurt anybody; I hope we didn't. We bounced around for a short while, and then he hauled back on the wheel. We barely cleared the trees, circled to gain altitude, and then headed to Allahabad. It was only about eighty miles away, so we made it there in short order, and the other plane followed.

When we landed, folks there told us that a bombing raid was going on in Assam, right where we were headed, and the whole of India had been put on radio silence. We refueled and took off. It was around noon, and we still had seven or eight hundred miles to go. We had no knowledge of what happened to the other planes. Later, we learned all seven of them had made forced landings and were damaged. None had completely cracked up; they were just unable to fly.

We roared on for hours. As we approached the Brahmaputra River, we could see smoke and fire. I got up in the cockpit again and saw Japanese planes in the distance. They were unpainted aluminum and easily visible, flashing bright in the late afternoon sun. Since they were still buzzing around, the pilot decided to fly close to the ground. Our sister plane followed us. We cruised up the river at maybe a hundred feet and stayed low until it looked like the ruckus was over. The airfields being bombed were Chabua, Dum Duma, Tinsukia, and I forget the other names; they hit practically every airfield in that part of Assam. Fighter planes were supposed to protect the airfields, but apparently, they'd been completely surprised, practically none of them even got off the ground.

When the pilot felt it was safe, he climbed back up to a decent altitude. Just as the sun was going down, we passed over Chabua. We could see airplanes burning all over the field. Some of the large buildings, shops, and hangars located adjacent to the airfield were also on fire, and there was smoke everywhere, so the pilot elected not to land there. He headed northeast to another airfield. Most of the airfields were named for the tea gardens nearby, and the one that he finally chose was called Sookerating. Just at dark, we came in sight of it. There were two planes burning, both P40s, but neither one was blocking the runway. He circled one time and came in for a rough landing. We bounced along, but rolled to a stop, all in one piece.

The Tea Garden

We piled out of the plane, unloaded our gear, and decided to dig gun emplacements that very night. We managed to find a shop building close by that was guarded by Indian troops. They got us a whole gang of shovels and picks. By then it was dark, but we dug gun pits all night long. None of us slept; we just picked out placements and set to work. All the time, those two P40s kept burning. Nobody tried to put them out. An airplane burns for a long time; even the aluminum burns when it gets really hot, and those planes burned the whole night. They provided an eerie, flickering light for our labors. By dawn, we had guns in place, ammunition ready, and squads in position.

We had to beg some food from the Indian troops. They had a telephone, and we got in touch with the Air Corps headquarters at Chabua, who instructed us to hold on until they could get us transportation. In a couple of days, we were moved to another field called Mokalbari, which was also on a tea plantation. It was inhabited by a group of fighter planes. The airstrip was an old rice field where they had knocked down dikes that held the water between rice patches. We set up at Mokalbari and stayed there until almost Christmas time.

If there hadn't been a war, Mokalbari would have been a beautiful place to live. "Tea garden" was a very descriptive term; the tea grew in perfectly trimmed banks covering the valley. There were several high-level bombing raids in the vicinity during that time, but none of them hit Mokalbari. They came against Chabua and Jorhat and Tinsukia and Sookerating, all tea plantations as well. They hit Mohanbari, not very far from us, and really tore it up. In all those cases, the Air Corps was pretty much caught on the ground. That changed a short time later, after air warning stations were established out in the Naga Hills east of us in Burma. They set up nine stations, each up on top of a mountain, manned by soldiers who identified planes by sight and by sound in the dark. A twenty-four-hour watch was kept, and they were able to notify our fighters by radio in time to get planes in the air.

After we got established at Mokalbari, the rest of our outfit came up by rail. We had sixteen guns when everybody got there. Captain Pidgeon was back in charge, and he had his hands full with our crowd. Once he said, "Look, we haven't fired these guns, so the first chance we get, let's test fire them to make sure they're operating." It wasn't very long until there was an alert, and the Japanese began to bomb nearby airfields. Captain Pidgeon said, "This is your chance, just fire a few rounds." So our men shot just one burst. But then a great big bird came flying across the airfield, and they all began shooting at that bird. Those machine guns make a big noise. The gunner swings around shooting, and all of our fellows began swinging around, shooting at the great big heron. With sixteen guns, that's a lot of racket. Pidgeon was beside himself trying to get them to stop. They finally hit the bird, and only then did they stop. With all that noise, the workers on the tea plantation panicked and ran in every direction. It was not an auspicious beginning for our stay at Mokalbari. Mr. McDonald, who ran the plantation, was not pleased, since he had to round up all the workers who had disappeared during the racket.

Mokalbari was surrounded by a forest of tall trees. While we were there, we built a platform high up in a big tree, put in a field telephone to each gun, and kept a lookout. Our guns were manned all hours of the day and night. We had many alerts, but no direct attacks. Up in November, it would get cold when the fog settled in, and the men began standing around a fire at night. Somebody found an old milk can, and they cooked tea in it. I don't think they ever emptied it out; they just kept putting more water and more tea in, and it was really strong tea. At 2:00 or 3:00 in the mornings, it looked to me like there were too many people milling around that thing, and the guns were not being manned.

My sergeant, name of Schlarb, was a good fellow. One night I said to him, "Let's sneak around and see who's at their gun and who's not." So we got together that cold night, and went around to gun number 1. No one was around. It struck me; the barrel was very easy to remove from the gun. (If a barrel gets too hot, you pull it off and put another one on. They had handles to keep from burning your hands). So I told Schlarb, "Sergeant, let's take the barrels out of every gun that's not manned, maybe that will teach them a lesson. They have two more barrels to put on if anything actually happens." So we went around to every one of the sixteen guns and took the barrels off. Nobody was there. They were all down at the tea can visiting and keeping warm.

As the sun came up, the conversation buzzed over the telephone lines when the men discovered that their gun barrels were missing. When we determined that every one of them had noticed, I got on the line and told the patrol leaders to report to the center of the airfield. When they got there, I said, "Boys, did anything unusual happen during the night?" They each said, "Our gun barrel is gone." And I said, "Well, where were you when your gun barrel disappeared?" They all finally admitted that they were down at the teapot having tea.

We had covered all the barrels up with a blanket and taken a piece of chalk to mark where they'd come from. I jerked the blanket off, and said, "All right. Come up and get your barrel and go back and screw it in the gun where it belongs, and don't let me ever catch anybody off his post anytime anymore. If something had happened and you weren't there, we'd be in the big soup." We didn't have any trouble from that point forward.

Feast of Lights

At Mokalbari there were about a dozen fighter planes, a full squadron. The planes were scattered around, and on each one, the Air Corps had a twenty-four-hour guard. There weren't any revetments to protect the aircraft, mainly because the planes were supposed to get off the ground if anything happened.

The people of Mokalbari had a Feast of Lights in October. They told me it was a celebration of light over darkness, knowledge over ignorance. During that festival, the Indians paid no attention to the fact that there was a blackout. The whole countryside was lit up with little oil lamps. It looked like a fairyland. They put them all the way around their houses and on the trails. If the Japanese had come, it would have been lit up like Christmas all over the place, and there was nothing we could have done about it.

One guard was on duty that night protecting a plane near the village. There were several thousand people there, working on the plantations. There was a school, a small hospital, and a temple. On the festival, they parade around with those lights. This guard's plane was right on one of their trails, the way they had gone for ages, long before the airfield was there. That night, the guard looked up, and here came all these folks with torches, right straight at him. He ordered them to halt in English, but they kept on coming. He didn't know a damn thing about Indian customs, so he began firing into the air. At least he didn't shoot directly at them, but understandably, they all panicked and ran away. Mr. McDonald was very unhappy; he had to round up all his employees for the second time. Not a victory for knowledge over ignorance that night.

Trip to Ramgarh

Around Christmas, Captain Pidgeon got the officers together and told us that planes were bringing Chinese recruits to India. They were still taking supplies to China over the Hump, but on their return trips, they started bringing recruits to flesh out the Chinese 22nd, 38th, and 50th divisions, the ones that had retreated out of Burma early on. Those divisions had lost a whole lot of people. Many had starved to death or died of malaria coming through the mountains. So, the Hump planes came back loaded with recruits. They took the men to a place called Ramgarh, farther west in India, for their training. Captain Pidgeon said, "They need a few men to teach those recruits how to use machine guns." So he put the finger on me and two others. One was Marion Hair from Charleston, South Carolina, a graduate of the Citadel. The other man's name was Shine, I forget his first name. He was from Alabama, went to the University of Alabama. They were both reserve officers like me. The three of us headed down to Ramgarh. Pidgeon said, "You won't be there but three or four weeks."

That was my first real experience on Indian railroads. We took a meter gauge train to the town of Guwahati, then rode a ways down the Brahmaputra River on a ferry. We caught another meter gauge to Parbatipur, I think it was, where we transshipped to a broad-gauge railroad. The trains were packed with people.

People hanging on top and underneath and everywhere else. They didn't have dining cars on the trains. They'd just stop the train, and everybody would get off at the station and eat, a little like Fred Harvey's deal with the Santa Fe Railroad in America, but less fancy.

When we got to Ramgarh, we were given motorcycles for transportation, military motorcycles painted olive drab. None of us three had ever ridden a motorcycle. It was a comical weekend, us madly trying to learn how to use motorcycles to travel fifteen miles to the shooting range. We managed to borrow a sidecar, which helped, like training wheels on a bicycle. We got out on a British tennis court to learn the controls and managed to get good enough to make it to the range.

We weren't there more than about two weeks instructing recruits, when the Japanese launched an offensive in the Arakan, down to the south. It was early January of 1943. The Allies were anxious to establish a road across northern Burma into China. In the middle of those efforts, when the Japanese launched this offensive, the Allies sped up their plans and the 22nd and 38th Chinese Divisions were ordered to take up positions as soon as possible in the Naga Hills between India and Burma. Very quickly, trains were lined up to move troops from Ramgarh to Upper Assam.

Ramgarh to Ledo

We were reassigned right then and there. They said, "You are now with the Chinese. You are liaison officers." In vain we protested, "We are supposed to go back to our outfits." "Well, that's all changed now. You've got to do this." So I became attached to the 112th Regiment and was told I was in charge of getting them to Assam. The train was ready at the marshaling yard. There were several trucks to load stuff. We also had a hundred horses, about a hundred tons of ammunition, two or three boxcar loads of hay for feed, and a piece of rope about three hundred feet long for use as a picket line for the horses.

Right quick, I tried to get things going. First, I went to check on the horses. They were all tied to one rope that ran from one stubby tree to another, each horse about ten feet from the other on either side of the rope. A Chinese sergeant went with me walking up and down the line. He didn't know a damn thing about handling horses, and neither did I. As I was standing there trying to talk to him, I turned my back on a horse. All of a sudden, that horse hauled off and kicked me in the rear end. I crashed to the ground and thought, oh, my God, my back's broken. I had a bruise about as big around as a dinner plate, but I managed to get up and keep going.

Then we started loading. Fortunately, we had a platform to load the horses directly into the boxcars, the goods wagons, they called them. It wasn't too much of a problem to get them in—each horse had a halter—it was just a manhandling job. While we were there, some of the men came to get me, gesticulating madly; I could tell something bad was wrong. So I followed them and found one of our trucks way down at the bottom of a hill. A fellow had missed a curve and rolled the truck. It had landed bottom-side up at the base of the hill. The trucks had these hoops with canvas tops over their beds, and this one was smashed. The driver wasn't hurt; he had bailed out on the way down. We got together a bunch of folks and rolled the truck right side up. We tied the picket rope onto the front of the truck and then with at least a hundred Chinese folks pulling, we dragged the truck up the hill, just with people. You can do almost anything if you've got enough people. The same fellow got back in the driver's seat, turned the key, and the damn thing ran.

While we were loading stuff, it began to rain hard, and that was a real problem. The local people call it the *chota* monsoon, which means "little" monsoon. Everything's been dry as the dickens in November and December, and then all of a sudden around late December or early January, it rains for about a week. Well, this monsoon didn't seem "little." It rained practically the whole trip. In Parbatipur, we transferred from broad gauge to narrow gauge while it was raining cats and dogs. The meter gauge train was lined up in the yard when we arrived, and we pulled up parallel and transferred everything across. The same horse that had kicked me refused to go up the ramp into the train. It was nighttime, and the only light was from kerosene lanterns. Each horse had a halter on with a band just above his eyes and a bunch of strings hanging down, designed to keep flies away. I thought maybe the strings were interfering with his vision, throwing funny shadows in his face. So I stepped forward and began tucking those strings up in the headband to get them out of his eyes As I was messing with the strings, that horse struck out just like a snake and bit me right in the chest. I mean, he took a mouthful. I staggered back. Without thinking, I hauled off and hit that horse with my fist right on the nose just as hard as I could. It didn't bother him at all. Then I backed up, still in the rain, just dripping wet. I opened up my shirt and saw he had drawn blood. Eventually it turned into a gigantic bruise right on the front of my chest. That was one mean horse, a real devil, and I had two gigantic bruises to prove it. Finally, with four men on him, two on either end of a bamboo pole, we pushed him, bucking like the dickens, into the boxcar.

We arrived at Dhubri in the pouring rain, in the dead of night, a thousand men, a hundred horses, and all the rest of the supplies, guns and ammunition. We had to get off the train while it was still raining buckets and move ourselves better than a mile onto two steamboats. I remember one of the boats was named the *Buzzard*, and one was the *Vulture*. Apparently, buzzards and vultures are highly regarded in India because they clean up the place. All the hay, the ammunition and everything else had to be carried by people across a wide mud flat to those boats. There was a bridge decked with bamboo crosspieces and dirt on top of it going to one boat. Horses don't like bridges anyway, and in the dark, with nothing but lanterns, in pouring down rain, the biggest problem we had was those damn horses. And it was cold. The place is subtropical, but it could still get cold.

While we were messing with the horses, an Indian fellow came running up to me hollering in Hindi or Urdu. I figured something bad was the matter, so I followed him as fast as I could. He was barefooted and could make better time through the mud than I could, but I stumbled along. By the light of lanterns, I could see we were headed for the second boat. It was a side-wheeler steamboat, great big one, with a walking beam engine, and that whole boat had tilted over so far that the port side paddle wheel, a wheel about twenty feet in diameter, was sticking clean out of the water. We had to climb up to get on the deck. Turned out, the Chinese had loaded 100 tons of ammunition all on the far side of the deck and stacked all the hay on the near side. The fellow who was hollering was the *sirdar*, the captain. It was his boat, and it was in real danger of capsizing into the river, which was now a swollen torrent. Luckily, the ammunition hadn't slid off. The rail and the superstructure held it on, but it was a precarious setup. Those ammunition boxes weighed 110 pounds apiece. We quickly got enough folks together to move the boxes down into the hold. While they were working, the ship began to right itself.

When we finally got ready to go, we had about a thousand men, all the horses, and the whole business on the two boats. Then, still in the dark, we headed up the Brahmaputra River. The river was at flood stage, and it was the scariest thing you ever saw, a muddy rush of water, with great logs and stumps and all sorts of things floating down. I went up in the pilot house on the *Buzzard*. The pilot wheel must have been twelve feet in diameter, it was huge, and it was located below the pilot house. The top of the wheel stuck out, and the pilot sat on the floor, steering with his feet, the wheel handles out in front of him. Another handle up above him controlled the direction of the spotlight. He didn't use the light except when he wanted to find the bank. He would turn the light on, see how far it was to the bank, and then turn it off. And he'd look and find the other bank. The man knew that river. It was amazing. He was going upstream against terrific current, and the steam engine ran just smooth as silk, with those paddle wheels chunking. They were independent wheels; one advantage of side-wheelers over stern wheelers is that you can use the wheels at different speeds. Like tractors, stop or slow one wheel, keep the other going.

We were on those ships two nights going up the river, and landed at Guwahati, a big ferrying point for the railroad and other traffic. We loaded onto another meter gauge and headed up north to Ledo. When we finally got there, it was so crammed with troops, we couldn't unload. Eleven days it had taken us to make the trip, and we had to wait three more until we could let those poor horses out.

New Orders

Ledo was headquarters for the NCAC (Northern Combat Area Command), under General Stilwell. The Americans had assumed the major responsibility for the northern sector of Burma. The plan was to push the Japanese out and build a road across upper Burma to join the old Burma Road. Stilwell was in charge, and Chiang Kai-shek had given him the command of Chinese troops to help. The British had set up their main effort further south at Imphal, extending all the way down to Chittagong on the coast. They made a barrier to keep the Japanese out of India and were planning to drive the Japanese back across the middle part of Burma.

We got off the train at Ledo in the rain. It was situated in flat river-bottom territory. The camp consisted of bamboo lean-to shacks, *bashas* they called them, very primitive pole sheds with thatched roofs, woven bamboo walls, no floors, just dirt. They did mostly keep out the rain but were right in a swamp. We established ourselves there in the mud and water, hoping we'd soon be sent back to our coast artillery platoons. I shared a tent with a man from California by the name of Donald Ducey. He was from somewhere around Los Angeles.

One day, I forget the occasion, I had to go to headquarters, which was still under construction. On the way, I ran into a colonel by the name of McNally. We got into a conversation, and it turned out that his daughter had been taught by an aunt of mine, Aunt Zet, at a school called Gunston Hall in Washington, DC. Apparently, McNally's daughter thought a great deal of my Aunt Zet, so right from the start, we had a common interest and a good conversation. In the process, he said, "By the way, we've got a job that we need done. We have been ordered to move two Chinese battalions up into Burma. We'd like to use horses for transport to support those troops." The civil affairs officer up there for the British was named Johnny Walker, just like the whiskey. McNally said, "Walker has told us that he doesn't think that animal transport is going to be very useful, but we need to get our own people in there to check it out." McNally asked if I were interested, and I said, "Of course." I asked, "When?"

and he said, "Now." At the time I didn't think much about it, but in retrospect, that spur-of-the-moment conversation determined the better part of my entire wartime experience and beyond.

McNally warned me that the Japanese had been reported probing around in the area and directed me to take my tent mate, Donald Ducey, as well. The two of us were to equip ourselves with whatever we needed and head up to an outpost in the mountains of Burma at a place called Pebu. He gave me a map and marked our destination on it. One thing the British always did whenever they took over some part of the world was to send survey crews and make good maps. They had better maps of India and the surrounding primitive regions than we had of Mississippi on my survey crew. The maps were old, however. Most were made at the turn of the century. The villages had often moved, and trails changed, but the geographical items like the hills and rivers were pretty dadgum accurate. I took the map, and I headed back to tell Donald Ducey that we had been assigned a job.

We hurried to get ready. I got a medical kit from a Polish doctor, who gave me supplies including opium, ipecac, and quinine, and I took a Springfield rifle, Model 1903, and a .45 caliber semiautomatic pistol. I had what, at that time, the army called a pack, really just a harness with belts and buckles to hold a rolled-up blanket. The next day we started out with the map, what rations we could carry, and ammunition, but we were totally unprepared. We should have gotten a local guide to help, someone who knew something about the territory. The only information we had been given was that somewhere near a village called Ranglum, was Pebu, an abandoned village where there was a small British outpost of Punjabi soldiers. We were to find them, check out the area, and come back. That outpost didn't have any radio communication with the base, so they had no idea we were coming. For a while, up in that country, there were no radios. The only way to communicate was by runner.

The rain had slacked off. We struck out along with a couple of Chinese soldiers, but we had difficulty communicating with them. They didn't seem to understand that we were in a hurry. We tried to encourage them, but at some point, we just got separated. I never knew what happened to them. I reckon they turned around. We walked until about 3:00 or 4:00 in the afternoon, when we realized we had made a wrong turn. We had passed a fork several miles back, and it took us a while before we noticed that the trail was taking us east. We were supposed to be headed almost straight south, so we turned back toward the fork. We thought we'd run into our Chinese friends, but we saw no one. We were in real jungle by that time, a fascinating place, unfamiliar trees with huge vines scrambling up them, thickets of bamboo with stalks as big around as your leg. It was muddy from all the rain, so we slipped and slid.

By the time we got back to the fork, we decided we might as well stay there for the night. Everything was steep and rocky and covered with dense forest, so we picked a spot right on the trail.

It was getting cold, so we started gathering wood for a fire and clearing off a place to sleep. While we were working in the dim light, I looked up the trail and noticed two figures standing, just looking at us. I said to Ducey, "Maybe we ought to go up there and introduce ourselves." We had heard a little bit about the people in northern Burma, but not much. We knew the mountains were inhabited by Nagas, very primitive people, reportedly some were head-hunters. The British had not firmly established any sort of administration up there; they had just tried to keep the peace. In that area also were Kachins, a group physically very similar to the Nagas but with quite different language and customs. Kachins had fought alongside the British before, and some had recently been fighting the Japanese on their own. I had, at least, been informed that there were Kachins and Nagas up in this country and that they might be sympathetic to us since they were longtime enemies of the Burmese, who were firm allies of the Japanese.

We saw these two characters a little ways away. One of them was obviously a big, tall fellow, and the other was just a child. The man was carrying a long spear in his hand. Ducey stayed back and cocked his rifle. I had picked up a smattering of Hindi and Urdu in Karachi, so I walked up to them, smiling big, and greeted them with, "*Raam raam*," a Hindu greeting. Thank goodness, they smiled back. Then they uttered something in return. Of course, I couldn't understand, so I asked something else, "Where's water?" I asked, "*Pani kitter ho?*" The man smiled again and pointed down the hill. Then he turned to this child, obviously his son, and uttered a command. The boy, who must have been about ten years old, had a big knife with a wide scalloped end on it. At the man's order, the child ran off. We could hear some chopping sounds down in the woods below, and in a few minutes, he came back with a big bamboo tube about five inches across, which he had obviously just cut. It was about 3 feet long, really just one big joint of a very large bamboo stalk, and it was full of water. He handed it to me. I said, "*Shabash*," and they seemed to understand. They lived close enough to the major part of India to where I reckon they knew some Hindi or Urdu.

Then we began talking to each other in rudimentary sign language. This man, who I found out later was a Naga, pointed down at the ground, pointed to me, and then made the universal sign for sleep. I guess all people of whatever origin know that sign. And I said "*Hi, hi*," which means yes. He pointed down the hill, and made a sign for "house," and then pointed to himself, indicating he was inviting us to go down to his village. I said, "*Hi, hi*" again. We immediately picked up all of our things and followed him.

Naga Hospitality

We came upon the Naga village in the gathering dark. There were fires going inside every house. I was to become well acquainted with Naga and Kachin houses. The thatched roof of a house came down very low, so there wasn't much wall, maybe two feet of woven bamboo. There was no chimney at all. The smoke rose right through the thatch. Each house was built off the ground on stilts, with an open area at the front like a porch. A log leaned up against that porch with notches cut in it, and you could step on those notches and climb it like a stair. Inside, the floor was made out of bamboo, which had been split and then rolled out, making flat pieces about a foot wide, like planks. When they would sweep the house, everything just dropped through the cracks. In the middle of the room was a box in the floor. The box was square and filled with dirt, and the fire was laid on top of that. Above the fire, a rack hung from the rafters. On the rack, they put all sorts of stuff that they smoked or wanted to keep warm. The whole inside of the house was shiny black from smoke and soot that poured through the rafters and thatch. There really wasn't a ceiling as such. The house from a distance looked like it was on fire, but it was just the smoke coming through the roof. The rest of the interior was separated by a wall. We discovered later, the houses usually had several rooms. Some houses were up to a hundred feet long, all under one gabled roof. Often two or three generations lived in the same house.

We ended up on our friend's porch. To him, we must have seemed a couple of strange, pale looking fellows dressed in funny clothes. Just about the whole village came crowding in. They all squatted down. People over there didn't often sit on the ground or floor. Fortunately, I was able to squat flat-footed like they did, since I'd spent lots of time out in the swampy woods of the Pearl River; squatting keeps your rear end dry. Ducey sat on the floor. We started in on our can of corned beef, but they invited us to eat what they had. They didn't have utensils or bowls; they ate with their hands. They handed us each a leaf, wrapped up like a package, which unfolded to reveal some kind of meat with rice. Then they gave us a kind of soup also in a leaf, something like a small version of a banana leaf folded to form a cup. We ate what they gave us, and believe me, it was hot as fire, highly seasoned with chili peppers. In my part of the country, we eat food that's pretty spicy, but not like that. The pepper was so strong that it gave me the hiccups. They gave us water and tea, which helped. They all drank strong green tea served in bamboo cups. So we had our first meal out in the boondocks with the Nagas.

After a while, we got out our blankets. We didn't have sleeping bags or anything fancy like that, just plain old army blankets. With everybody still staring at us, we laid down right there by the fire. Our host finally laid down on the other side of the fire. He didn't bother with a blanket; he just went to sleep. I guess the other people drifted off during the night, but when we woke up the next morning, they were all back waiting for us to wake up. I somehow managed to get across to them that we wanted to go to Ranglum, so our host went with us to get us started on the trail. He took us several miles to be sure we were headed in the right direction. Our first experience with the Nagas had gotten us off to a good start.

Strange Celebration

We kept on the trail all day and watched the contour lines on the map very carefully this time. As it began to get dark, we heard the faint noise of drums. They got louder as we went along. Every now and then a gun would go off. Obviously, the din was coming from a village in the general direction we were headed. We heard people shouting, clanging gongs, and the wailing of pipes that sounded a lot like bagpipes. When we came on a trail branching off toward the village, we decided to go check it out since we'd gotten such a royal welcome at the other place. We walked down the hill and came upon a crowd obviously involved in some kind of religious celebration. Drums were beating, and people were gathered around a fire chanting. There was a man in the middle holding some branches of bamboo with the foliage still on them, waving them around. Some ceremony was definitely going on, but when they saw us coming, they came up to meet us.

No one in the crowd had hardly anything on except little breechclout-looking things. But they had swords and lots of other accoutrements. The chief, I guess it was, had on a headdress with boars' tusks coming out of it and some feathers. We greeted them as we had done before, with smiles and peaceful signs, but something about them made us uneasy. I remarked to Ducey, "These people don't look right to me. I think they're drunk." He replied, "I get the same impression." We quickly came to the conclusion we'd better keep moving. We stayed for a little while to be polite but kept repeating we were going to Ranglum, Ranglum, Ranglum. They did appear to recognize that name, so we figured we were on the right track.

We got back on the main trail and kept going in the dark for a while, but we didn't ever get out of the range of the sound of the celebration that night. It went on and on, the drums beating, the sound of a gong, "gung, gung, bum, bum, bum, bum," and the chanting and the wailing of the pipes. Every now and then a gun would go off. Those guns were probably a hundred years old. They were flintlocks or matchlocks, some of them, and others used percussion caps.

We were probably less than half a mile away from the village as the crow flies when we stopped. This time we got off the trail and found a flat place up among the trees. We made our own little fire and cooked up some C-rations. We laid awake late, until finally the whole business just died away. The last thing we heard was a gong, then a gun going off, "boom," and finally there was dead silence.

Language Lessons

At daybreak, we headed out, hiked all day, and in the evening came to a place where we could see ahead some distance. Much of the time in the jungle, it's hard to see anything, but here it opened out. Near the path, there was a village on a ridge with smoke coming out of the roofs of the houses. We decided to go on in, and luckily, we got the same reception that we'd gotten at the first place. When we appeared at the edge of the village, everybody turned out to see these peculiar foreigners and asked us in. We ended up in the front end of a big house, same as before. They invited us to eat, and we did not bother to unpack our stuff. We just ate what they had.

The village was called Manmauk. There was a big, tall man there. His name was N'gumla. He was not a Naga, but a Kachin who was traveling through. I read later that the average height of the men there was about 5 foot 4 inches or so, and the average height of women was less than 5 feet. But this man was a good 6 feet tall. I had a notepad, and I started trying to learn the language from him. I managed to get pretty far that one night. I would point at something and indicate that I wanted to learn how to say it. For example, a piece of wood. They called wood *pun*. That was one of the first words I learned. Water was *hka*, and rice was *shot*. I pointed at various and sundry things. Finally, I learned how to say, "How do you say this?"—*n'da gaw ganing tsun ai gun*. *Ganing* makes a question out of it, asks "how?," *tsun* means "say," and *gun* emphasizes the fact that it's a question. "*N'da ganing tsun ai gun*?" And N'gumla would tell me the way to say it. A crowd was listening, men, women, and children.

The men were all in the inner circle around the fire, and the women and children and very old folks in rows behind that. I spent a good while writing down my own phonetic interpretation of words. Later on, I learned that a Swedish American missionary named Hanson had devised an alphabet for the written language. What N'gumla was teaching me was Jinghpaw (Kachin). He spoke both Naga and Kachin, but he had sense enough to know if we were going further, we'd be dealing mostly with Kachins. Jinghpaw was the lingua franca of that part of the country, where Nagas and Kachins both mingled.

I never learned any Naga language to speak of, but I started off right away with Jinghpaw, or the Hkahku version of it; each area had its own dialect. *Hkahku* means the headwaters, and this was headwaters country.

I asked a lot, "How do you say the sun? How do you say the moon?" everything I could think of. Then I asked, "How do you say sleep?" and N'gumla told me, "*Neru neru.*" Everybody chuckled a little. Not knowing any better, I repeated the word. I said, "I go *neru neru.*" Then they all just rolled, howled with laughter, men, women, and children. I shut up quick and went on to something else. He had apparently told me some dirty word. I never used the words *neru neru* again, but I learned then, they were jokesters. They had certainly tricked me, this big "important" white man. It was all in good fun, and I learned a lot that night. I wrote down a whole bunch of words. I've still got that notebook somewhere.

N'gumla became one of my advisors later. He was with me through '43 and part of '44, about a year. During that time, a tragedy occurred. It happened much later, but I'll tell it now, briefly. He had left his family behind in the Hukawng Valley when he joined us. His wife was pregnant at the time. While we were on the march, we heard that the Japanese had come up pretty close to his village, and the whole village had cleared out, several hundred people. They fled north. We were going south, and happened to run into them on the trail. They had already traveled thirty or forty miles on foot. It was the rainy season; the rain was pouring down.

N'gumla's wife was in the group of refugees. She had the child with her, who had just been born a few days before. He didn't know she was coming; he just met her as she walked up the trail with their tiny baby. He held the baby briefly and then told his wife goodbye and continued on with us. We all thought they'd be all right since they were with the whole village. I remember that little child. He was very tiny, and she had him all wrapped up. N'gumla was so proud of that baby. When we heard later that the child had died, it was pretty hard on everybody. N'gumla stayed with us, nevertheless. But that was all much later. This time, Ducey and I left alone the next day, but I had gained a beginning knowledge of the Kachin language thanks to N'gumla.

Pebu

After that, the two of us headed on up the trail towards bigger mountains. We were getting into Burma now. We had crossed the invisible border. We made it up to five thousand feet pretty quick and passed by the turnoff to the first of the air warning stations. It was called KC9. The people in Manmauk had told us where it was. We didn't go up to it; we noted the location but kept going since we were behind time. All told, it took us eight days just to get to Ranglum. From there, we went on to the abandoned village of Pebu, where the Punjabi contingent was camped. As we approached, a sentry ordered us to halt. He was a Punjabi soldier and could speak some English. We learned from him that the Japanese had been patrolling nearby.

It was nightfall when we arrived in Pebu. An Indian Army lieutenant or "leftenant" as the British pronounce it, a tall Punjabi whose name I do not remember, was in charge. His soldiers were all Muslims, regular soldiers in the British Indian Army. He invited us to stay and served us hornbill for supper. One of his soldiers had shot the bird, which I learned later is almost sacred to the Kachins. Unlike the Hindus, Punjabis eat meat, except pork. The Hindus principal diet is rice. The Punjabis eat rice too, but they eat a lot of whole wheat flour they call *atta*. They make *atta* chapatis, a little like flour tortillas. So we had hornbill and chapatis. The lieutenant had a little bamboo *basha* and made room for us to sleep on the floor.

We sat up half the night asking questions. The lieutenant spoke fair English, and we learned a lot about the local situation. He told us that further down this same trail, directly south of us, the allies had just established another air warning station, KC8, at a village called Hkalak Ga. We also learned about the two main refugee trails. Both came up from a large area called the Hukawng Valley in Burma and went over into India. They branched off at a place called Shingbwiyang; one went almost straight north through Pangsau Pass, through the Patkai range of mountains, and it ended up at Ledo. That's where the main thrust of the refugees, tens of thousands, had come to get away from the Japanese. The other trail branched toward the west from Shingbwiyang and went up over a higher pass called Okatohap, about 8,000 feet, then across the ridge and came out at a military outpost at Tirap. That branch, mostly Indian and Chinese troops followed. According to the lieutenant, many had died on both those trails. Later on, we traveled on each trail at one time or another. They were both lined with dead bodies, sometimes right in the middle of the road. We were stepping over them, stepping on them, it was the ghastliest thing you ever saw. Folks had died from exhaustion, died because they didn't have anything to eat, from malaria, from floods, since it was raining all the dadgum time. They had died by the thousands. Nobody will ever know the number of dead from that first rush to get out of Burma.

At Pebu, in addition to the Punjabi lieutenant, I first encountered someone from OSS Detachment 101, a man named Harry Hengshoon. He went by the alias "Skittles." The OSS (Office of Strategic Services, the American intelligence group) had recruited him in Calcutta. He was half Chinese, half Burmese. He'd been trained back at OSS headquarters in Nazira, India, and had two men with him, also with code names. One was called Perry and the other, Dennis. They were both Anglo-Burman. Perry was blond and blue-eyed. He could speak good English and Burmese. Skittles and his men showed up just about the time I was getting ready to leave Pebu. When I saw them, they had just tried to penetrate deep into Burma with a radio, but hadn't managed to get far.

Liaison Officer

We turned around at Pebu, went through Ranglum, and headed back. We were late. We figured we'd get back in just a couple more days, but when we rounded a corner on the trail, we ran into a Chinese battalion of the 112th Regiment, 38th Division. They had gotten tired of waiting for us. The trails were so slick that it was difficult for a human being to negotiate, much less a horse. Our recommendation would have been to hold off using animals until conditions were drier, usually from February on up into May. But here they came, mules and all.

When we ran into them, they were already struggling. They had lost two mules over the side of the steep trail, and mules don't often fall. It didn't help that these particular Chinese really didn't know how to handle horses. A lot of Chinese folks knew how to handle them, especially the ones in the caravan business, but these soldiers were raw recruits, and they didn't know much. The mules had both been hurt badly, so they had killed them, butchered them right there on the spot, cooked them up, and eaten them.

We heard all that from an American colonel who was with them, Colonel Coughlin. When we ran into him, he was struggling up the hill himself. He looked up at me and said, "Is your name Lutken?" And I said, "Yes, sir." He said, "Well, you're now liaison officer with this battalion, and I'll turn them over to you." I was taken aback. There was nobody with the battalion who could speak English, and, of course, I knew practically no Chinese at all. I knew a greeting, *hao bu hao. Hao* means "good," and *bu hao* means "no good." Instead of saying, "How are you doing?" you say, "*Hao bu hao?*" That's about all I knew. But there I was. When I turned around to accompany the Chinese, Coughlin turned back to headquarters and took Ducey with him. I presume that Ducey at least got to give a thorough report when he got back; he had good judgment.

I never got back to my original artillery outfit. I was assigned to the Chinese battalion but stayed with them only a few weeks. We went back to Pebu, and since we were planning to be there for a while, we put pickets out on the trail and a few machine gun placements, expecting that the Japanese, who had been patrolling the area, would probably be coming up sometime to pay us a visit. I met the headman of Ranglum around then. We called him "Two Hats";

he wore his own turban and a hat. He had been along one of the two refugee trails where so many people had died, and had picked up a broad brimmed Gurkha-type hat, off of a dead fellow, no doubt. He wore that on top of his turban, so we nicknamed him "Two Hats." He was the Naga headman, or the *gampura*, of Ranglum, and he and I became fast friends.

In the meantime, the Chinese set up defensive positions, but I couldn't get them interested in patrolling. It worried me that nobody was going along the trail any further to see what might be happening. I asked Two Hats to help me recruit a few Nagas. He found two men to assist me in scouting out the area. I nicknamed them Henry and Zeke. They were both real skinny, as most Nagas were. In the battalion, there were close to a thousand Chinese, so there was some extra equipment. I got a pair of rifles for Henry and Zeke and showed them how to use them. The rifles were U.S. Model 1917 Enfields. They came from an armory in Canada that had made rifles for the British and Canadian armies in World War I. When we got into the first world war, apparently we didn't have enough rifles, so the Canadian armory was called on to bore some rifles to fit the 30–06 of the Americans. Everything else was the same. Plenty were left over from World War I, and that's what they armed those Chinese troops with, and they were good rifles. So I showed Zeke and Henry how to operate them, and the three of us began patrolling the area.

We learned a good deal in a very short period of time, just by roaming around. We went down the trail toward the south ten or fifteen miles and checked out where other trails went. I started with those two men, but gradually added more, until I had what you might call a private little army of about twelve or fifteen men. They came and went, so I never knew exactly how many. But with that little group, we put out a pretty good, continuously operating screen around the Chinese position. If anybody came in there, we knew about it. We arranged with surrounding villages to communicate with us, so we had our own little information system going.

At Pebu, one of the ways I attracted Nagas was by teaching them songs. They thought I was a real funny fellow because I sang these absurd songs. One was "Old McDonald Had a Farm." I taught them all about the ducks quacking and the pigs oinking, and the cows and chickens and everything. They understood, of course, and were amused. Quite a while later, David Darlington, who was an English clergyman, came into that part of the country to investigate a plane that went down. He told me he was greeted by all these Nagas singing "Old McDonald Had a Farm," and they all had a good laugh.

I took lots of scouting expeditions with my recruits. Once, we came upon a bunch of Garo porters. The Garos are a tribe of folks that come from the Khasi Hills, a branch of the Naga Hills in the southwest near the Brahmaputra River.

They had been hired by the British as coolies. As my group came around a corner, we looked across where the trail zigzagged up a ravine and saw a number of Garos, some other Nagas, and an Englishman with them. This Englishman was sitting in the middle of the trail at a table and chair that had been built on the spot. There was a tablecloth, china, a cup and saucer, and he was having tea in the early afternoon.

We went up the trail to the tea party, and I introduced myself to Rufus Thompson. He had been working in India for many years as a tea planter and was a member of what they called the Territorials, a group that I was to run into frequently. They were like the National Guard in our country, part-time soldiers who lived in the area, and had been called to active duty with the war. Rufus Thompson had been assigned to command the porters, with directions to support our Chinese battalion. Right then, he ordered the Garos to build me a chair. I sat down, feeling awkward, as they poured me a cup of tea. It was a surreal experience, having tea with my English friend out in the middle of the jungle.

When I went on back to my battalion, the Garos encamped just down the hill. The Chinese planned to move to an outpost further south, and the Garos were supposed to help them. Thompson, in the meantime, had other orders and left his men under the command of one of their people. They were supposed to come up to the Chinese position on a certain day. Early on the scheduled morning, I heard several shots fired, went running out to see what happened, and discovered that the porters had encountered a Chinese sentry who hauled off and shot at them. I never got the whole story but found out that one of the porters, a Naga, had been hit. That fellow took off back to Ranglum after he got shot.

I went to Ranglum to see about the man. He had been shot in the left side of his chest. The villagers had already stuffed the bullet entrance and exit holes full of some kind of chopped-up leaves, and Two Hats told me, "He'll be all right." Turned out he was right, the fellow recovered. But the Chinese had incurred the extreme unhappiness of the Garos. They didn't appreciate being shot at, and they very quietly packed up their stuff that same night and left.

Dogfight

On another of my outings, I heard the unmistakable sound of Japanese bombers. I was on a high ridge overlooking the Brahmaputra Valley, and as I remember, was by myself. I moved to a place where I could see through the trees, and sure enough, there they were; two formations, bright in the sun, about twelve planes in each formation, like flocks of geese in V shape, and with a bunch of fighter planes accompanying them. They were all headed almost straight north. I watched until they went out of sight and then turned around and kept doing whatever I was doing. After a while, I could hear a terrible rumble, rumble, rumble. The planes had obviously gotten to their destination and were dropping bombs. After some more time, I began to hear them returning. I didn't know where they had been, just the general direction, but found out later that the principal place they attacked was Sookerating, the airport where we had first landed. By that time, it had developed into a much bigger operation, an inviting target, and the Japanese unloaded a whole bunch of bombs there. When the Japanese planes returned, unfortunately for them, they flew right over the town of Digboi, which had an oil field and a refinery and lots of British anti-aircraft guns. The British let them have it. I could see off in the distance, the sky darkened by black smoke from anti-aircraft guns. As the airplanes continued toward me, I heard the sound of American airplanes; our aircraft must have gotten the alert, gone aloft, and hidden in the clouds.

The P40s came in after the Japanese, and it was really spectacular. They did what their commander Chennault taught them to do: get up above and dive and just keep going down toward the ground, not to engage, because the Zeros could outmaneuver them. First, I saw two Japanese bombers start smoking and come down in a slow decline. They didn't blow up, they just came down, losing altitude and smoking all the time. Every now and then another Japanese plane would burst into flames. I didn't see any American planes hit. The final report that we got through the grapevine was that our folks got almost all of them.

That was, I guess, the first great success for our side, due in large part to the establishment of those air warning stations. I talked to one of the folks from KC8 later, and he said his group had reported the planes. That was the first time our side had caused much damage since the AVG left. The American Volunteer Group (AVG) was there when the war began, actually, before it began in Burma. A volunteer group of American pilots had gone to help the Chinese. They were located up by the China-Burma border. The planes were shipped there in pieces and were put together before the Japanese took over Burma. Those "Flying Tigers" took part in the earliest Burma campaign and got a great reputation for what they did. But later the Japanese had established air superiority, until this battle, when it seemed to me, the tide began to turn.

Attack on KC8

Not too long after that, we got the word that KC8, the air warning station south of us at Hkalak Ga, had been attacked by Japanese ground troops. We heard the news through the jungle grapevine. Word seems to travel that way faster than people can move. Hkalak Ga was several days' march from where we were, and I had not yet been there. In the wake of their defeat, the Japanese probably figured that KC8 warning station was responsible, so they went for it. For some reason, they didn't go after KC9, which was not too far away from us.

I had no way of verifying that KC8 had indeed been attacked because we had no radio. But I knew if I could get to KC9, they could find out since they did have one. So I struck out before daylight the next day. I didn't even carry a rifle. I went, as the Kachins say, *kunkuman*, which means "naked." I did have my shoes and clothes on but didn't carry anything else. I wanted to get there as fast as I could, and it took me all day, going as hard as I could go. It was probably about 9 or 10 at night when I came into their camp. It was up on top of a mountain, with a little place cleared off where they could look around. When I arrived, I surprised them; they didn't even have a guard out; they were just looking at the sky.

I asked them to find out what happened to KC8. They had to encrypt the message, of course, so it took a little time. They radioed the Air Corps, and the reply came back that KC8 had indeed been attacked. The KC8 folks had barely gotten the word to command before radio communication had broken off. We were told they were retreating northward. I turned around like Pheidippides and ran right straight back to Pebu. When I arrived, I grabbed my impromptu army of twelve or fifteen Nagas, and we set off down the trail to meet them.

About halfway down to Hkalak Ga, I encountered Captains J. R. Wilson and Hector Meston, of the British Army, and the KC8 radio men: Sergeant Kunz the American in command of KC8, and his men, including Martin "Killer" Thrailkill, Bob Phillips, and several others. J. R. Wilson, who was to become my future commanding officer, had been stationed with Meston and a contingent of Assam Rifles and Kachins at KC8. When the war broke out, J. R. was around forty years old. He had been working in India for the India Tea Association when he was called up to fight. He and the other Englishman, Meston, were with the Assam Rifles and served as a small guard for KC8. Not too long before the attack, a company of Punjabis had marched down there under the command of a new British major who had taken over the defense of Hkalak Ga from Wilson and his Assam Rifles.

All the folks I met on the trail, Wilson, Meston, Kunz, and the rest, were mad as hornets because the new fellow had ordered them to retreat. The new company, all heavily armed, had set up at the pass of Shamdak Ku that separated Hkalak Ga from the Hukawng Valley. They had a pretty good position with all sorts of booby traps and machine guns and should have been able to hold out, according to Wilson. But the Japanese went around both flanks of the Punjabi outpost and got behind them. The British major then ordered everyone including the KC8 men to pull back. Nobody wanted to retreat because the Japanese force was apparently not very large. But the major thought differently, and he was in charge, so they pulled back to various positions and finally ended up in a full-scale retreat. The station folks destroyed their supplies before they left and tried to hide their elaborate radio setup. They moved it out in the jungle and left it. Of course, the whole village of Hkalak Ga panicked and left at the same time.

When I got through talking to Wilson and Meston, they headed on back to report to the British 116th Brigade. I suggested to the KC8 gang that they stay at Pebu, until this thing was resolved one way or another. So Wilson went on back to Assam full speed, and the Americans stayed at Pebu. They weren't there long but did stay until I got back. I continued on with my group down to Hkalak Ga. It took us a few days to get there, since we were not exactly running. We approached cautiously and came to a place on the track where there were several empty cartridge cases lying in the trail. We got to checking around in the jungle and found two Punjabi soldiers from the major's group. They were dead, lying on a blanket. They had several wounds, but each had also been shot in the head. Apparently, the two fellows got left behind because they were wounded, and the Japanese found them and killed them.

We went on down to the village. The Japanese had gone. Amazingly, we found one woman there, an Indian woman. We heard a noise, a moaning sound, went into a house and found her by a briskly burning fire. She had firewood and some water. The Japanese had not hurt her. The village people had obviously given her food and wood and water, but she couldn't walk, so they had left her. The Japanese didn't harm her either, and they were bound to have known that she was there. I couldn't talk to her much; she was Indian. I left her with almost all the food we had and gave her a bunch of quinine. I told her to stay put, that people would be back. Then we scouted out the whole area. No Japanese were anywhere around. We went over to Shamdak Ku pass. Nobody was there either, so we turned around and went back to Pebu.

The Americans including Thrailkill and Kunz were there when we arrived. Thrailkill was an interesting character. He was from Orange, Texas. When he was at KC8, he was a sergeant. He got a field commission and was later made second lieutenant on account of his performance. I got to know him; he was a tough fellow and a great storyteller. Like me, he learned to speak Kachin. The main thing I remember about Sergeant Kunz was that he had a big mustache, which he waxed with C-ration coffee. The coffee was in powder form, instant-style coffee, but in the damp climate, it became just like wax or glue, real sticky. So he would twirl his mustache in that stuff. That was Sergeant Kunz. In the course of events, Kunz and the rest of them left, but Thrailkill stayed at Pebu for a while.

Deadly Air Drop

Around that time, air supply was initiated. We still had no radios; a messenger arrived to tell us to prepare a drop ground. We had to find a spot and make a panel that could be seen. We used a bunch of banana leaves for the panel, but after that first drop, we used the material from a white cotton parachute. I made the panel in the form of a "P" for Pete. That very first drop, we didn't know much; we didn't even know exactly what they were going to send. We were just told that they were going to drop supplies.

In those early days, the airplane crews really didn't know much either. The year before, British planes had dropped sacks of rice on the trail to try to keep the refugees alive, so there were some experienced pilots, but for this plane, it was apparently the first time. We were standing out on a knoll where we had cleared off the brush. The knoll was on a ridge that came into a canyon near Pebu, and the canyon was huge. I forget the name of the river at the bottom, but it was a sizable stream. Folks sometimes got fish out of it by dropping hand grenades in it.

When the plane arrived, he circled a few times and then pulled around and made a run. He was so low that as he came in, we couldn't see him at all; we could just hear the engines roaring. All of a sudden, he burst up very close to the ground near where we were standing. He shot across the field and dropped a load, free-fall. He dropped a few parachutes from higher altitude and then dropped more free-fall loads on low passes. On the last pass, he went so low he actually knocked the top out of a tree. Not much of it, but he hit it as he was leaving. Thrailkill and I both stood there watching. We remarked to each other, "The guy must be nuts. He doesn't have to come that low."

After he finished his drop, the pilot turned and headed straight down the canyon, out to the east. We actually didn't pay too much attention. But then Thrailkill said, "Look yonder." So I turned around. The C-47 was headed straight toward another ridge that came out from the side of the canyon. The plane was painted olive drab on the top, but the bottom was white or blueish, so we could clearly see as he turned almost belly up. Then to our horror, we watched him drop straight down.

I don't know what in the Sam Hill he was trying to do. Maybe something had happened to the steering when he hit that tree. Probably, nobody will ever know. But the plane turned up sideways; then down it went. I said to Thrailkill, "If he comes out of this, he's the luckiest person that ever lived." Just then, a column of flame and smoke went up like a bomb. The sound took a few seconds to get to us. It was this sickening "whomp," like a combined impact and explosion. I turned to Thrailkill. "Go grab all the first aid stuff you can find and bring people to help." Then I struck out by myself, running to get to the plane.

I had to go clear to the bottom of the canyon and back up to the site of the crash, and I was running as hard as I could go. I had just a knife with me, a big Kachin-style knife. It took me nearly two hours to get to where the plane had gone down. When I arrived, the wreckage was burning fiercely, I mean a blazing-hot, ferocious fire. Some Nagas from Ranglum had beat me there, but they hadn't been able to do anything. They just stared. It was so dang hot, no one could even approach the thing. The tips of both wings had been torn off and had fallen away, but the body of the plane was a furnace. The tail section was pointing down. It had broken at the doorway. There was a man hanging there. Strangely enough, even while he was being cooked by the fire, he still had his hands around something. Everybody on the plane was obviously dead and were being consumed by the flame.

We hung around for a while. Thrailkill came up, and we searched the surrounding area to see if we could find anybody or anything. All we found was one undamaged sack of shoes, British ammunition boots. It looked to me like every one of the shoes in that sack was for a left foot. Apparently, they put all the left feet and right feet in different sacks. While we were still searching the area, another plane came out to see what had happened. They circled around a few times, and we waved at them, so they knew somebody was down there looking, and they went on back. We had to wait until it cooled off, so we struggled back to camp. We didn't have a radio yet, so we sent a messenger with the news and the number of the plane.

Next day we went back to the site. The pilot and copilot, or what remained of them, were face down on the ground. The pilot looked to be a redheaded man, seemed like hair should have all burned away, but you could still see the coloring a little. Otherwise, there wasn't much to tell. All I came away with was his pistol, which was still so hot that I had to drag it out with a stick. Those planes had crews to move the stuff and check it out. I counted a total of nine people in the body of the plane.

The two engines had hit hard. Each one had knocked a hole in the ground, and one of them had bounced out and lodged down the hillside. The propellers were twisted up into nothing. We fished out what we could of the remains of the crew. It took us a couple of days. We scraped all the remains into the hole knocked out by the engine and covered them up as best we could. The remaining load on the plane was apparently more shoes, but most everything was all burnt up. There was nothing left except hobnails and toe and heel plates, tons of them. I suppose they're still there, out in the jungle, thousands of shoe plates.

Bill Cummings

As you can tell from my account so far, I had done a lot of things, but not much in the way of liaison duties with the Chinese. I spent most of my time finding out information about the Japanese, which I hoped was helpful to the Chinese, but I didn't spend much time with them. After that air drop, I hiked to another village to see a fellow named Bill Cummings who I had encountered when I was at Ramgarh. He was a third-generation missionary. His great-grandfather named Roberts, "Saraw" Roberts, the Kachins called him, originally came from Arkansas. Roberts was involved, so the story went, in the Battle of Pea Ridge, a hard-fought struggle between the North and South during the War Between the States. In the middle of that battle, things got so intense that Roberts apparently decided he'd better do a little praying. So he prayed and promised the Lord that if he lived through the battle, he would become a missionary. When the war was over, he managed to make his way to Burma and fulfill that promise.

There was a story the Kachins told about Roberts. He had to petition the king, probably Mindon, the most famous king of Burma, or it might have been Thibaw, I'm not sure. In those days, when someone approached the king, they had to prostrate themselves, get down on their stomach and crawl. Roberts managed to make his way in to see the king, and after approaching him appropriately, he asked permission to work among the Kachins. Mindon said, "What do you plan to do when you get there?" Roberts replied, "I would like to teach the Kachins to read." Mindon pointed to a dog over in the corner of the throne room and said, "First teach my dog to read, then I'll give you permission to teach the Kachins." To this day, the Kachins tell the story that they were compared to dogs by the king of Burma. But Roberts kept after it and finally got permission to work among the Kachins, and he did teach many to read. His children, a number of them, became missionaries.

I had met Bill at Ramgarh. He had received a similar assignment to mine, but unlike me, Cummings was prepared for the job, born and raised in Burma. He had been an agricultural missionary himself and could speak Burmese like a native. He also knew Kachin. He had toured Kachin territory, taking vegetable seeds and distributing them among the villages to improve their diet. Cummings was one of the reasons that the Kachins had a favorable impression of the Americans. He was a good man, and I kept in touch with him and his family after the war.

I got the word one day that Cummings had come up to Tagap Ga, a village on the refugee trail. So, I decided to pull another *kunkuman*. I struck out before daylight, and I walked until I got to the village. J. R. Wilson also happened to be at Tagap right then. He had been assigned to what they called the V Force, British special forces in Burma. As I mentioned, he had been at Hkalak Ga at the time of the attack and had gone back and made his report. They'd bumped him up from captain to lieutenant colonel in the V Force and sent him back in. He established his headquarters at Tagap. As a result of my meeting with Cummings and Wilson, shortly after I made my way back to Pebu, I got the message that I was being transferred to the V Force, British special forces. I was no longer a liaison officer with the Chinese. I was to work under Wilson's command.

PART III

WITH THE V FORCE

March 1943–April 1944

First Assignment

It was early March 1943, when I cut loose from Pebu. Somebody else was assigned as liaison officer; I don't remember who. I went up to Tagap Ga, where the V Force was preparing the way for a major offensive involving all three Chinese divisions. The divisions were eventually to move from Assam over the old refugee trail, down into the Hukawng Valley, and on across upper Burma. The engineers were to follow and build a road from Assam through the major town of Myitkyina and on to connect with the Burma Road. Our outfit was to provide intelligence for the operation.

My first mission with the V Force under Wilson was to reconnoiter the Hukawng Valley, to check out the upper reaches of its river system, see if it was navigable, and find where the enemy was. The Hukawng was a huge, sparsely populated area at the time. It was mostly jungle, and maybe fifty miles square, with mountains all the way around it and the river coming out at the south-western end. Two Kachins had been with Wilson a long time. One was named Goitum Kamai, and the other, Nawji. He assigned those two men to go with me into the Hukawng. To begin with, we planned to explore the upper reaches of the Tarung Hka, a river that comes into the valley from high up in the mountains. It starts up north around Chaukan Pass between India and Burma, at near ten thousand feet. There was a Kachin village up there, Tarung Hku. Somebody had given headquarters information that a lot of people from the Hukawng had fled there when the Japanese came into the valley, so we headed there first.

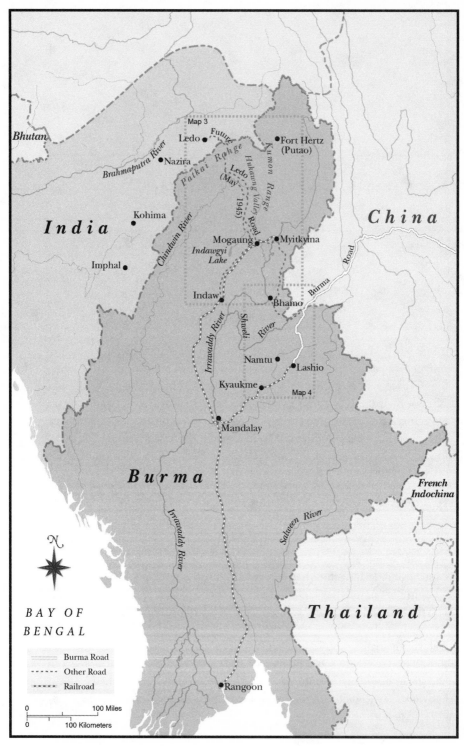

Map 2: Burma (now Myanmar) showing areas covered in Maps 3 and 4, and the future course of the Ledo Road under construction at the time.

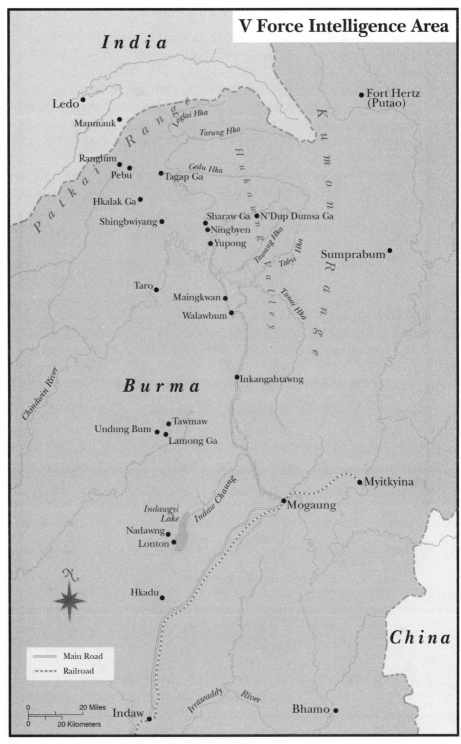

Map 3: The area in northern Burma where Pete Lutken conducted intelligence-gathering activities with the V Force and early assignments with the OSS.

Our plan was to walk to Tarung Hku, get what information we could, then build a raft and ride down the Tarung Hka River, get out somewhere in the middle and do our reconnoitering. So we stocked up with rations, weapons, ammunition, and a map and then started off on foot toward the village. To get there, we had to cross some tributaries of the Tarung Hka. The first, called Nam Yun, ran west to east, right north of Tagap. The water was pretty high, but we roamed up and down and finally found a ford. The river was roaring, but with staffs to help us, we managed to get across.

When we reached the other side, it started raining, and for several days, we walked in the pouring-down rain. Along the way, we ran into a group of Nagas headed in the same direction. They had on these great big hats called *kabans*, which resemble umbrellas without stalks and are worn with a strap under the chin. Going through a village, I got me a *kaban*, too. I had started off in India with only a cap, but it afforded very little protection against rain. While in Assam, I had encountered an American nurse wearing a campaign hat. When I saw that campaign hat with that big, broad brim, I complained about the fact that I didn't have one, so she said, "I'm going to be inside most of the time. I'll just give you this one," and I wore it for the rest of the war. But the *kaban* was better in the pouring rain, so I used it during this trip. I remember walking with this great big hat on as the rain poured off, and thinking what a great idea it was.

We walked in the rain along with the Nagas, seven of them. They were headed toward a Naga village just up the hill from Tarung Hku. Nagas didn't like to come down low. They said they all got malaria, so they lived in the highest places. We had quite a crowd then: me, Goitum Kamai, Nawji, and the Nagas, all with our *kabans* on. In the midst of the constant downpour, we came to another tributary of the Tarung River, which came down from the northwest, called Loglai Hka.

Crossing the Loglai Hka

When we got to the Loglai Hka, it was a raging torrent, about seventy-five or eighty yards wide, moving so fast you could hear the rocks rumbling, "bump, bump, bump," big rocks actually moving around in the current. We couldn't figure how in the world we were going to get across. Somebody in our crowd pointed out a raft on the other side. I could barely see it, high up on the bank. I figured maybe I could get over there and bring the raft back to our side. The water was swift as the devil, and most of my gang couldn't swim. They were mountain people. So it was up to me, and I didn't see another way to get across within a reasonable length of time.

I took off everything but my shorts and walked upriver barefooted, with a large knife in a scabbard slung around my shoulder. The bank was matted with vines and stickers, so half the time I walked in the water. I finally managed to scramble about a mile upstream, then gritted my teeth, cast off, and swam as hard as I could to the other side. By the time I made it across, the current had carried me to a spot about even with the rest of my crowd. I climbed up the bank to the raft. It was about twenty feet long and about five feet wide, made out of bamboo lashed together. There were a couple of paddles on it. Somebody had obviously been using it to get back and forth across the river when it was a much milder stream. I cut a vine and tied it to the raft and then struggled for probably an hour to pull the raft up across from the place where I had taken off swimming. Then I cut a long bamboo pole with a hook on it where a branch came out, figuring that I could use that for the men to grab and pull me in. The pole was about fifteen feet long. I put it in the raft, tied the extra paddle onto the raft, and set sail. And, man, I had a ride. It was terrifying. I wasn't sure whether I'd to be able to stop that thing or not. I went racing along, and I got pretty close to the men. As I went by, they were able to catch the end of the bamboo pole. I managed to brace myself and hang on, and they swung me around and grabbed the raft when it hit the bank. There we were.

We went to work, made more paddles with what we could find, and fitted everybody with one. We worked and scraped, dragging the damn raft up through the rapids until we finally got roughly a mile back upstream. Then we all got on. There were too many of us. We were ankle deep in water, just barely floating, but being foolhardy, I made the decision to go ahead. I did tell everyone, "Whatever happens, hang onto the raft. Don't let go, or you'll be a goner." I was the last one holding the raft while folks got on. Then I jumped in, and off we went.

All of us paddled furiously, but as we approached the other side, a current came boiling out from the bank, pushing us away. Trying with all our might, we just couldn't get close enough. We had the pole with the hook and got to where we could reach something on the bank. Although three or four of us held that pole tight, it was jerked clean out of our hands by the muddy torrent. The vine was still tied to the raft, so in desperation, I tied the other end of it around me. I had foolishly put on all my clothes before I got back on the raft, including shoes and everything, so I jumped off of that raft with all my clothes on and the vine around my waist, and made my way close to shore. At that particular spot, there was no bank to speak of, just tall grass growing in the water, so I grabbed armfuls of grass trying to stop the raft. I uprooted huge clumps, but it slipped through my hands.

All the time, I could hear a roar ahead where the Loglai Hka branch we were on was running into the Tarung Hka, the main river. If we didn't stop quick, we were going to be carried into the Tarung Hka and all the way to the other side of it, away from the village. By that time, everybody had stopped paddling. They didn't know what to do. I yelled and screamed at them to paddle, but in spite of their best efforts, we all went sailing out into the Tarung Hka, a huge river, at least three times as big as the Loglai Hka and all rapids, nothing slow moving, no pool, just powerful fast-moving water.

The Tarung Hka was at flood stage, and the bank where we were headed was underwater, but there were a lot of trees. With all my clothes on, the knife hanging on me, and vine still tied to me, I swam like a dog to get to the bank. I finally managed to get close enough to where I could grab a hold of a tree about a foot in diameter. The water was roaring past it. I grabbed that tree and wrapped myself and the vine around it. When the raft hit the end of that vine, I hung on for dear life. The vine jerked the raft to a stop and then jerked everybody off of it. They all went overboard into the water, and the vine broke at about the same time. I was completely exhausted, and I just hung onto that dadgum tree until I got my breath back. The raft and all of my buddies were in the water. Every now and then, I'd see a head come up as they went around the bend. It was a helpless situation.

I half swam and half walked up onto solid ground. By that time, it was getting dark, so I began walking as fast as I could downstream. I had lost everything I had except my map, my knife, and whatever I had in my pockets. It was slow going because of dense jungle, particularly on that side. There wasn't human habitation anywhere near. East of the Tarung Hka, for miles there was nothing, nobody, no nothing. About every fifty yards, I would let out a whoop, hoping I'd get an answer. I kept walking until I guess about ten at night, bungling my way through the jungle in the dark. At last, I heard an answer to my whoop; somebody hollered, and I yelled again. Somebody else whooped down the way. That kept up as I got closer and closer.

Finally, I came to my bedraggled group. Two of the Nagas were missing, and we just had to assume they had drowned. The group told me that most of them managed to grab back onto the raft and sailed on downstream maybe seven or eight miles from where the two rivers came together. There was a great big, bushy tree still connected to the bank, with lots of limbs down in the water. As they came whirling around a bend, they ran right into that tree, and the men were able to climb onto the limbs and get out. They just let the raft go.

We had a few things tied on the raft, but the men didn't have presence of mind or strength to get them; they were exhausted, so whatever was on the raft was gone. Everybody, including me, had lost his rifle, all except Nawji. He had managed to hold onto his. But the overwhelming tragedy was that we'd lost two men. We whooped and hollered and hoped that maybe they would answer. But we couldn't go downstream any farther. It was pitch-black dark, and we needed to get up onto the bank, where we weren't in danger of being flooded out.

To Tarung Hku by Land

High up on the river bank, we found a place flat enough for a shelter. There were lots of big plantain trees around, which are a lot like banana trees. We cut forked sticks to make a framework and used those wide banana-like leaves to cover the structure. Then we gathered wood. I had a pocketknife, my big Kachin knife, and my Boy Scout Waterproof Marble Matchbox still in my pocket. I kept that thing for years. I suppose it's gone now, but that matchbox was among the few things that saved us. We split good sized wood to get to the driest parts at the center, and even in the driving rainstorm, we managed to get a fire started. And I'm telling you, that was the most beautiful fire I'd ever seen in my life. We were all dripping wet and freezing cold. The lean-to wasn't waterproof by a long shot, but it knocked off most of the rain. And with the fire, we were okay.

Then at daylight, Nawji, the man who had managed to preserve his rifle, went out to see what he could get for food. His gun had ten cartridges in it. A British Short Magazine Lee Enfield holds ten rounds. We heard one shot, and he made his way back with a little brown monkey. We gutted him and, hair and all, put him face down on the fire. I guess we could have tried to skin him, but we were so tired, we elected just to roast him whole. It was the most unappetizing thing you can imagine. It looked like a little baby being roasted. The hair all burned off of it, and it smelled like the dickens. But we ate because that was our meal for the day; we didn't have anything else, just one small singed monkey to share between eight of us.

I still had my map. It was in the case but completely drenched. We could just barely make things out, but we knew that we were on the south side of the river and downstream from Tarung Hku, the village. It took us almost two days just to get back up to the confluence of the two rivers and then another day from there. At that point, the river was running almost east to west, and Tarung Hku was on the north side. We whooped and hollered when we found ourselves opposite the village. They heard us and came down to the bank. They knew what they were doing and ferried us across easily. They had stout poles, a very big raft, two men operating it, and they took half of us and then came back and got the rest. We were wet and cold and hungry and tired, and thankfully, they took us in. I guess we stayed there about a week. They were happy to give us whatever information they had about the Japanese, and while there, we worked to build a really good raft with a stout rudder on the back. The first raft had been slap-dash. Looking back, that crossing had been a crazy fool effort. We should have camped for a week at the riverside and prepared. Another bitter lesson: if you don't prepare for the worst, it'll be there waiting for you.

Surprising to me, the Nagas who had accompanied us were very grateful, even though they'd lost two men. One of the survivors was the headman of their village up on the hill. They invited us to come there, way up, a couple thousand feet above Tarung Hku. They had a feast, and the whole village celebrated the fact that we had arrived safely. Even though we'd lost the two, the others were grateful to be alive.

After that, we went back down and finished our raft. There was plenty of giant bamboo, and the folks there didn't mind us taking whatever we needed. As a matter of fact, the whole village pitched in to help. The raft was a monster, about twenty feet long, with a platform in the middle about a foot above the main structure. We made extra paddles and poles. Since there were only the three of us, we could sit on the platform and ride like kings. But we still didn't have any weapons or ammunition except the one rifle, all because of my poor judgment.

Rafting the Tarung Hka

We cast off where the Tarung River ran east to west. After it joined the Loglai, it began to curve around to the south and came within a day's march of Tagap Ga. So we stopped at the spot closest to Tagap, and Nawji and Goitum Kamai, and I got out and hiked there to get re-equipped. We got rifles and food, mostly salt and rice. They had just come out with a new thing called a D ration. It was supposed to be a survival food. Each bar was about the size of a cake of soap, wrapped in wax paper and packed in a box. One of those bars a day was supposed to be enough to keep you alive, not a meal, more like a big candy bar consisting of oatmeal and maybe some other kind of grain, chocolate, and a lot of sugar. Since we planned on being gone a few weeks, I thought we could use them as a backup ration. It was my great experiment.

We gathered our supplies and struck out to the raft. Once we got on the river, it quickly got even faster and bigger. It was the most spectacular thing you can imagine, almost one long rapid the whole way. Every now and then, we'd run into a pool of quiet, deep water, but most of the time it was a long, rocky ride with huge standing waves and rapids, the biggest, roughest river with the most vicious white water I've ever been in. But we managed to stay afloat on our stout raft and stopped each night to camp on the bank.

At one point, the Tarung Hka ran alongside a cliff that looked like it might be a thousand feet high. A river called the Gedu Hka came in from the east there. As we approached the junction, there were waterfalls coming over the top of the cliff that never reached the main river; they just turned into mist before they hit. Traveling under that cliff was stunning. The sun shining through the mist made a beautiful circular rainbow. Shortly after that, we encountered one rapid after another. We were barely able to stay right-side up, working like dogs to keep in the middle of the river and avoid rocks and all sorts of obstacles. We didn't know whether we were going to run into waterfalls or what. There were no people, no villages, just wild jungle, and the map was not that exact.

We saw huge fish as we went along. Later I learned they were mahseer, a kind of giant carp. They looked like porpoises; some of them must have been six or eight feet long. We'd be paddling along steadily, and all of a sudden one of those things would swim alongside us, its back coming up out of the water. I'd never seen anything like them before. Of course, Nawji and Goitum Kamai knew what they were and assured me that they were not man-eating creatures.

When we passed the Skadu Hka River, there was a big rumpus where the two rivers came together. All of a sudden, we began to hear a deep roar. The rapids make a lot of racket anyway, but this was louder. It didn't sound good, so we decided to head for the bank. We hoped to get out and plan a route, but the water was too swift and powerful. In spite of frantic efforts with poles and paddles, we were fast approaching an area where a big rockfall had come off the cliff and dammed up the river. As we got nearer, we could see that there was a narrow place where the river had overtopped and washed out a sluice in the middle of the rockfall. We realized that we were going to go through that sluice, no matter what we did.

When it became apparent that we had to let the river take us, we grabbed a hold of the platform in the middle. Then the raft breasted the top. And I'm telling you, it was a long and wild ride. The water went down several hundred feet, not a straight fall but a long steep slope of smooth, swift water. At the bottom of the whole thing was a giant standing wave, and we were headed for it. I don't know how many miles an hour we were going, but I know we were traveling at a high rate of speed. Down we went. We hit that standing wave just like a submarine. The raft and everything and all of us went completely underwater. We were torn off of the raft, and tumbled every which way, struggling for air.

I guess I was the first one to get my head above water, and I commenced to looking around. I was amidst big waves, couldn't see very far, and was still traveling fast, but I spotted the raft. It was upside down, but I could see it. And then a head popped up over here, and then another one popped up over there. Thank goodness both of my men had gotten their heads above water. I hollered at them to try to get to the raft. They spotted it, and even though they had said they couldn't swim, they managed to thrash around and get to it. Then with the aid of the waves, we turned the raft right side up.

The raft was crosswise of the river, but we managed to get on it. The extra paddles and the poles and everything we had tied on had stayed with it. We hadn't lost the sweep either, nothing but the paddles in hand. So our preparation had paid off. The rifles were still lashed to the raft. I don't think we really lost anything. Even my shoes were still tied on. We made it through, and that was the last really bad spot.

The mountains tapered off from that point, and the cliffs and the rugged terrain on either side began to ease up. As we moved into more gentle territory, the water smoothed out, and we coasted along, still at a pretty good clip. We didn't have to paddle much; the current of the river carried us. And we began to see a lot of magnificent wildlife. I remember we went by a gravel bar, and there was a great herd of pigs, wild pigs of some kind. They spotted us, grunted, and took off into the bushes. We saw deer, big deer called "sambar." They almost looked like elk. There were bunches of them along the bank, and they would pick up their heads and stare at us as we passed by. The most spectacular sight we saw was a herd of elephants. We came around a bend, and there they were out in the water, about belly deep. You couldn't count them; they were all bunched together, but there must have been at least a dozen, maybe more. When they saw us, they trumpeted and charged out of the water and into the woods. The great big bull stayed behind, he flapped his ears and watched us, and then he wheeled around and disappeared into the jungle.

Pretty quickly after that, we figured from the map that we were getting near civilization, so we quit traveling in daylight. The first village along the bank was called Sharaw Ga, which means "Tiger Town" or "Tiger Village." The folks at Tarung Hku had told us the Japanese were there, so as we approached it, we moved only at night.

First Stop at Sharaw Ga

We kept a close watch since we knew there would be paddy fields along the river upstream of Sharaw Ga. Paddy huts were always some distance from the villages. That time of year, March or thereabouts, women and children were usually out in the fields preparing to plant rice. The men did the clearing. They'd cut the trees down and do the heavy stuff, and if they had oxen or buffaloes, they would plow, but the women did most of the weeding and tending. We stopped at the first firelight we spotted. I sent Nawji by himself to check with the inhabitants of a paddy hut, hoping he could sound them out while we waited by the riverbank. He wasn't wearing a uniform, and he didn't carry a gun, just his knife, like any Kachin. He was gone for about an hour.

We already knew from the folks at Tarung Hku that the headman of Sharaw Ga, Sharaw Tang Hkam, had fled with much of his village when the Japanese came in, but a few folks were still around. Nawji found out there was a Japanese contingent of around a hundred men in the village and a much larger force about ten miles further down, in a village called Ningbyen. That village was actually half Shan and half Kachin. That whole countryside had at one time been inhabited by folks called Hkamti Shans, but long ago, the Kachins had come out of the north and gradually pushed most of the Shans out of the Hukawng Valley. There was only one village left in the Hukawng that had any Shans in it, and that was Ningbyen, and it was approximately half Kachin and half Hkamti Shan.

We learned that the Kachin chief, or *duwa*, was a fellow named N'ding Zau Awng. The Shan chief was subservient to him. I found out later, there was a similar situation at the village of Shingbwiyang. The Shingbwiyang *duwa* was not only the head of Shingbwiyang, but also of several Naga villages around, including Hkalak Ga. Whenever the people killed a deer, they were supposed to give a thigh to the chief. The set-up was called *magee shi. Magee* means the thigh. So the Shingbwiyang *duwa* was the eater of thighs from many villages. Well, N'ding Zau Awng, he's the one that got the deer thighs from the Shans in Ningbyen.

When Nawji returned, he suggested we all go meet the folks in the paddy hut. They disliked the Japanese and wanted to help, so they arranged to send one of their boys down to Ningbyen to get hold of N'ding Zau Awng and bring him back up to see us, all in secret. They had some canoes, so this boy paddled down to Ningbyen, several miles away. During the intervening time, we learned a lot from the folks in the hut about the Japanese locations, strength, trails, and patrol patterns. Finally, the boy came back and brought N'ding Zau Awng. It was the middle of the night, but brighter, since the moon had risen.

N'ding Zau Awng

I met N'ding Zau Awng in the paddy hut. The very first thing he said was, "I'd like for you to come with me to Ningbyen. We need to talk to the Shan headman, too." So he and I and Nawji and Goitum Kamai and the boy got in long dugout canoes. In the bright moonlight, we paddled down river to Ningbyen. After Sharaw Ga, the river was placid, winding through a level plain, with a few humps of hills here and there. Sharaw itself was on the west side on a long ridge that went parallel to the river. The ridge extended past the village and then leveled off. There was a large open field between Sharaw Ga and Ningbyen.

It was a quick trip to Ningbyen since the water was fast. We pulled up on a gravel bar. I could speak some Kachin by this time, and I asked N'ding Zau Awng, "Tell me, which direction are the Japanese? Where is the camp?" He said, "It's right over yonder," and pointed to it. Then he pointed another way and said, "We're going to my house." So we walked. I held tight to my rifle as we went past a bunch of houses in the moonlight. We had no trouble at all seeing where we were going. Every now and then a dog would bark, but otherwise it was quiet. We got a good look at the large open field between Sharaw Ga and Ningbyen and then came to N'ding Zau Awng's house, a real headman's house, Kachin style.

The thing that separated a Kachin headman's house from all the other houses was the center post in the middle of the front porch. It was like a Greek column, carved very carefully, smooth, just like something off of the Parthenon, bigger at the bottom, with this graceful curve to the top. We entered up a log that had toeholds cut in it and went past the front part of the house into a room back behind a wall, so we weren't exposed to the outside world. When we got there, several others were waiting for us. They had a fire going. N'ding Zau Awng introduced me to the two or three Kachins that were sitting there, and he said, "Now I will go and get the Shan chief."

We had been warned about the Shans. They were Buddhists like the Japanese and pretty much supported the Japanese; not all, but many did, so it was almost like we were fixing to confer with the enemy. I put my rifle across my knees. We carried on a little idle talk while we waited. I asked a few questions in my limited Kachin, like how many Japanese were there and did they know the number of the unit and what was the rank of the man in charge. They said there was a major in charge. They knew that much. That gave me some idea of the size of the operation, probably a battalion. They said most of them were right there in Ningbyen, but there was also the outpost up at Sharaw Ga, another bunch at Yupong, a river crossing further down, and another at Ningam Sakan, a place halfway between Yupong and Shingbwiyang, on the refugee trail.

I sat there until the Shan chief came. He could speak Kachin, so we talked in Kachin. I tried to make a speech. I said roughly, "I'm the first of many Americans who will come here. The Japanese have taken most of Burma, but it is the intention of the British Indian Army and the Americans and the Chinese to drive the Japanese out, and we would appreciate any help we can get. I'm here as a scout to check into the situation, and I'm asking you to help us if you can and to keep your people out of the way if you can't. We don't want to hurt anybody. The battle will come to this place because the Japanese are here. So please be warned, when this begins, and I don't know when it's going to begin, but it will, my advice to you is to either help us or go back into the jungle for your safety." They all seemed to agree. At least they didn't disagree. But the Shan chief pretty much had to do what N'ding Zau Awng told him. The conference lasted for maybe half an hour.

When we left it was still night. The moon was moving into the west by this time. We went back down to the river, got into the canoes, and poled our way back. Before we got to Sharaw Ga, the river made a big loop, so we took a shortcut, left the canoes, and went back on foot to the paddy field and hid nearby. We waited until the next night and then set sail again on our raft. The river was relatively smooth from this point, so we went on down without any trouble. There was an island in the river. We managed to go around the east side of it, away from settled areas, and on down close to Yupong, where we'd been told there was a Japanese cantonment. We pulled out before that, at a place where there was no sign of anyone, dragged the raft ashore, dismantled it, set the pieces adrift, and continued on foot.

Graffiti

We made a gigantic loop through the jungle after we scuttled the raft. We skirted around along the banks of the Tanai Hka at daybreak, reconnoitering the river to see what it looked like. The land was entirely different, almost level. In the deep forest, there were huge trees but not much undergrowth, so it was not too difficult to travel. We went along the Tanai for quite a piece, then cut north towards the village of Ningam Sakan, near the Japanese outpost that N'ding Zau Awng had told us about. We assumed they would have patrols out, and we were on the lookout for them.

We approached Ningam Sakan the next morning before daylight and came on a clearing. We had been told that the Japanese had made a parade ground there. We could see a shelter on the north side of the opening, so we proceeded carefully. The field wasn't very big, just an open space in the jungle with one tree in the center of it. The Japanese camp was farther to the north. It didn't look like anyone was in the shelter. At that point, I was feeling my oats, and in the gray, misty dawn, I decided I'd leave a message for the Japanese. The big tree had smooth bark like a beech tree, so I hurriedly scratched on it with my knife; I hate to use bad words, but I was young and didn't know any better. I carved a message that said, "Kiss my ass, you yellow bastards!" Then we departed. Not all that bright a move, but satisfying at the time. And by the way, that anecdote got written up in *YANK* magazine.

We continued on toward Shingbwiyang, and by this time, we were down to our emergency rations, the so-called D-rations. Come to find out, those bars were disgusting. The mixture of oatmeal, or rolled oats, chocolate, and I forget what else, quickly got to be too much. Eating one occasionally would have been fine, but we were trying to live off of them. The Kachins didn't like them at all. They didn't like sweet things very much, claimed sweets gave them tuberculosis or respiratory problems, cough, and sore throat. Besides that, they were used to consuming a great volume of rice. They normally got the standard Indian Army ration, the rice version primarily given to Hindu troops, which consisted of two pounds of rice per man per day. That's a lot of rice. Anyway, we ate those chocolate D rations for nearly two weeks. My compatriots, Nawji and Goitum Kamai, complained bitterly. They were busy trying to gather edible plants from the jungle as we went along, so they could at least chew on something that had a little more substance to it.

We scouted out the jungle in the southwestern corner of the Hukawng Valley, including the river that comes through Shingbwiyang and goes south to the Tanai. It appeared to be navigable. As it turned out, later on, our side ended up using it to great advantage. By the time we got to Shingbwiyang, we were powerful tired of eating D-ration bars. Every time we belched, it tasted like chocolate, when we broke wind, it smelled like chocolate, and when we went to the bathroom, it resembled chocolate kisses!

Shingbwiyang had been burned to the ground by the Japanese when they moved out. Nothing was left of it when we got there but the charred remnants of houses, mostly the vertical posts. Those big uprights were still standing, but everything else was completely consumed, and everyone had left. By now it was April, and things were beginning to grow. There in Shingbwiyang, we found a wonderful surprise: tomatoes! The Kachins had obviously planted them. The vines were all over the ground, and as we walked through the ruins of the town, little tomatoes were everywhere. I reckon Bill Cummings must have brought the seeds. Man, after having eaten nothing but those disgusting chocolate oat bars for a couple of weeks, we plunged into them. We just sat in the ruins of Shingbwiyang, "hrrg, hrrg, hrrg," wolfing down the best tomatoes I ever ate.

The Refugee's Plight

From Shingbwiyang, we went up to Shamdak Ku to check that trail out; then we started up the main refugee trail. We climbed onto the mountain barrier that surrounded the Hukawng Valley. The narrow gorge at the southwest corner of the valley looked like a perfect place to build a big dam; you'd end up with a huge lake of maybe a thousand square miles. Of course, you wouldn't want to do that because an incredibly beautiful area would be lost, but Burma is full of those bowls. I don't know what kind of geological formation they are, but the Hukawng Valley is the biggest of them.

We went through the mountain barrier on a path of hairpin turns and came to another bowl, Dalu Valley, or Taru, some people call it. It's a good deal smaller, but still with mountains all the way around and a narrow exit. We continued climbing through the mountains north to Chingloo Sakan and headed for Tagap on the Refugee Trail. By then, there was just a trickle of refugees, but we saw evidence of the earlier tragedy of epic proportions, now mostly forgotten by history. As we followed the trail north, we ran into a series of parallel rivers running east and west, and we encountered refugees, just a few, but we saw literally thousands of the dead.

The bulk of the refugees had made their attempt during the previous monsoon. So in 1943, we saw a few stragglers, and the dead, mostly from the year before, when the main exodus had occurred. There were places on a hillside where the travelers had built lean-tos, each maybe one hundred feet long. They had constructed them up off the ground, made them out of poles, and covered them with leaves. Folks had stayed there waiting for the rivers to go down. But they had starved while they were waiting. We saw skeletons lying side by side. Probably a hundred people in each shelter, all reduced to rotting remains, with tattered clothes still hanging on them. Every now and then we'd notice baubles that the women wear still decorating a corpse, but most had been looted. Buzzards were all over the place. I can't describe how awful it was.

Most of the folks had come all the way from the southern part of Burma, running from the Japanese. There were different groups: civil servants, moneylenders, folks with other unpopular occupations, and foreigners, mostly Chinese and Indians. When the British were driven out, these folks had to get out, too, and there was no way out except to walk. The Japanese had closed off most exits, so the refugees ended up in two general areas. One was on the western side of Burma towards Imphal, to the south of us. There was just a track there, not a real a road, and Nagas, some of whom were headhunters, lived there. Imphal itself was in a big bowl, like the Hukawng Valley, in the middle of the Naga Hills. Most of the British Indian Army went out that way, but the Chinese Army and many civilians went north.

Every now and then we'd run into something odd. A tailor, whose livelihood was his sewing machine, had lugged that darn thing up to the Okatohap Pass, eight thousand feet. In the end, he didn't make it. He dropped his sewing machine and died right there by it. We also saw bicycles and other things that you wouldn't think anybody would carry in flight from a brutal enemy, but they couldn't bring themselves to let go of their most valued possessions. Nobody was equipped to handle themselves in the jungle, and they got sick, they got malaria, they ran out of food and starved to death. There were so many skeletons along there, it was too sad to even think about.

The British and the Americans had tried to help. For a while they manned aid stations about a day's march apart, with first aid teams and supplies. But in a way, it was a grim joke. So many people died, others would pick up skulls and stick them on sticks just to mark the trail. Children, women, old folks, nobody will ever know how many died there; it's bound to have been in the hundreds of thousands. In some of those camps, I would just guess, there could have been four or five thousand corpses in the rudimentary shelters that we saw. It had been raining like the devil and the river as impossible for them to cross as the Atlantic Ocean. They died waiting.

On to Tagap

We climbed up to Chingloo Sakan and camped off the trail. While we were busy getting ready for the night, we heard a noise. Two Chinese soldiers were coming down the trail. The nearest Chinese at the time were at Tagap, seven- or eight-days' march away. I walked out and stopped them. I said "*Hao bu hao,*" and they grinned and replied "*Hao.*" I tried to talk to them with what little Chinese I knew and wondered what I should do about them. They were obviously deserters, but taking prisoners was an impossibility in our situation. It passed through my mind that we might ought to shoot them since the Japanese would probably eventually catch them, and they might give away information. But I finally decided that the men had no idea what was going on, and the Japanese wouldn't to be able to get anything of value from them. So I bid them goodbye, and they headed off. Maybe we should have shot them. But on the other hand, c'est la guerre, we let them go.

After that, we made our way back to Tagap which, by this time, was occupied by an allied battalion. A big quartermaster setup was there. A fellow named John Allen was in charge of the drop down. He had about four or five Black soldiers under his command. The army was still segregated, and there were a bunch of Black outfits in Burma, mostly quartermaster staff and some of the engineers who were building the Ledo Road through extremely rough and dangerous territory. Also, Dr. Gordon Seagrave, another Burmese-born American missionary, had set up a hospital there at Tagap. It was down in a draw on the east side. The Chinese occupied the higher ground that overlooked the trail coming up from the Hukawng Valley.

I got back to Tagap and made my report, wrote it by hand. Long after the war, a man I knew from Houston called me. He said he had run into a fellow named Ben Gearhart from Marfa, Texas, who still had a copy of my report of that first reconnaissance in the spring of 1943. They had typed it up and given copies to all of the American liaison officers in that area. He faxed it to me. I don't know where it is now, but it's here somewhere. I got in touch with Ben himself later. He was a veterinarian and a rancher and had worked with animal transport over there. Over the phone he remarked, "I followed you down through there," and he jokingly said, "The only reason I didn't catch up with you was that I had those damn mules with me."

When I got back to Tagap, Colonel Wilson was ensconced there in a *basha*. He had a cook who was half Naga and half something else, Indian, I think. His name was Katchka. Everybody liked to go and visit Wilson because Katchka was a real good cook. He could make anything. At that time, Wilson had just gotten a radio. Wilson and I visited for quite a while and went over the intelligence I'd gathered. Johnny Colling was also there, another fellow I had met in Ramgarh. He was a reserve officer who had been born and raised in China. He had come back to the United States, gotten a commission, and ended up in Burma because he could speak Chinese. He had also recently been assigned to the V Force. We crossed paths many times after that.

The Power of Nature

Tagap was V Force headquarters for a long time, and I got back there every once in a while. Seagrave had his hospital there, with several nurses and a contingent of Friends, or Quaker corpsmen. The Friends were Englishmen. They were ambulance drivers and medics who had gotten caught on the wrong side of everything. When the Japanese drove north, the Friends retreated with the British forces. They had to abandon their ambulances and walk out on foot. They fell in with Seagrave, who had volunteered his whole hospital to be a part of the Chinese American operation. So they were at Tagap, working at his bamboo hospital down in the valley.

A lot of hilarity went on down there. Those Englishmen loved to sing. With what little recreation time they had, they were always putting on skits and plays and singing songs. One of their favorite songs was "Green Grow the Rushes, Ho." They never sat down to a meal without singing it. And the nurses would sing too. It was like a big party, in spite of the war and all the hard work. And they always seemed to have something good to eat. When I was passing through from time to time, the crew down at Seagrave's hospital would invite me to supper, and it was always a great treat.

My shoes would often give out, and all through the war, I kept sending messages back, "Send me some shoes, size 12," so I got the nickname from these hospital characters of "Bigfoot." There was a wonderful Burmese nurse there by the name of Than Shwe, who loved to make jokes. She is still alive today, and we have exchanged letters for many years. She called me Bigfoot, so I said, "Well, if I'm Bigfoot, you're Little Foot." So she got the nickname Little Foot. She was the only Burmese nurse. Koi, who was the head nurse, was a Shan.

As I mentioned, the Chinese battalion was stationed there at Tagap, also the American quartermaster unit, and the engineer group. Lieutenant Hardison, who was laying out the trace for the Ledo road, was the head of the engineering operation. He had a group of dedicated soldiers with him, and a compass, a map, and a clinometer. His instructions were not to exceed a grade steeper than 1 in 12. Basically, they had to go where the compass and the clinometer carried them; they couldn't just follow any trail. Those engineers did an incredible job.

The engineers lived up top. The next hut down was the V Force hut, on the side of the mountain. One side of the hut was on the ground, and the other side was about eight or ten feet up on stilts since it sat on a very steep slope. Seagrave and his hospital were at the end of the line, down the hill by the creek We were all facing the same direction, toward the Nam Yun Hka, the river at the bottom of the canyon.

One night, while I was back there, we were asleep on the floor of our hut. The only light inside was the flickering fire in our firebox. The moon was nearly full, very bright, the night as clear as could be. We were waked up suddenly. It felt like some gigantic hand had taken a hold of the hut and was giving it heck, whipping it back and forth. It was an earthquake and gives me the chills to think about it even now. The building that was supposed to be stable was acting like some giant hand was shaking the living hell out of it. We woke up everyone who wasn't already awake with cries of, "Get out of here!" and we all jumped up and ran outside, as though that would do any good. Even if the whole bamboo hut had fallen in on us, it couldn't have hurt us very badly because there wasn't much to it in the first place.

Anyhow, we ran outside like bees out of a jostled hive. Across the canyon, which was covered with forest, we watched a huge landslide take place. A section of the side of the hill just peeled off, followed after a slight delay by a tremendous roar. Trees and dirt and everything went sliding down the side of the mountain and toppled into the river below. There were several different shocks. It seemed to me that the earthquake lasted on and off maybe fifteen or twenty minutes. Seeing the other side of the canyon come thundering down, we wondered if our side might go down too. But it didn't. Luckily, it was dry. If it had been raining, there's no telling what would have happened.

All this took place in the glow of bright moonlight in the depth of a still night. In the midst of war, having seen and heard bombs, gunfire, and crashing planes, this seemed somehow more powerful, more awesome. Later on, when I did get down to the valley floor, I saw where the landslide had dammed up the river, forming a lake. Fortunately, the water didn't back up to where the main trail crossed the river. This dam, though, it must have been nearly a hundred yards long, made of a mass of dirt and huge trees tilted at random angles. The landslide had been terrifying but beautiful in a strange way. Out of the whole incredible event, the thing I remember most was the cloud of dust roiling upwards. It obscured the landslide as everything went down. The huge column rose up into the sky just like smoke and took a long time to drift away. It just hung in the air, lit by the moon.

Other Enemies

Earthquakes were not the most dangerous aspect of mother nature we had to face. In the rainy season, there were clouds of mosquitoes. They were everywhere—we couldn't keep them off—and they carried serious and sometimes fatal diseases, cerebral malaria probably the most feared. Soldiers I knew died from it. I kept covered up as best I could with green fatigues, a jacket, really more like a long sleeve shirt, which hung outside of my britches, and long pants. Nevertheless, the mosquitoes bit anywhere they could get at me. I eventually got malaria myself, but not the worst variety.

And there was an absolute plague of leeches. No one could get away from them. There was one variety on the land and a different type in the water. On trails, they weren't too bad, but in the jungle itself, constantly fighting the undergrowth, we couldn't escape them. They varied in size from maybe one to two inches long. They didn't seem to have eyes, but they could tell folks were coming, maybe by vibration or smell or something. As we walked through the undergrowth, why, every leaf or frond seemed to have one on it. When they detected someone's presence, they stood up on one end and began waving around, preparing to glom on.

Sometimes we'd use sharpened pieces of bamboo to scrape them off. But to really get anywhere, we just had to ignore them. They would get inside our britches; they'd get inside of our socks. We wore British puttees, wool strips about three feet long or so. We'd carefully wrap them tight around the top of our shoes and stick our britches into them, but the leeches would somehow get inside. They'd cut little triangular holes in us, like little three-pointed stars, and merrily suck our blood. A leech no bigger than a pencil lead would swell up as big as your thumb, bulging with blood. Frequently, they'd fall down into our shoes, and we'd squeeze the blood out of them as we walked, squishing along in shoes filled with our own blood. We used to joke about folks who experienced trouble in the genital region. When the leeches invaded some soft part, it would turn purple and swell up. But the worst thing was when they got in your mouth or your nose. Once I woke up with a leech way down in my throat. I practically had to get my whole fist in my mouth to pull him out.

We went to extreme lengths to fend them off at night. We'd cut four forked sticks, drive them into the ground, stretch a couple of poles across the head and foot, then place a bunch of small flexible poles lengthwise to make sleeping platforms up off the ground. If we could build a fire, we would take the ashes and pile them around each one of those forked sticks. The leeches couldn't cross those ashes; salt will dissolve things like snails and leeches, and so will ashes.

We had no sleeping bags, just blankets, and pieces of canvas to keep off rain. Later, we were given ponchos, but they never completely kept the water off. We just got wet. At some point, I got hold of a mattress cover and slit it halfway down one side to make an impromptu sleeping bag. It was long enough to where I could pull it up over my head, and made of heavy enough cotton to where mosquitos couldn't bite through it. I slept in that cotton mattress cover for most of the war. There were strings to tie it together, but I never used those. I just climbed inside and held it shut.

The conditions there were not like in the Rocky Mountains where the air is dry and clear and beautiful and there are not too many varmints. It was a jungle, and there was plenty of life. When I put my shoes on in the morning, I had to watch out for scorpions. Everybody talks about snakes, but snakes were not so much of a problem. I'd come from Mississippi where I could go down to the Pearl River any Sunday afternoon and see more snakes than I saw the whole time I was in Burma and India put together. The snakes were there, all right, but the jungle was so vast and dense, we rarely saw them. We did have two occasions where our soldiers were bitten, but it was rare, considering we were out days and nights for three years.

The village of Pebu had been abandoned by the Nagas. The empty houses became infested with rats, fleas, lice, all sorts of creatures. Nevertheless, when we were there, we mostly stayed inside of the houses. It was better to be dry at night. One time while I was sitting in a house, something dropped down my back and immediately began stinging me. After dancing around a bit, I jerked my coat off, and a big centipede came out. It had dropped down from the thatched roof. And that dadgum centipede stung me or bit me, I don't know which, but it hurt. I finally managed to kill him. Meantime everyone had a good laugh watching my struggle.

At Pebu once, Skittles, Dennis, and Perry, the fellows from the OSS, came through and stayed for a while. We all slept in an abandoned house. I had a flashlight at the time, which was not always the case, since batteries gave out pretty quick. During the night, I was awakened by a rat that fell out of the rafters and landed on the side of my face. I hopped up and spotted him with the light. He ran under Dennis's blanket. All of a sudden, Dennis just exploded, he must have come three feet off the ground. I don't know how he did it, but he rose straight up. There were several of us in there, Kachins and Nagas too, and Dennis's leap woke everybody up. We got a tremendous laugh out of it.

A fellow named Colonel Rothwell Brown came through the area one time. Colonel Brown was probably fifty-some-odd years old, but he was a pretty tough old goat. I accompanied him to Tagap once. To us in our twenties, he seemed like an old man, close to retirement, with graying hair and a beard. I got to know him pretty well in the short time that we were together. I mention him now because he had a real sleeping bag. We were having a big problem with fleas at that time. They would get all over us at night, and they'd bite. One night I heard this huge rumpus. Brown was cussing and swearing. By the light of the fire, I could see he was doing something, so I said, "Colonel, what's going on?" He said, "I'm trying to turn my sleeping bag inside out. I'm going to get back in and see if I can go to sleep before the fleas change sides." It wasn't only the Japanese that kept our attention. Various creatures like leeches, mosquitoes, lice, fleas, rats, and the elements were also formidable enemies.

Floating in Fear

From Tagap, Colonel Wilson sent me back down to reconnoiter the big field near Sharaw Ga. I had reported earlier that it might be a good location for an airfield, and the higher-ups were interested. Again, I went with Goitum Kamai and Nawji by raft. It must have been almost a month after the first trip. We got there without incident. I paced off the field by moonlight as best I could and drew a map. It looked to me like the best possible spot for an airfield in the valley.

The next night, we went downriver past Ningbyen. We tried to get to the east side of the island like we had the first time, to avoid going past the Japanese camp. But the flow of water was such that it took our raft to the west. We paddled as hard as we could but couldn't make it over. We were stuck on the wrong side.

It was night, and the rising moon was shining bright. We were in a terrifying situation. When it became clear we couldn't make it, we just quit paddling and coasted down river. In front of us, we could see Japanese soldiers coming down the bank to wash dishes. One man was carrying a lantern. Some soldiers were already set up at the river's edge, but a few were still coming down to the bank. We could hear them talking and clattering around with their dishes. While we were watching, the soldier put the lantern out on a big rock out in the water and they commenced washing pots and pans in the river.

So there we were . . . Goitum Kamai, Nawji, and myself floating down river. We were going to drift right by the Japanese, and there was nothing we could do about it. I moved quietly, and whispered to the men, "Lie flat on the raft. Stretch out one arm, look underneath it to see what's happening if you need to, but don't make a noise." We couldn't paddle, we couldn't steer without giving ourselves away, so we just lay as still as we could and floated quietly by in the moonlight. As luck would have it, the lantern had been placed out on a rock between us and them, and it was shining brightly, effectively obscuring us. The Japanese never knew that we went by. If the lantern had been sitting back on the bank, I'm sure we would have been spotted. Thank God for that light. I'd say we were no further than about twenty feet out in the water in front of them. They were scrubbing and chattering and clanging pots while we drifted right on by, with our hearts pounding in our ears.

The Deerslayer

After we got off the river, we hiked back to Chingloo Sakan and into the territory around Shingbwiyang again. We ran across a huge deer there, a sambar, standing right out in front of us in the trail. Goitum Kamai and Nawji both said, "Shoot him. Shoot him." And I said, "No, no, there might be Japanese around. If we start shooting, they'll hear us," So I didn't shoot. But this dadgum deer just trotted ahead of us, and maybe fifty yards further, there he was standing on the trail, great big horns sticking up. "Shoot him, *duwa*. Shoot him. *Gapo, gapo*," they repeated. I answered, "No, no, we don't want to shoot him." We went on again, and he did the same darn thing. He was not afraid of us at all. He'd just trot off and then stand broadside looking at us, and he was a great big thing, almost as big as a horse. I finally thought, oh well, okay, I'll shoot him. So I picked up my rifle and took dead aim. When I shot that deer, he jumped up like a scalded dog and took off. The two Kachins laughed at me, "Ha, ha, you missed him. What kind of shot are you?" that sort of thing. Here was this huge animal, as wide as a kitchen cabinet, and it looked like I'd completely missed him. I said,

"I can't possibly have missed. Let's go see." So we commenced following his tracks. And we began to see a drop or two of blood and more blood and more, and when we got about a hundred yards farther on, we found the deer. He was dead; he had run all that way shot right through the heart.

We decided to make camp that night and feast on the deer. He was a giant, so we just sawed off a few chunks and cooked them. We hadn't had any substantial amount of meat for a long time. In the middle of the night, I woke up with terrible diarrhea, sick as a dog. And it wasn't ordinary diarrhea. By firelight I could see it was pure puss. Eventually, I got so sick I could hardly move. My two compadres discussed my situation. They use opium for all sorts of stomach disorders over there, so they decided to give me some opium. They rolled up a little ball about half as big as a marble, held me up while I swallowed it, and gave me some water to wash it down. Then I went to sleep or passed out or something.

The next thing I knew, I halfway waked up in the middle of the night and felt like I was paralyzed. I couldn't move, couldn't speak. All I could do was make a noise, a kind of a grunt, but it woke them up, thank the Lord. They came over and got to looking at me. One of them said to the other, "I told you, you gave him too much. He's going to die." They debated back and forth. Meantime, I was on the ground, lying in my own excrement, unable to communicate. I could hear, and I was vaguely conscious, but I had no control.

One of the men finally left for a while and came back with a fist full of some kind of leaves. He squeezed the juice of them into my mouth. Amazingly, whatever was in that juice woke me up, it must have been some natural antidote. Later they gave me water to drink, but I was still very sick, so they decided that one of them would stay with me, and the other would go for help, back to Tagap Ga where Seagrave's hospital was, maybe five days' march.

Nawji struck out for Tagap. At the time, a fellow named Ray Chesley happened to be there with Seagrave. Chesley was not a doctor; he was a scientist, an expert on epidemics. They had him there because he knew all about diseases that afflict armies, so he got in on the discussion. Nawji told them what my symptoms were. Apparently, Dr. Seagrave said something to the effect that, "He's got cholera; he's dead by now. With no treatment, he's just bound to be dead." Chesley argued, "No, I don't think it's cholera." Chesley later told me Seagrave got mad at him and said, "Well, if you're so damn smart, why don't you go out there and cure him?" So Chesley said, "All right, by God, I'll go," and he grabbed some medical supplies, and he and Nawji took off. It was practically all downhill to where we were, so they made it back in about half the time.

When they got there, it had been at least a week, but I hadn't gotten any worse. As a matter of fact, I was able to sit up. But I was not well by any manner of means. Chesley diagnosed me as having, he said, "plain old dysentery." He gave me sulfadiazine, as I remember, and it cleared me up in a matter of days. So Chesley won that argument, and he wouldn't let Seagrave forget it. But I was glad somebody won it, because he and those Kachins saved my life. I kept up with Chesley after the war; he was a great fellow, and I'll always remember what he did for me.

In the meantime, we had built—I say "we." I wasn't doing any work because I was pretty sick, but Goitum Kamai had built a lean-to on top of a cliff where we could see way down into the Hukawng Valley, a couple of thousand feet. It was a beautiful view. Every morning, I'd drag myself out to look, and the valley would be filled with clouds, white clouds just like a blanket of cotton wool. The fog would lift about ten o'clock in the morning. But up until then, it was a sea of white clouds. That's where I convalesced.

Food

We did occasionally eat wild meat on the trail, when we weren't worried about nearby Japanese. Our diet was diverse, and I enjoyed most of the local fare and didn't get sick from any food after that. One of my favorite foods was jackfruit. Generally, each village planted a jackfruit tree in some convenient location. It was called *malong pun* amongst the Kachins. The tree grew to be large and had a distinctive look, a lot like a magnolia. We would often describe the location of a Japanese installation in relation to the village jackfruit tree. The bark was relatively smooth, and the leaf was big, shiny, and elliptical. Instead of growing out on the ends of limbs where fruit normally grows, it grew right out of the trunk. The fruit was shaped somewhat like a watermelon, ten or maybe twelve inches in diameter, with a very rough pebble-like surface on the rind.

Often, we'd be walking down the trail, and a cry would come from the point man, "*Malong pun!*" The whole march would come to a halt, while somebody went up the tree to throw down some jackfruit. It was absolutely delicious. We'd break it open, and on the inside, the aroma was fantastic, a sweet fragrance, similar to but more pleasant than a banana. The fruit had a core with very large seeds, maybe 3 inches long, lozenge-shaped and covered with a creamy white flesh, the edible part. When we ran into a jackfruit tree, the whole war stopped while we sat down and feasted. Since that time, I've found jackfruit in this country, but only in cans, and I haven't seen it very often. But when I do run across it, I imagine us on the trail, waiting while someone climbs the tree and throws down fruit. I can hear it busting open when it hits the ground and picture everybody proceeding to gorge themselves.

Out in the jungle, we also found sour citrus fruits. The Kachins liked things that were sour and bitter. It was a job for me to keep them from cutting down small fruit trees to get at the fruit. I would try to convince them, "Wait a minute, now. Don't cut it down. We can shake it or take a stick and knock down fruit. Save the tree for other folks." It made me doubt some of the stories about primitive people always being natural conservationists. At least in this case, they paid no attention to that sort of thing. If they saw something edible, they would make use of it right then. It had to do with abundance, I suppose.

One of the most common fruits we ran into was wild banana, a sort of plantain. One blow with a knife and down came bananas and all. The bananas there had big seeds in them, as big as number 2 shot and just as hard as a rock. When you were eating, you had to be careful, or you'd break a tooth. Some of them were red bananas, bright red on the outside. The local people regarded them as a delicacy. When I was leaving for the United States at the end of the war, several people gave me whole big bunches of those red bananas as presents. Sadly, I had to give them away because I couldn't take bunches of bananas that weighed twenty-five pounds apiece on an airplane. Fruit in Burma was plentiful and a bright spot in my memory.

We also ate some meat. Southeast Asia is the birthplace of the chicken, and there are both wild and domestic chickens. People didn't seem to pay any attention to the joints when they cut them up. They'd just put a chicken down on a block, and with this big knife, just "whack, whack, whack," chop it up, bones all. The Kachins usually made stews, although they did eat a few things kabob style. They'd make a kabob out of pork and eat it rare. It's good that way, if you're not scared of trichinosis. They also prepared pork by chopping it up into small pieces and mixing it with cooked rice. They'd stuff the mixture down into a bamboo tube, pound it in there real tight, and then put a leaf over the top of it and set it way up over the fire. It stayed nice and warm up there, and smoke got into it. The rice fermented in the warmth, so they'd end up with half-fermented rice together with almost raw pork. Doesn't sound very appetizing, but I ate it many times.

We ate a lot of insects, especially ants and termites. They'd collect ants, pound them, and make a kind of a sour relish out of them. They also fried a mixture of bees and their larva, the grub-looking thing that comes on before the actual bee flies. Big beetles that fed on bamboo, we ate them, too. The Kachins knew how to take full advantage of whatever was available in the jungle. When we'd run out of rations, why, we could always send somebody out into the bushes to dig a few roots. "*Nai tusha*," they would say, which means "You're reduced to eating roots," a sign you're poverty stricken. They also ate rats and dogs occasionally, but not unless they needed to. The animists among them sacrificed animals to the *nats*, the spirits, and put the heads on poles, even chicken heads, after they'd eaten everything off of them. On top of bamboo poles in a cluster at the entrance to the village, there might be the skulls of dogs or other animals. Both the Kachins and Nagas did this.

There is a legend I was told about how two groups were separated because of their method of food preparation. The Kachins believe that they and the Nagas both came down from the north from a place they call Majoi Shingra Bum. That name means a naturally level mountain, a plateau. Way back before any recorded history, tribes began migrating down from the north. If you ask a Kachin about the history of his race, he'll go back to Majoi Shingra Bum. I suppose the migration was caused by drought or famine. The legend goes that two groups were traveling together. They were hunting and trapping as they moved toward the south, and one group chopped up their meat really small, almost like hamburger or hash. The other group cut it up into bigger pieces and cooked it either in a stew or kabob. These two groups got along pretty well, except the crowd that chopped their meat up in big pieces always took longer to cook the meat and get going. The group that cut their meat up in small pieces prepared theirs in a much shorter time.

Finally, they all came up against a big river. The story varied as to what river it was, but probably one of those that empty into the Irrawaddy. This river was so wide and deep that they had to build a bridge to get across. They stopped and made camp on the backside of the river, and working together, they built a stout bridge of bamboo. Then they got up bright and early and started cooking. The group that cut their meat up small were ready to go in short order. The other group was slower; they were still cooking up into the morning. The early group got tired of waiting, so they crossed. When the second group finally finished eating, they walked down to the river, and lo and behold, the bridge had been destroyed. The others had decided they wanted to get away from the people who were slowing them down. They had knocked down the bridge and left them behind.

The slower group was justifiably angry. They'd helped build the bridge and here these so-and-sos had left and torn it down. They decided they'd send a scout to find out where the first group had gone. There was some tall bamboo growing on the bank—it can grow to tremendous heights. So they quickly sent a boy who wasn't too heavy up that bamboo and then cut it down and lowered the little fellow across the river. He hit the ground pretty hard on the other side, and it knocked him out. But when he woke up, why, he immediately headed down the trail to try to find out what had happened.

The mud was soft there, so the first group had left footprints. The boy followed for quite a piece but couldn't catch them. He came back and reported that the other crowd had gotten far away. Chins and Nagas were the folks who crossed and kept going. They still live mostly down south. The Kachins call them Kongni, the footprint people. The word *kong* means "footprint." To this good day, the Naga Hills all the way south to the ocean are inhabited by Kongni, the footprint people. The Kachins themselves are Jinghpaw. The word *jinghpaw* just means the "people." The other people are footprints. *Kachin* is actually a foreign word, and people don't agree as to what it means. Some say that it's really a Chinese or possibly a Tibetan word, and they will point out that in Chinese there is a similar word which means "jungle man." *Kachin* is a term by which they're known to others. To themselves, they are Jinghpaw. But the Nagas and the Chins who went the other way, they're called footprint people, and they still cut their meat up small.

Hkatyaw

When I came back to Tagap, Colonel Wilson decided to divide things up as follows: Cummings was to stay at Tagap with Wilson and help manage things, Johnny Colling was to move to Hkalak Ga to take care of the western flank, and I was to go east to a place called Hkatyaw, about a three days' march toward the Tarung Hka River. I took some twenty fellows that I had recruited. Colonel Wilson assigned a Kachin named Mahka La to my outfit, who had been with the British Kachin Rifles. Mahka La became a key man in operations that followed and stayed with me until I left Burma. Dr. Abdul Halim Banday was another man assigned to my outfit at Hkatyaw. He was from India and was a soldier as well as a doctor. He became a great friend; I keep in contact with him to this day. Dr. Banday was invaluable in many ways, being a medical man. He helped with the local people. They'd find out he was a doctor, and, although they had their own methods of treatment, after they had done everything they could do, they'd come to him. He performed some miracles along the way. I remember one time he was called to see a village woman who had been in labor for many hours and unable to deliver. He catheterized her, and the baby was quickly delivered, and her life saved. Doc was a big part of everything. He ended up being my second in command for the time he was with me, which I wish had been longer.

Early on at Hkatyaw, Doc went out for a hunt to try to augment our diet a bit. He was looking for one of those great big pigeons, imperial pigeons they are called, damn near as big as chickens. In the process, he somehow bumped into a hornets' nest. Boy, they lit into him and stung him so badly that he lost consciousness, just passed out in the jungle. He finally waked up and staggered back to camp. His head had swelled all up like a melon. Those hornets nearly killed him, but he pulled through.

Another fellow who joined us at Hkatyaw had an interesting story. This Kachin, whose name I'm not sure I remember correctly, I think it was Maru Tu, he was fighting the Japanese long before he found his way to us. He had a gun that he had picked up from some British soldier along the way, a Short Magazine Lee Enfield. One time his former outfit ambushed a Japanese column, and he was hit in the hand. The bullet shattered his thumb. In the chaotic retreat, he became separated from his group. Rather than take a risky short route back to the main road, he decided to take the long route back across a mountain.

It was his left thumb that was injured, and rapidly, it got all rotten and infected. He knew something needed to be done, or he might die, so, out there in the jungle by himself, he placed his hand firmly against a tree trunk, took careful aim with his machete, and "whack," cut his own thumb off below the infected area. He kept traveling, and over some days in the jungle, the remaining portion got infected again, and filled with maggots, so he chopped it off again. Three times he cut his thumb off, progressively closer to his palm. Ended up, he cut it off to where he had no thumb at all, just right down through the lower joint. He finally made it to a Kachin village, and they applied native remedies. By the time he came with us, he had no thumb, but the area was well healed. In spite of his disability, he was an excellent soldier. He became a member of our group when we were at Hkatyaw, and he stuck with us until down at Hkadu. At that point, he had to go home; harvest was approaching, and he had to help his family. So I gave him my watch. I scratched my name on the back of it with the point of my knife so he wouldn't forget and gave it to him because he had been such a great soldier.

With Hkatyaw as a base, we sent Kachins into the Hukawng Valley to bring back reports on the Japanese—how many were there, a description of their weapons, names, numbers, and whatever else they could find out. Several of our spies were opium addicts because they were often willing to take risks. We were supplied by headquarters with opium for that purpose. It was the consistency of coal tar or gum, and came in blocks, approximately two pounds to a block, wrapped in paper, and tied up with a string. I had a little scale, a balance made out of bamboo. When we recruited folks, first thing, we'd determine whether or not they used opium. Then we'd negotiate as to how much they needed to keep them going. Payment would be one rupee weight a week or some measure that we agreed on, and for that they would go down and deal with the Japanese.

For other folks, the pay was in rupees. I think it was twenty rupees a month. A rupee was worth about thirty cents, so that's about six dollars a month, standard pay, which was a handsome sum as far as they were concerned. At first the rupees were silver. When the British began adulterating the coins, the Kachins didn't like it, but they eventually got used to it. The final payroll that I conducted was with paper money, but early on it was silver, and they'd drop it to us in sacks, a thousand coins in a sack. They'd just throw it out of the planes.

One fellow we recruited at Hkatyaw, named Jatdu, was an addict who was very familiar with the countryside. We used him regularly as a spy. Once, he went down to the paddy house north of Sharaw Ga to question people, but he got drunk and stayed there for several days. The Japanese were patrolling up in that direction along with some Burmans from the Burma Defense Army. They caught Jatdu there, and they killed him. They just shot him. So the Japanese became aware that something was going on, and they commenced doing regular patrols farther up the valley.

Lost Crew

We operated out of Hkatyaw for some time. One day, I got an urgent message that a B25 had gone down about eighty or maybe a hundred miles to the east, up the Gedu Hka, the river by the cliff we had passed on the first big raft trip. They sent the coordinates of the plane and notified us that they were sending Hector Meston's brother, George, I believe, another V Force man, to conduct a search. An unfortunate error had been made. Apparently, a rescue plane had located the lost airplane. As far as they could tell, the whole crew had survived the crash and had jumped out into a completely uninhabited area, no villages anywhere around. So a plane dropped them supplies, arms, maps, survival equipment, rations, and so forth and gave them instructions to go *east*. But we were the closest friendly folks, and we were eighty miles to the *west*. Somebody had made a huge mistake. The closest place to the east was Sumprabum, where the Japanese were. Our Fort Hertz was northeast, but there were big mountains up there. They'd have to cross a pass ten thousand feet high. In the next few days, somebody figured out the error. Frantically, they sent the plane back to try to find them. But they never found them. They circled and circled, but the canopy was impossible to see through.

In desperation, headquarters dispatched Meston. He was a big, tall fellow, taller than his brother. He took two Gurkha soldiers with him, and they knew how to take care of themselves in the woods. They stopped at our place, and we helped them get across the Tarung Hka River. From there, they headed up the Gedu Hka. They spent three weeks looking for the survivors but came back empty-handed. They found the plane, found where the crew made camp the first two or three times, but when they got to the Kumon Mountain range, they lost the track completely. They even went looking down near Sumprabum, where the Japanese were. They contacted villagers near there, but nobody had seen the men. To this good day nobody knows what happened to those men. There were about eight or nine of them, and they just disappeared from the face of the earth. Meston was devastated. He damn near ran out of rations, he went everywhere he could think, but finally he and the two Gurkhas just had to come back. That was an unhappy event at Hkatyaw.

The Engineer

By September 1943, we'd been in Hkatyaw for about five or six weeks, when I got word from headquarters that they were sending an engineer to inspect the area near Sharaw Ga that I had recommended for an airfield. I had paced off the area and given them the general azimuth, but they wanted a bona fide engineer to take a second look. Two other Americans came with him. I knew one slightly; I had run into him when he was coming out of Hkalak Ga. The two of us figured we had been in the same convoy when we came over by ship because he had gotten a tattoo on his arm that read something like "Durban, South Africa, June '42." For the reconnaissance trip, I arranged for Goitum Kamai and Nawji to accompany them. A few days later, the Kachins came back to us alone. And they told a terrible story.

The group had made it to the location and checked out the field by moonlight, but apparently, the engineer wanted to see it in the daytime. Nawji and Goitum Kamai said they tried to talk him out of it, but I reckon there was no real communication; the Americans couldn't speak any Kachin, and the Kachins couldn't speak much English. The Americans were certainly aware the Japanese were nearby, but they took the risk and walked near Sharaw Ga in the daylight. When they saw smoke coming out of a house, they quickly cut into the jungle and headed back north.

The going was rough in the jungle, and the Americans wanted to get on the main trail to make better time. The Kachins warned them against this, but they went ahead, and in short order, they found footprints in the soft ground. Goitum Kamai pointed them out, "These are Japanese footprints. We've got to get back into the jungle." They did, but after struggling a while, they decided to return to the path. Again, they found more footprints, and back into the jungle they went. The third time they returned to the trail, some Japanese and Burmans were there waiting for them.

Nawji and Goitum Kamai scrambled for cover. The Americans apparently didn't make it. The engineer ended up dead, with all the notes he'd made about the airfield still in his pocket. The Kachins laid low until the Japanese finally left. When they were able to look around, they found the engineer. The Japanese had looted his body and left him there. But they couldn't find the other two. After a while, they came back to Hkatyaw and reported what had happened. I think that event tipped off the Japanese and changed everything.

Battle of Sharaw Ga

Not too long after that, my men and I were assigned the job of advance guard for the Chinese battalion. The plan was for the Chinese to push the Japanese out of both Sharaw Ga and Ningbyen. The battalion was coming from the north and was to meet us and continue on down the same trail where the tragic event had occurred. Another battalion was to come along the trail from Ningam Sakan and advance to Ningbyen from the west. The whole operation got going in late October 1943.

By that time, there were a total of about forty men with me at Hkatyaw. I left Doc Abdul in command of half of the men and took Mahka La and the rest with me. We struck out toward Sharaw Ga with the Chinese following us. On October 29th, we went past a salt spring about midway along the trail and arrived at the spot where the ambush of the engineer and his group had taken place. We found one rotting body there. The head had been chopped off, and the hands and feet were missing.

We buried the engineer off to one side of the track with as much decorum as time allowed. The story we heard later was that the enemy had put his head, hands, and feet on poles somewhere. With the exception of some who had been converted to Christianity, the Kachins were still mostly animists at that time and believed in sacrificing animals to the *nats*, or spirits. At the entrance to an animist village, there were usually poles sticking up with the skulls of dogs or buffalo or chickens or pigs on them. So the Japanese, in mock fashion, had apparently stuck the fellow's head on a pole somewhere, signifying, "This is what's going to happen to the Americans who try to come here." We buried his body, and we looked all around, but we couldn't find any evidence of the other two men, so we continued on.

Scouts we had sent on ahead determined that the Japanese were on the back side of a paddy field near Sharaw Ga, so we hid in the jungle and waited for the advance elements of the Chinese battalion to catch up with us. On October 31, when they did, I said to the captain in charge, "The Japanese are in this field. They've got a wide-open field of fire in front of them. My suggestion is to avoid them, go around the field and on past Sharaw Ga." I told him I had information that there were about a hundred Japanese entrenched in or around Sharaw Ga. I thought we should go on toward Ningbyen, where the main force was, but this guy didn't agree, and he was in command.

He just said, "Well, let's go see," or words to that effect, and started walking right out into the field. Face is very important to the Chinese, so I figured I better go with him. We started together out into the field, just he and I. About that time, a voice yelled out from the other side of the field, "*Nagaw*?" which means "Who goes there?" When the Chinese officer heard that, all of a sudden, he believed me. We rapidly turned around and ducked back into the jungle, as the Japanese opened fire. The officer then decided to start a fire fight from the edge of the jungle. I took my men, and we circled around toward the river. Some Japanese near the river spotted us and began to shoot. We all did belly flops on the ground and commenced returning fire.

It was a beautiful, clear afternoon, and the sun was bright. I remember lying in a tall patch of weeds similar to milkweed. Maybe it was milkweed. Anyway, as I looked up at the sky, every now and then something shiny would drift down. When I looked closer, I noticed, as bullets hit the pods of those plants, little feathered seeds would come floating down, shimmering in the sun. That picture of bullets flying and shining seeds drifting through the air has stayed with me all these years. I can see it just like I was back there now.

After the shooting slacked off, I hollered at Mahka La, and we moved to a position with better cover. It didn't take us long to determine that the Japanese had left. We went up into the edge of the woods and found their campsite. They had gone, but there was a fire still burning and a big wad of mosquito netting on the ground, soaked with blood. Somebody had been hit, but it was almost accidental; we had just fired in their general direction. We followed their trail to the river bank and could see where canoes had been dragged off into the water.

From there, we continued down the trail toward Sharaw Ga. Our spies up ahead told us that the Japanese had dug foxholes, fortifications in and around the village, and that they had done some clearing for a field of fire toward the trail. As we began to get closer, sure enough, we found where they'd chopped brush away to get a clear view of whoever was coming. We took up a line under cover and waited for the Chinese to catch up with us. And they caught up.

When the captain showed up, he just started walking out into the open like before. I hurried alongside but kept my eye on the village on the slope above us. We were in high grass. As we walked, I saw two Japanese run between some houses. I grabbed the captain by the arm and said, "Japanese." About that time, they opened fire. We dropped down right where we were, underneath a large banyan tree. I took off my pack, one I'd made myself. I didn't like the army packs very much, so I had fixed up a sack which coolies used to carry thirty-five pounds of rice. It was made out of heavy waxed canvas, and I could stuff everything that I owned in it. I pulled that pack off, put it in front of me, and rested my rifle on it.

The Chinese and the Kachins behind us in the edge of the jungle began returning fire. About that time, there was a loud crackling noise. We looked up, and a branch of the banyan tree broke and came swinging down. We'd heard a lot of stories about Japanese snipers, so my first thought was maybe there was somebody up there, but the branch had just been hit by bullets and swung down in front of us. We stayed in that awkward position for a while and then went back. The captain wanted to wait for reinforcements. There was a second company coming, so he decided to set up a perimeter and hold his position. He organized the men in a rough semicircle to the right and sent us to the left.

Wounded

I managed to get the word out for my group to scatter. The shooting kept on going as it began to get dark. Every once in a while, I would crawl around amongst my men and encourage them. I crawled over to the Bren gunner at around 10:00 p.m. that Halloween night. All of a sudden, it felt like somebody had hit me with a hammer right in my tail. I knew I'd been shot. My first reaction was to try to move my legs. Thank God, I could move them. Then I reached around to try to feel where I'd been hit. There was an unfamiliar hole in my britches. I stuck my fingers through that hole, and I found the new hole in me. Apparently, the bullet had first hit the ground behind me, and tumbled. Then it had hit, between my anus and tailbone. I could stick three fingers back in there without any trouble, so it hadn't gone straight in. The doctors later told me I was the luckiest man in the world. They said, "An eighth of an inch higher and it would have hit you in the tailbone and wrecked your spine. Or if it had been half an inch or so lower, it would have torn all your plumbing to pieces, and you probably wouldn't have lived at all."

I figured later that at least three bullets came my way. One hit me, the next tore up my cartridge belt, and the third one went through my canteen. I must have caught a burst of fire from some automatic weapon. The water ran out of my canteen. I saved that canteen, and still have it today, bullet hole and all. In my pocket, I had a little metal container, like an aspirin box, that held sulfanilamide tablets. The instructions said, "If you get wounded, take one of these every five minutes until you take them all." There were twenty-four tablets in there, as I remember. I had no water, so I just chewed them up and swallowed them.

I punched the Bren gunner and told him what had happened. He went to try to find some help. We had no aid man, and Doc Abdul didn't arrive until later. The gunner found a Chinese aid man. In the dark, the man crawled up, pulled out a flashlight, and turned it on. I yelled at him to shut it off, which he did, but not before the Japanese saw it, and for a few minutes, we were under heavy fire. But they were just shooting in the black dark toward where they had seen the light. We lay there until it stopped; then the aid man got a bandage and fixed me up. The bandage came in a little tin container. He pulled it out and tied it on me. I was bleeding, but no major artery was hit. There was blood all over my britches, though; something for me to think about as I lay there the rest of the night.

During the night, the Japanese brought mortars up from Ningbyen. We could hear the men making a lot of racket, talking and yelling. Just at daybreak, they opened up on us. Mortars make a coughing noise; the shell goes way up high, comes down, and explodes when it hits. They mortared us pretty heavily that morning. We stayed in position, but the Chinese withdrew. Every now and then, a bunch of them would just get up and run back into the woods. Finally, we figured out what they were doing, and I gave the order to move back. I managed to crawl into the edge of the woods along with the rest.

The other company still had not come up, but the Chinese captain decided that he was going to go ahead and launch an attack. I lay in the bushes in the edge of the jungle and watched. I couldn't believe what I was seeing. The Chinese lined up practically like they were on a parade, on the edge of the jungle with fixed bayonets. Then the bugler blew, just like in the days of Napoleon, and they charged across the open space. The Japanese stopped shooting, but they didn't run. They waited until the Chinese were within twenty-five yards of them and then opened up and mowed them down like wheat, not only with rifle fire but automatic weapons as well. That didn't last very long. The Chinese that were left standing turned around and ran like blazes back downhill into the edge of the jungle. They left about half of their number up there either dead or wounded. That was the first charge.

The other company came up the next morning. After that first ill-fated attempt, amazingly, when the second company came up, they did the same thing, lined up on the edge of the jungle, sounded the charge, and went up the hill. We could hear the bark of the machine guns as the Japanese cut them down. The Chinese managed to drag some of their wounded back down the hill that time, but most were left up there lying in the grass. In the meantime, we stayed where we were. I did not have my men participate in those attacks.

The Chinese attempted one more foray with the whole battalion. There were three companies in the battalion and a heavy weapons company, a machine gun company. This time they managed to get up into the village. They never did move the line directly in front; they swung around the right flank and made some headway. When they got up there, they dug in. One thing the Chinese could do big time was dig. They made connecting trenches six feet deep, and pillboxes and logs all the way around, like a real fort. Obviously, they were planning on staying for a long time. In the meantime, the Japanese had lost a part of the village, but they were still there. The advance into the Hukawng Valley had started in the middle of October, and the first contact for us was on October the 31st, 1943, Halloween, the day I got shot. After settling in, the Chinese 38th Division didn't get up and get moving until after Christmas. They just stalled out in a situation akin to World War I trench warfare.

Help Arrives

In that first action, the official count was forty-eight dead and nearly two hundred wounded. There are a little less than a thousand in a battalion, so the casualties were significant. On the third day, Captain Miles Johnson showed up. He was an American doctor, one of Seagrave's. He had one medical orderly with him, a Chinese fellow. The medical supplies they had were only what they could carry on their backs, a big load for them, but in terms of the number of wounded, a pitifully small amount. Miles told the lieutenant colonel in command, "We've got one bottle of plasma. Who do you want me to give it to?" The lieutenant colonel said, "Give it to the machine gun company commander." That man had been hit in the face. The whole side of his jaw had been torn out, and he had bled a whole lot. So Miles gave it to him. Undoubtedly, other men died because they didn't have more. But that machine gun captain pulled through.

Miles told me later, "When I got there, right away, I noticed you lying on the ground. All the Chinese were dressed in khaki uniforms, but you had on green fatigues, and you were considerably taller than they were. I looked up and down the line, and there you were, one long green guy amongst all these short ones." He said, "I divided up the wounded the way they tell you. Those you think are going to die, set them to one side; there's nothing you can do for them. Those that you think are going to get well regardless, not too serious, set them to another side, and then try to tackle those that you think you can help." He said, "You looked bad. I saw where you had been hit, and your stomach had begun to swell up, so I figured you had peritonitis. I put you with those that were going to go on out." He may have been exaggerating, but that's what he said. My men took care of me until he tended to me later. Fortunately, it was not raining.

Miles didn't get to me for about three more days. When he did, he told me, "I saved the last few drops of ether for you, so I can knock you out and then see what's really going on." He put this thing over my face and said, "Take three deep breaths and hold them until I tell you to let them out. It's all the ether I've got, and you've got to be asleep by the time I use up these drops." So, I took one big breath and then another and then another, and I didn't know anymore. They rolled me over and propped me up where he could get at me. Apparently, the bullet had broken up, so he got some pieces out and probed up as far as he could. He told me later, he believed fragments had broken into my abdominal cavity and probably messed up some things in there, but he couldn't do anything about that.

Then he took about three yards of gauze and Vaseline, and he worked the Vaseline into that gauze so it was all gummy. He shook sulfa powder all over it and stuffed all that up in the hole. The idea was to get it to heal up from the inside out. Every day after that, he'd pull the old gauze out and then stuff some more back in there. He used something, for lack of a better term, like a Kotex pad with strings on it to cover the wound. I had a belt and tied the strings to it. I had to wear that thing for a long time, but after about two weeks, I changed the dressing myself.

We were in a forest with great, tall trees and undergrowth down in the bottom. The undergrowth got trompled down quickly, so then we were in the relative open, no shelter, no nothing, under the trees. The battle was still going on that whole time. The biggest weapon we had was a 60 millimeter mortar. The Japanese, however, had big guns, and we could sure hear them. Most of the shells burst in the trees. The Kachins made a stretcher for me out of bamboo, and they'd pick me up and carry me around. At first, I was out of my head with fever, but finally, I came around and carried on with sending out patrols and gathering information from that stretcher. And I continued to slowly improve. During that time, we moved to a different place, back up the river a piece from the Chinese front, where they were engaging the enemy sporadically. Mainly they were busy building those enormous defenses. The structures, pillboxes, and trenches were so big that I reckon some of them are still there.

Because of the fighting, a village nearby—I've forgotten the name—evacuated en masse. They just picked up and got out of there. I saw that sort of thing happen more than once. In this particular instance, about eight hundred villagers—men, women and children—circumnavigated the battle and came into our little camp on the way out. Of course, we didn't have enough to feed them. There were air drops, but nobody had anticipated eight hundred people coming to our spot.

We had pickets out at night, and occasionally the guards drifted to sleep. One such fellow—I don't remember his name—fell asleep at his post and was waked up in the middle of the night by a wild elephant right there at him. He didn't know what it was, I guess, so he opened up with his machine gun and poured a stream of bullets into that elephant, which was very sad, but as it turned out, it was a godsend because we were able to feed those refugees. We turned the villagers loose on the elephant, and they skinned him and cleaned off the meat to where there was absolutely nothing left.

Purple Heart

General Stilwell had set up his headquarters at Ningam Sakan, trying to encourage the Chinese to move, but they wouldn't move. They were dug in. The battalion that was supposed to attack Ningbyen wasn't moving either. Another group trying to take the ford at Yupong also stalled out. It wasn't until later in January 1944 that any of them moved. In December, shortly after I had become truly mobile again, I got a message direct from General Stilwell. He sent orders that said, "If you can move, come down and meet me at Ningam." It was about a forty-mile trip, and, of course, the Japanese were in control of the territory, so I took a Kachin soldier with me. I was still wearing that pad, the wound didn't want to heal, but I was able to walk.

We made it to Ningam Sakan, and I met with General Stilwell in the dugout. It was the first time I'd ever seen him, and he wanted to know what the hell was happening over there. The Chinese were using up ammunition like it was going out of style. The allies were madly trying to keep up the supply. They couldn't fly down and drop direct to the Chinese, so they built an airfield back at Shingbwiyang in the heavy forest. They got bulldozers in there and managed to clear it off. It was the damnedest airfield you ever saw; trees a hundred feet high on either side. The airplanes that came in there had barely enough room to land.

Stilwell kept me in the dugout for a couple of hours talking and asking questions, and I told him what had happened as I saw it. When all that was over, we climbed back out. He assembled the troops that were there, had a ceremony, and presented me with the Purple Heart. As he approached me with the medal, I tried to keep a straight face and said, "Pardon me, sir, but I understand it's the usual custom to pin the medal over the wound." He laughed and said, "Lieutenant, we will dispense with that part of the ceremony." Then he went ahead and gave me the medal. They also gave me the Bronze Star; I think the citation reads that they carried me around for about three weeks on a stretcher bed and that I refused to relinquish my command in spite of being wounded. But I didn't actually get that medal until later.

Early in the war, by the way, the United States had a rule that they would not give noncitizens any medal higher than a bronze star. They changed that rule later. The British never had any such rule. Many Gurkhas have won the Victoria Cross, and the French have given the Legion of Honor to anyone who deserved it, but the United States at that time, did not. Several men under my command got the bronze star, but some deserved more.

Swim Party

Sometime in December of '43, while we were stalled out at Sharaw Ga and I was still somewhat disabled, a memorable incident took place. Our little encampment was very close to the Tarung Hka River. Some American sergeants named Tuggle, Van Arsdale, and Buck were with us by then. On a day when the sun was shining brightly, and they felt particularly dirty and crusty, they got the idea to take a swim in the Tarung Hka, so they asked me if they could have a few minutes to go over and take a dip. I reminded them that there were Japanese around, but, "Oh, yeah," they said, they'd be careful. So I said okay. They took off, and it wasn't very long before I heard the rattle of machine gun fire from their direction.

Different weapons have different sounds. The .30–06 had a deeper boom than the Japanese rifles. The sound of the Nambu machine gun was high pitched. Of course, the noise also depends on the direction. If it's coming your way, you'll hear the crack of the bullet go by before you hear the initial pop of the shot. A battle always seemed to me a little like a symphony; pop, pop, pop, crack, crack, boom, in various patterns, along with rumbles, roars, howls, whistles, and mortar explosions like bass drums in an orchestra. Artillery makes swishing sound in the air and then a terrible thunder. Those sounds were seared in our minds, and I knew this was a Nambu machine gun that had opened up, possibly on my buddies.

Half an hour later, here they came back, Tuggle, Van Arsdale, and Buck, obviously unhappy, but safe. As they told it, they made it to the river and undressed right on the bank. The "sandbar" was typical for that area, not made of gravel or sand, but boulders about the size of a football or bigger, very hard to walk on and particularly hard to run on, especially barefooted. Even with shoes, you'd have a devil of a time. All three of them went out in the water, gamboling about and having a grand time, throwing water all over each other and laughing, when this machine gun opened up from the opposite bank and bullets began spattering all around. They turned and fled, I mean, they ran pell-mell across this rocky bar and plunged into the woods. At that point, why, Van Arsdale turned to Buck and said, "Our clothes! Our clothes! We left all of our clothes! Go get them! Go get them!" So Buck, without thinking, tore back out across the bar, stumbling, falling, scrambling. He made it to the clothes and swept them up. Somehow, he managed to get them all. He turned around with the bundle in his arms, raced back and plunged into the bushes full of brambles and stickers. And there he was plumb buck naked. He thought for a moment, raised his head and said to Van Arsdale, "What are you doing hollering at me to go back and get the clothes? I might have got killed for some old clothes!" Then he started after Van Arsdale, and they were just before having a big fist-fight, when Tuggle, who was bigger than either one of them, managed to get them apart. Finally, they began laughing about it. They really were lucky to be alive, and not just Buck, but all of them. When they arrived back at camp, with their feet all crippled up and bodies scraped from thorns, they were the most bedraggled looking crew you can imagine. There were no more requests to swim in the river after that.

Basel Alexandrovich Schervoshedza

As it got along near Christmas time, an American medical battalion came down and brought with them a real Red Russian whose name was Basel Alexandrovich Shervoshedza. He was an interesting fellow, claimed he was a Cossack, and I'm sure he was. He had been a Red Army pilot, and in the fracas between Japan and Russia, along the border of Manchuria back about 1935 I think it was, he had been shot down and captured by the Japanese. When they finally worked out a peace agreement, he got instructions to stay in Japan and to enter the University of Tokyo. So when the war started, he was neutral as far as Japan was concerned. He managed to get on a Swedish ship that was taking a lot of the neutral people out of Japan, a whole lot of Swedes, and Portuguese and Swiss and others that were not involved with the war.

This ship dropped him off at Calcutta, where Basel immediately took advantage of the fact that he could speak Japanese, and Chinese by the way, and got a job with the US army. Somehow, he ended up in Sharaw Ga. He was a colorful character and at least as far as the Chinese were concerned, a troublemaker. Sometimes he would go up to the front lines, climb up on a parapet, grab somebody's submachine gun, and start shooting at the Japanese. Of course, they'd immediately start shooting back, and the Chinese didn't exactly appreciate that. I remember, he also played chess with Doc a lot. Most of the time, Doc would beat him, and it just infuriated him. Here he was a Russian, supposed to be such great chess players, and here this Indian fellow would beat him. Of course, he probably didn't realize that the Indians invented chess.

Around the time I got crippled up, we had gotten a radio and a radio operator, an American named McCullough. We also got a code machine that we used for a while. It had little wheels, and it printed a tape, like a stock market deal. It would print the message out as you wheeled these wheels around. McCullough came to me one day and said, "Lieutenant, look what I got." The message on this particular tape was from Northern Combat Area Command. It ordered me to arrest Basel Alexandrovich and to take him immediately back to Ningam Sakan, under guard. There was a lot of enemy territory between there and us, and in the meantime, we'd all become good friends with Basel.

I just went straight over and showed Basel the message. He read it, and he didn't flinch. He just looked at me and said, "Well, what do we do about it?" I said, "Basel, we can't send you under any kind of guard from here to Ningam Sakan. The Japanese are roaming around, and I can't conceive of having you handcuffed out there. I believe I can trust you, so I'll make a deal with you. I'll send a Kachin with you and give you both arms and ammunition. You may have to fight your way to Ningam Sakan, but when you get there, you've got to turn yourself in, on your word of honor." He said, "I will," and we shook hands. The next day, I equipped him with a submachine gun. I instructed the fellow with him, "Do your best to get this man to Ningam Sakan." And they didn't let me down. They made it there, and Basel turned himself in. He must have pulled some strings because the last I heard, he was a free man, associated with the Russian consul in Calcutta and was cutting a wide swath among all the available ladies. He was a character. I wish I could have crossed paths with him again, but that was the last I saw of Basel.

One Found

Right before Christmas, there was an airdrop for us in the paddy field about two miles back from the action. The Chinese were getting drops there as well. Interesting to me, when the Americans retrieved a heavy box of ammunition, they would cut a bamboo pole and hang the box in the middle, with one man on each end of the pole to carry it; two men, one box, and they would grouse and complain about it. The Chinese, who were picking up the same sort of stuff, they'd have one man with a bamboo pole and a box of ammunition hanging on each end of it, and he'd trot along like it didn't bother him at all; one man, two boxes. The Chinese were pretty damn good at it. But these particular Chinese were mostly country folk. They were used to carrying things, and most of us Americans had never carried much of anything heavier than a few school books.

On that day, after we'd got our supplies, the plane dropped a streamer. Streamers were used to send messages. They would tear off a big strip of cloth from one of the cotton parachutes, tie it to something heavy—a bolt or whatever—and wrap the note around it. Well, last thing they did at this drop, they waggled their wings and dropped this streamer. Our people picked it up, and on it was a note, with a little hand-drawn map of the bend in the river and an "X" mark-the-spot. They wrote, "There's a body lying on the bank at approximately this spot on the river. Looks like it's probably an American because his uniform is green." (Both the Chinese and the Japanese wore khaki.) The message said, "Please investigate." I asked Doc to go and check it out. He took two or three men and went over and found the body. The man was considerably decomposed, but on his wrist was tattooed, "Durban, South Africa, June '42." He was lying half in the water, and the flap of skin with the tattoo on it had remained intact. When Doc told me he'd seen the tattoo, I knew damn well it was that fellow who had accompanied the engineer. We never did find out for sure how he died. Doc tried to examine him, but he said the body was too far gone for him to tell much. So we reported the fact that we found him and buried him beside the river. We never found the other man. The Graves Administration, I think it was, who try to find missing people, they came back at me several times about that, asking me where the site was. I gave them the coordinates on the map. I also told them who they might ask to help find him. But to my knowledge, nothing ever happened.

Sanip Hka Journey

The battle of Sharaw Ga dragged on. Thankfully, when I was in better shape, Colonel Wilson sent my group east towards the Sanip Hka River to reconnoiter. It was good to get away from the stalemate, and the area was one of the most beautiful sections of any country I've ever been through, a real jungle paradise. All kinds of animals were in there, and the forest was tall and green and magnificent. At night, we'd sometimes be disturbed by herds of elephants tearing up trees. The Sanip Hka itself was a shady river with clear water and fish; we'd see tons of them just swimming out in the open, not scared at all. We stopped at one pool where great schools of fish were milling around, and decided to harvest a few, so the Kachins showed me their favorite method.

We built a temporary dam above and below a particular spot to create a small pool. Then they collected some roots of a particular plant. They pounded those roots on the rocks. Then they took an old piece of gunny sack, put the pulp in that sack, tied it on the end of a long pole, and thrashed it up and down in the water. Some compound in the roots stunned the fish, and they just floated to the surface belly up. We waded out into the water, picked them up, and threw them up on the bank. We got probably a hundred pounds of fish in no time at all, and we feasted upon them for the short time that we were there. I wish I knew the name of that plant.

Another fish story: One of our soldiers had a British rifle, Short Magazine Lee Enfield, a distinctive weapon with a cutoff look where the bayonet stud sticks out beyond the end of the barrel. The water was so clear along the river that he decided he was going to shoot some fish. He concealed himself on the bank, and when a big fish roamed around in the water just below him, he carefully took aim at the fish and pulled the trigger. Unbeknownst to him, he had stuck the barrel into the water, so his gun just blew up. It bloodied his nose, and his ears were ringing to beat the band. When he pulled his rifle back out of the water, six inches of the end of the barrel had just opened up like a flower.

In an effort to get him back in business, I sawed the end of the barrel off with a file and managed to put the bayonet fixture back on the shortened barrel. We decided to test fire it, so we set up a piece of paper on a tree about one hundred yards away and tried it out. The muzzle blast was pretty fierce because the powder was designed to burn up in twenty-four inches, but the barrel was only about eighteen inches long, and we had to change the sight setting to bring it up to where it hit the center. He served the rest of his time with that extra short-barrel Lee Enfield rifle. At least he was armed. And I sure won't forget him. When he came to me with his ruined rifle, he had actually killed the fish, and even though he had blood pouring out of his nose, he brought that fish back with him.

Once, we were walking along a creek near the Sanip Hka, and the men up front saw two small animals up on a limb, engaged in mortal combat. One of the men just hauled off and shot them. He hit both because they were embroiled together, and they fell "whop," right down in the water in front of him. He was practically under them. Very foolishly he reached over and grabbed one of them by the tail. When he grabbed it, this thing just climbed right up his tail and bit him, bit him in the hand pretty hard. He managed to shake the animal loose and kill it. I'd say both animals were about as big as small dogs, ten or twenty pounds apiece. They were both tree-climbing animals but different species. I have since looked them up and believe the one that bit him was something called a slow loris. Not sure about the other one; it was different. They had big squirrels over there, but this was not a squirrel, at least it didn't look like a squirrel, more like a mink or ferret or something.

This loris bit the man, his hand was bleeding, and I told him to wash it off. The water was clear water. He did that, but then he immediately went over and sat down and said, "I've been poisoned, I'm going to be pretty sick." I asked what he was talking about, and he said that this loris, or whatever it was that bit him, was poisonous. Right there while we were looking at the soldier, he began to swell up just like he was violently allergic to something. His face swelled all up, his eyes practically closed, his lips got real big. I felt his pulse, and it was almost like his heart was fluttering, it was going so fast. I had no idea what to do about it. We didn't have any Benadryl or anything like that—I'm not even sure they'd even invented it by that time. So we just decided to stay there and wait it out. We waited the rest of that day and the following night. The next day, he was still feeling bad, but he said, "I believe I can keep going," and he went on with us. Without any treatment, he survived what seems like it must have been anaphylaxis. The Kachins were tough.

Mihelich's Decision

Americans could be pretty tough, too. On the Sanip Hka, John Mihelich, my radio man at the time, began getting a toothache. He tied a rag around his head and tried to gut it out. Finally, he came to me. I think by this time, I was a captain. The joke was that if you needed ammunition or supplies, and they couldn't get them to you, they would promote you, so I'd been promoted. Anyhow, Mihelich was feeling very bad. And he came to me, and said, "Captain, I don't believe I can go any further. This tooth is killing me." His jaw was swelled up, and he was obviously in great pain.

At that time, we had arrived at one of the prettiest spots I've ever seen, a big pool in the river surrounded by a forest of huge trees. The Sanip Hka usually wasn't any more than about six or eight feet wide. It was the dry season, and there wasn't much water in it. But here was a big, deep pool, and out in the middle, just like a chimney, was a rock spire that rose up at least fifty or sixty feet with some trees on the top of it. We stopped right there and made camp near that beautiful pool. I told Mihelich, "Looks to me like you've got two alternatives. I can give you a couple of men, and you can walk back someplace where there's a dentist or at least somebody that knows what they're doing to take care of you. You might have to go as far as Shingbwiyang; that's over a hundred miles. The other alternative is to let me try to pull it with that pair of pliers in your radio repair kit. If you can point it out to me, I'm willing to give it a try." He thought a minute and said, "I don't think I've got any choice, I can barely get around, I hurt so bad." He said, "Pull it." So I said, "All right. Let's do it now." I got Casey Migon, another American soldier with us, and I said, "Casey, I'll sit on his stomach, and you hold his head. Let's see what we can do." It was an upper tooth. I don't know what I would have done with a lower tooth. It would have been much harder to hold him steady.

Mihelich was a bartender by trade, from Pueblo, Colorado, which was a mining district, and I mean, a real tough place. And old Mihelich dealt with all those miners in the bar. He was a gritty fellow. So I sat on his stomach, Migon held his head, and I said, "Be sure you tell me the right tooth." He said, "Oh, I'll get the right one, all right." And he pointed to one of these great big molars in the back. I put my hand on his forehead and reached in there. And when I grabbed a hold of that tooth, man, he hollered; it hurt bad. He was saying something. At first, I couldn't tell what it was, but I finally figured out that he was trying to say: "Pull it out! Pull it out!"

I grabbed down on that tooth with the pliers, and I pulled with all my might and main, but I could not budge it. I really pulled hard, and he groaned. I tried again, and blood came out all around the base of it, and he hollered, but no tooth. Then I tried once more, but this time I twisted it just a little bit. And when I twisted it, it popped out just like a cork. All three roots came out clean, and one root had a little white sac on it. A dentist later told me, "That sac was an abscess, and you're the luckiest man alive. If you had busted that sac open or crushed his tooth, which you might have done with a pair of pliers, it would have been a mess." Anyhow, it came out just as clean as a whistle, but he was still hurting bad. You would have thought he was going to give up the ghost. We didn't even have any aspirin, nothing to help him out. We had opium, but I'd had a bad experience with that and didn't want to risk it. So we stayed by him all night long, while he rolled and tossed and groaned. We put wet rags on his head to try to get his mind off of the pain. Along came morning, and he began to feel better. We stayed there, and by the following day, he said, "I'm ready to go. Thank the Lord, it worked." So we took off in good spirits, on the way to the village of N'Dup Dumsa Ga.

Snake Bit

We cut across the top of the Hukawng Valley, to get over to the east and around the flank of the whole operation to the village of N'Dup Dumsa Ga. This village was what they called *gumlao mung*. *Gumlao* means rebel. Apparently at one time, some Kachins revolted against their *duwa* and deposed him. After that, the village functioned pretty much like a New England town. The whole village got together and conferred on any question that they had. They did not have a headman; they operated as a group. It seemed to me in my time in northern Burma that practically every basic form of government was represented throughout those hills. Some of the villages and the tribes were like absolute monarchies; others would have an oligarchy with a group of *salang ni*, or elders, who would run things. We credit the Greeks with the invention of democracy, but I think it's been around in one form or another ever since the beginning. I don't think anybody told these people at N'Dup Dumsa Ga about democracy, but they had the most elementary form of it, where everybody voted on everything.

We were camped out not far from N'Dup Dumsa Ga, when one of our Kachins came running back into camp with a snake. It was a little green snake, only about a foot and a half long. The snake had bitten him on the top of his big toe. He killed it, and brought it in. I took a good look at the snake. Its head was triangular like the rattlesnakes and moccasins in the US, and it had two fangs. Obviously, it was poisonous. So we went through all the rigmarole to try to do him some good. I cut holes and I sucked on his crusty toe to try to get the venom out. He looked like he'd never worn shoes in his whole life, I don't see how this snake got through that skin, it was so thick. But I sucked on his toe and spit out venom like they used to tell you to do, but it was to no avail. Up in the night, his leg swelled up so big that the skin split above his ankle, and oozing fluid came out. He was in terrible pain, rolling and moaning all night long. He was a little better in the morning, and we had to go on, so I told him, "I'll leave two men with you, and we'll leave you plenty to eat. Keep that thing still, and don't walk anywhere until it begins to go down. When you feel up to it, head back to the village." So we went off and left him with the two men to help him.

We continued on toward the other side of the valley. The three rivers over there were the Tawang Hka, the Tabyi Hka, and the Tanai Hka. Our plan was to cross the Tawang and the Tabyi over to the Tanai. Then we were going to follow the line of the Kumon range of mountains and head straight south, but on the way, I got an urgent radio message.

A Guide for General Merrill

The radio message was from Colonel Wilson, ordering me to report to General Merrill. The Chinese had been stalled for months, so in February of 1944, Stilwell went down there and just booted them out. He said, "You can't sit here in a hole and expect to win the war," and he moved an American regiment down there, the Galahad, 5307th provisional regiment that the newspaper people called Merrill's Marauders. The American regiment jarred the Japanese loose from Sharaw Ga, Ningbyen, and Yupong, forcing them south. I had vaguely heard that this was going on, but I didn't know much about it. Then I got this message to meet Merrill at a place called N'Dawng Ga.

N'Dawng Ga was southwest of us, a day or two away. The message said they wanted me to show up there with a guide who could take some of Merrill's regiment to the vicinity of Walawbum, a town on the main road which came down the Hukawng Valley and extended on to the railroad at Mogaung. The "road" was really more of a cart track, but it was the main Japanese supply line into the Hukawng. To get to Walawbum cross-country, and surprise the Japanese, the Americans needed to cross a stretch of jungle that was more than forty or fifty miles wide, with no tracks, no paths, no nothing. It was completely uninhabited. On the map it literally read "dense jungle," and there were no terrain features out in there, no hills or slopes or anything, just a mass of jungle. They wanted somebody that knew how to get across it, and I was directed to find that somebody.

I had several older Kachins with me. It was a practice I had initiated early on. When we'd get to a village, I'd try to persuade some of the older fellows to come with us as advisors, and I almost always had a few with me. So, I got my group of *salang ni*, or elders, together right quick, and I said, "Where can we find somebody who knows the area?" We squatted there on the ground, and I got the maps out and told them where the Americans wanted to go. The elders said, "There used to be a fellow around here who was a professional hunter. He would go out in that area and kill rhinoceros and tigers and sell them for big money to the Chinese." The Chinese liked rhinoceros horn and tiger bones; they'd grind them up and use them as magic potions. The elders said, "If that hunter were only here, he could lead them, but he died not long ago." One of them spoke up, "I don't know of anybody that knows how to get across there now." But another said, "I think the hunter had a son; he's bound to be twelve years old by now. He used to go with his father on those hunts. He might be able to do it." I thought, wait a minute, a twelve-year-old boy, what are we talking about? But they agreed amongst themselves: "If we can find him, we think he can do it." I said, "Well, if you think so, let's find him." So they sent folks to ask around at a few villages, and low and behold, within the next couple of days, they came back with this boy, the son of the hunter.

He looked like a baby, maybe twelve years old at the most. But they grow up in a hurry over there, I'll say that. I questioned the boy at length. He was an impressive youngster. He told about how his father did a lot of trapping and took him along, not just once but many times. The old men sat around and talked to him for a while, and they all came to the same conclusion: "He can do it." So I said, "All right. If you say he can do it, why, we'll use him as the guide." So we went to meet Merrill. We walked all one day and then stopped for the night. The next morning, we got up early and headed towards N'Dawng Ga. Along the way, a voice in English ordered us to halt. An American stepped out of the bushes. He said, "If you hadn't had that big hat on, I'd have shot you." I said, "Well, I'm glad I had the big hat on!" I had this little boy with me, and I told the soldier, "I need to talk to General Merrill. This boy's going to be your guide." The guard just laughed, but I repeated, "Take us to General Merrill as quickly as possible. I'm running late already." So the man took us to General Merrill.

When we approached, there was a fellow I knew talking with Merrill. It was C. E. Darlington, an Anglican clergymen, a missionary like his brother David. The Kachins called him Darlington Gam. He had been stationed in Shingbwiyang a while back to help handle the refugees and had recently been assigned as Merrill's chief liaison with the local population. He knew the Kachins well and could speak to this boy. We were lucky he was there. I don't think we would have sold Merrill on taking this little fellow as his guide if it weren't for Darlington. We still had a long, interesting discussion before we were able to convince Merrill that he should put this boy in front and have his men follow him. We finally did convince him, though, and all struck out immediately.

They put us with what they called an I&R platoon, information and reconnaissance. A big, tall fellow named Logan Weston was the first lieutenant, the platoon leader, and it was the funniest thing you ever saw. Here was this little barefoot boy maybe four feet high, and here was ol' Weston, six foot or more. And this boy knew where to go. There was no trail, but the little fellow was just like a bird dog. He skittered out front, going this way and that way and this way, looking for signs and maybe cutting a weed down with his knife or making a mark on a tree or something. He didn't have any compass, he didn't have anything. There were no streams out in there, it was just a flat, vast area with big trees and dense undergrowth. It took us a while to reach Tawang Hka, cross it, and head to the Tabyi Hka, not too far from where it joined the next river, the Tanai Hka. We went across both those rivers and through more jungle. Finally, after several days travel, the boy came to the stream right next to Walawbum. He was out front when he just turned around, pointed, and said, "Walawbum is right there." He had done his job. One twelve-year-old boy had led a significant force of men across the jungle and gotten them exactly where they needed to be.

Merrill's men immediately followed the creek down to the road and set up a roadblock. The Japanese by this time had begun to retreat. They tried to knock Merrill out of there, but Merrill's forces killed a ton of them. We didn't stay with them for that, though. We turned around and went back, and the boy went with us. They should have given him a medal of some kind, but it was war time, and everyone was in a big hurry, so he just disappeared into the mist of history. I was twenty-three then, and he was at most twelve, so he might still be around. He's probably telling the story himself. That little fellow was a real hero, but it didn't faze him. He just said, "I think I can do it," and he did. I heard that Merrill employed another young guide, maybe fourteen years old, on the approach to Myitkyina some time later. In light of that first experience, I imagine Merrill followed the boy without hesitation.

Billy Baird and the Buffalos

When we left Merrill, we continued south. We stopped for a while on the Tanai Hka, put out agents in the villages all around, and settled in. From the north one day, here came three people. The fellow in the middle, walking on crutches, was the man with the snake bite and the others, the two who had stayed with him. They had gotten scared just sitting there, so they headed out to find us. By the time they got to us, he had gangrene in that foot; it smelled like something dead. He was in terrible shape, so we decided we had to get him out. There was a gravel bar there on the river which we thought was big enough for a light plane, so we radioed for someone to come get him. The pilot that came was Billy Baird, an old friend of mine from Mississippi State. He made a point of trying to get to me every time he could. He took the man all the way back to Shingbwiyang, at least a hundred miles away, to the airfield in the forest. By that time, they had a hospital there. The man lost his whole leg, not just his foot, but he survived.

When Baird made that trip, he was based at Maingkwan, or Moonkum as the Kachins call it. The battle line had moved down since the Japanese had retreated south. The Chinese then established a little airfield at Maingkwan. When he came out to get the fellow, Billy mentioned they were having trouble with rations. He complained, "We get enough to eat, but we don't ever get any meat." We got to talking, and I said, "Back up the Tanai Hka, we passed an abandoned village, and there was a herd of buffalo near there." I said, "If you think we can land and take off on these rocky bars, maybe you and I could run up there and kill a buffalo and supply your outfit with some fresh meat." This was a diversion, I guess you'd call it.

So after Billy had flown out the snakebit man, I got a message over our radio that he was going to come back and see if we couldn't get that buffalo. He came in one morning, landed on those dadgum rocks, and we took off together. It was a hairy takeoff, like riding a bucking bronco, but he pulled it off. We flew down river, and sure enough we sighted the herd of buffalo from the air. On a long stretch of rocky bar, we managed to land in the vicinity. We got out and stalked the herd. There were some of the biggest bulls I had ever seen, with six-foot horn spreads, really enormous creatures, maybe two thousand pounds.

We picked out what looked like a half-grown calf. It was a small one, or at least small compared to the others. I knelt down and took aim and shot that calf right on target. He just walked off. I had to shoot that animal three more times before he finally dropped. This aroused the rest of the herd, so for a while, we retreated behind a big tree. Finally, they dispersed.

When we got up to the calf, he must have weighed eight hundred pounds if he weighed an ounce. The plane was small, maybe an L4 or L5, and it couldn't possibly get that whole calf off the ground, much less me and Billy Baird. So we decided to butcher him right there. We both had knives, and I had my Kachin sword. We thought we might be able to get away with two hindquarters. We skinned them and trimmed them, but we still had these two enormous legs and part of the back. Billy said, "I don't know whether we're going to be able to take off with them or not." Here we were all covered with blood. We'd been butchering in a hurry, because time was passing, and he had to get me back and then get himself back to Maingkwan, almost a hundred miles away.

The two of us hauled the airplane back across the rocky bar, backed it up against the trees at the end of the gravel bar, and then we made another trip back across those darned rocks to pick up the meat and carry it to the plane. Those pieces really were heavy. The pilot's position was in the back, the passenger in front on that plane. Outside the door was a strut that went up to the wing. Our idea was for me to sit in front, put one haunch on the floor by me, and hold the other haunch out the door. If Billy saw that we were not going to be able to get off the ground, he would hit me in the back, and I was to drop that leg. It must have weighed a hundred pounds. With two legs, we might not make it, but we were going to give it a try. So, we loaded the one leg in the cockpit where I was to sit. It made a big bloody mess. I picked up the other haunch and put it on the strut where I could grab it. Then I got down and helped him start the plane by flipping the propeller. When it started, I climbed back in and held the second haunch in position.

Billy set the brakes and revved up the engine as fast as it would go. Then he released the brakes, and off we went, bouncing and jumping across the rocks. We gradually picked up speed. I was sitting there hanging onto this buffalo leg, watching the trees in front of us get closer and closer and taller and taller. I kept expecting Billy to hit me on the back, the signal to drop that leg and just leave it for the tigers, but he didn't.

I remember that plane ride hanging onto that bloody leg more than any other ride I ever took. Good thing I had a belt on to hold me in the plane. At the very last minute, Billy hauled back on that wheel, got it off the rocks, and immediately turned while we were just six or seven feet off the ground. He got out over the water and flew down the river until he could gain enough altitude to clear the trees.

We made it, with me still gripping that haunch. Then we went back up the Tanai Hka and landed where we had plenty of men to help us pull the plane around.

The Kachins were sad to see all that meat go. But we loaded both haunches where I had been sitting, and Billy managed to take off and make it back to his home base. We heard from him later that his whole outfit out there in the middle of the jungle had a big barbecue and cooked that meat. He said it was a little tough, but it was meat, and they appreciated that.

Colonel Peers Takes Over

Merrill kept going down the main road, setting up roadblocks. My group went parallel to them, east of the main Japanese supply line. Late in March of 1944, we ended up near a place called Nawbum. While we were there, I learned that Colonel Ray Peers had taken over from Carl Eifler as the head of OSS detachment 101. I had never met either one, but I got a wire from Peers that he was coming in by plane and wanted to talk. At a paddy field there, we prepared a small airfield by knocking down some dikes, or bunds as the British called them, between sections of the field.

Peers came to tell me that the V Force and OSS 101 had been combined, that I was now in the OSS, and he was to be my new commander. He also let me know the overall plan. Several groups were to move south from different locations. A man I knew from Tagap named Vincent Curl, better known as "Knothead" Curl, was sent to Fort Hertz airfield. He was to come south along the eastern mountain range with a group of Kachins. On the upper reaches of the Irrawaddy River, the Kachin Levies under Stilwell were to come south along the river. I was to move west of the main road and go south from there. Peers assigned Johnny Colling's group even further west.

I told Peers, "I've got to get back to a hospital to get my wound cauterized. It hasn't healed up; I'm still having to put a bandage on it every day. I can start my outfit in that direction, but I think I need to go to a place that can fix me up." He gave me the go ahead, so I gathered my men, and we all started walking toward the west. When we got to the main track, I turned north and went up to Shingbwiyang by myself, and the rest of the men went toward a place called Dalu. My outfit at the time included a few Americans—Tuggle, McNabb, Sayers, Migon, Van Arsdale, Buck, a radio operator named Moffet—and about eighty Kachins—Goitam Kamai, Nawji, Labang Naw, and my right arm, Jemadar Mahka La. They all walked straight across to Dalu, or Taro it's sometimes called, on the lower Tanai River as it leaves the Hukawng Valley and runs into the Chindwin. We were to meet at Dalu after I got fixed up.

Colonel Peers was a gung ho sort of a fellow. He had been a football player and had broken his nose way back when. Although he'd been Eifler's number two man, Peers was not really very familiar with the territory. He had sense enough to make Cummings his chief of operations, but even so, I thought Peers suffered from lack of experience. He would tell you, "We want you to recruit all the men you can and give the Japanese hell. And we want all the information you can get. And we want you to blow the railroads up. And we're going to supply you. We've got the aircraft to keep things running." It sounded good, but sometimes the 101 supply folks would question why we needed this or that. J. R. Wilson had never done that. If we asked for something, hell, he would try his dead level best to get it there, even if he had to deliver it himself. He had been in the thick of it and knew what it was like.

Later on, Johnny Colling ended up in an intermediate station at Singaling Hkamti, relaying our radio messages because we were getting so far away that radio communication was difficult. Sometimes I would vent my frustrations in messages after unsuccessful requests. Years later at a reunion, Johnny told me, "I kept you from getting court martialed several times. I changed your messages before I relayed them in." Over time though, Peers got better. And ultimately, we made it through to the end with Peers in command.

Percy Jones, radio operator, picked up by Pete's group south of Bhamo. Percy had been hidden by villagers, after others in his group were killed in a Japanese ambush in October 1944. Picture taken at Namon. April 1945.

Curtis Schultz standing behind Kachin boys sporting Japanese uniforms and equipment captured by 7th Battalion Jinghpaw Rangers. Spring 1945.

At 7th Battalion headquarters, boys turn a generator crank for radio operator Russel. February 1945.

Dashi Yaw, one of Pete's advisors, 7th Battalion headquarters at Namon. March 1945.

Capt. C. E. (Chuck) Roberts, A Company commander, and Lt. John A. McCargar, B Company commander, 7th Battalion. Longtawk. February 1945.

Lieutenant Gordan A. Totten and soldiers of C Company 7th Battalion. February 1945.

D Company (left to right) Subedar B'rang Nu, Saw Abbey, Lieutenant Wesley Richardson C.O., Subedar Lum Dai. March 1945.

Near Hungwe airstrip. Major Hamm holding white object in left hand, then (left to right) Curtis Schultz, pilot Vince Trifletti, Singh with turban.

Longtawk headman. February 1945.

Kunhawt, a village on the
march towards Namyun.
February 1945.

A crowd gathered around an L-1 plane at Namon airstrip. March 1945.

7th Battalion taking a break on the way from Namon towards Hsipaw. April 1945.

Officers and medal recipients holding shotguns they also received as rewards. Front row: (left to right) Lieutenant Sao Hkun Tha, Jem. Marip Gam, Tagu Zau Tu, Hkangda Gam, Dashi Yaw (advisor), Ying Siang (interpreter). Back row: Captain C. E. Roberts, Major P. K. Lutken, Subedar Mahka La, Private McLeod, Ting Bawm (I & R platoon leader), Nhkum Zau Seng (clerk and advisor), Percy Jones (radio operator).

Soldiers of the 7th Battalion. Major P. K. Lutken commanding officer in foreground. Namtu. April 1945.

The "Three Musketeers" (left to right) Subedar Major Mahka La, Major P. K. Lutken, Ting Bawm (I & R platoon leader). Namtu. April 1945.

Final pay distribution. (left to right) C. E. Roberts, P. K. Lutken, Nhkum Zau Seng, and soldier receiving payment. The soldier is wearing his own sword, as many did. April 1945.

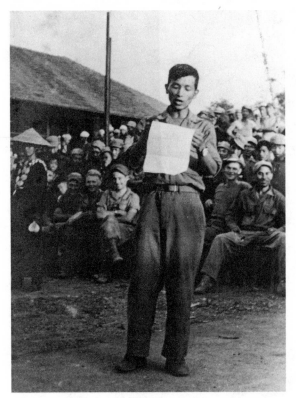

Saga of the 7th Battalion composed and read aloud at the Namtu *manao* (celebration) by Hbau Yam Gam, one of Pete's advisors. April 1945.

Jinghpaw dance leaders at the *manao* (celebration) in Namtu. Jemadar Tubu Gam, who previously had served with the British Burma Rifles and then with the Japanese before joining the 7th Battalion, is in uniform standing behind the dancers. April 1945.

Jinghpaw soldier performing the sword dance at the *manao*. April 1945.

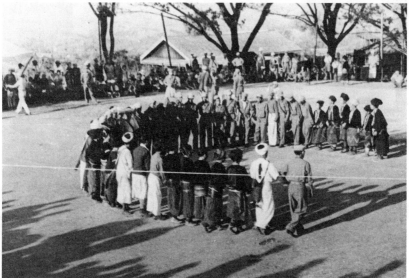

"Housebuilding" dance, both men and women participating. Namtu *manao*. April 1945.

Women at celebration serving *lao hku*, a fermented rice beverage, poured from the large bamboo vessel held by the woman on far left. McLeod, center, reaching for cup, then left to right, Dashi Yaw, Ting Bawm, Pete Lutken, Chuck Roberts. Namtu. April 1945.

Mahka La and others on the Namtu/Bawdwin Railway for a ride. April 1945.

Captain Tom Chamales (left) and Captain Phil Weld at army base in Calcutta (now Kolkata) area. June 1945.

British cruiser headed eastward through the Suez Canal, taken from Pete's transport ship, the USS *Gen. William F. Hase*, which was tied up, since eastbound traffic had the right of way. July 6, 1945.

Pete Lutken and staff at a farm in Myanmar sponsored by Project Old Soldier. 2005. Photograph by Dr. Ed Runge.

Pete receiving gifts, including a sword, at ceremony honoring the veterans of OSS Detachment 101 in Myanmar. 2005. Photograph by Dr. Ed Runge.

P. K. Lutken Jr. 2012.
Photograph by Rollin S.
Fraser.

P. K. Lutken Jr. 2012.
Photograph by Rollin S.
Fraser.

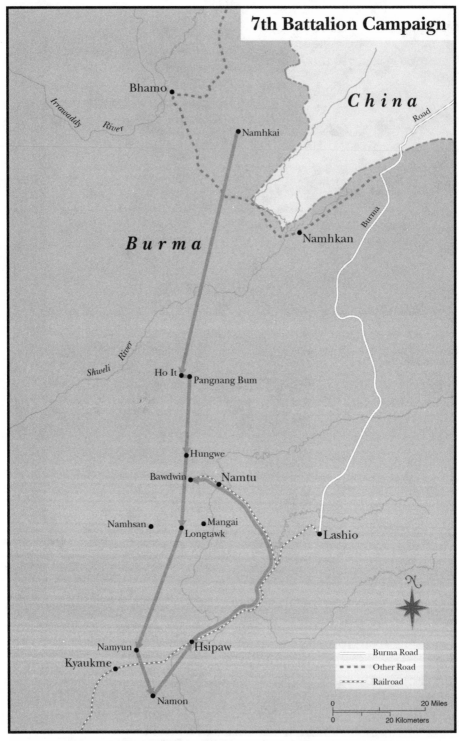

Map 4: The area south of Bhamo where Pete, Mahka La, and radio operator Paul parachuted behind Japanese lines. Arrows mark the route they took as they recruited soldiers for the 7th Battalion, subsequent route of the battalion's campaign, and final gathering for celebration at Namtu.

PART IV

WITH THE OSS

April 1944-May 1945

Rats

Shingbwiyang was the station area for the whole business by then. Command had planned for Ningbyen to be the main spot, but it didn't pan out. The road was finished at Shingbwiyang for one thing; at least it was passable for trucks and tanks, and they had made an airfield. There was an American field hospital right next to the airfield: thatched bamboo *bashas* with dirt floors, nothing fancy, just shelters. They cauterized my wound there. It was a relief not to have to wear a bandage and to be able use the bathroom without any trouble. While I was at Shingbwiyang, I picked up a jungle hammock. It had a roof on it, a mosquito net, and a stick to keep it from folding up—the first time I had anything like that.

After my treatment, I went south by boat. Some soldiers took me along the river at Shingbwiyang in a dugout canoe with an outboard motor on the back of it. The river joined the Tanai and looped like a corkscrew through a deep canyon. It was quite a ride. They let me out at Dalu, as far as they were allowed to go. By the time I got there, my outfit had left, along with an officer named Dow Grones. Grones had decided he was going to get them moving and that I could just catch up because the Chinese had pushed a little farther down. They were fighting with the Japanese between Dalu and a place called Tawmaw. I found two local Kachins willing to come with me, and we got in a dugout canoe to paddle down river after my friends. We had to be cautious because the Japanese were all around. They were still pretty much in control of the area, and we were looking out for them.

We hadn't gone too far when we came to a bend in the river and noticed smoke up ahead. There wasn't any village marked on the map, so we thought we'd better stop and investigate. We pulled the canoe up on the bank, climbed up a steep hillside, and found a site with a good view. The smoke was coming from near the riverbank. We could see some Nagas setting up a camp. It was unusual, because Nagas almost always lived on the top of ridges, not in low spots. But there they were, so we decided to go check in with them. We made a peaceful approach and managed to get into a conversation. I asked them, "What are you doing down here?" And the answer I got was one word, "*Yu.*" *Yu* means "rats."

Bamboo is odd. The plants in one grove have a simultaneous cycle, and when the grove hits a certain point in the cycle, why, the whole thing flowers and goes to seed. There are apparently many different kinds of bamboo, and for some of them, that cycle is many years long. The bamboo grows and flourishes, and then it flowers and seeds and dies, and it dies en masse. We hadn't paid much attention as we were going down the river, but the bamboo jungle off to the north, covering the whole mountainside for miles, was all dead.

Where these Nagas lived, way up on top of the ridge, the bamboo had all died, and any animals that lived off of bamboo had moved out. The whole jungle was full of rats. They came out by the millions and swamped the village. One man told me, "The rats ate up almost everything we had. We couldn't get rid of them. We killed them by the hundreds and cooked them and ate them. But you can't live off of nothing but rats." Their traditional method of defense against the rats, fire, didn't work; there were just too many. They were everywhere.

The people had a few storage containers way up off the ground, so they were able to save some of their rice. The folks told us, "We had a town meeting. We figured we had about enough rice for half the population, and therefore half of us had to leave." Nobody was mad about it. They drew lots to see who would have to go. The losers came down to the river valley. There were plenty of edible roots, and they were planning on living the rest of the year on those roots until they could grow another crop.

It was April, so the others were planting up on the ridge, but they wouldn't have a crop until the fall. This group was going to have to live down by the river until September or October, when there would be a harvest up above, and they'd be able to go back. Of course, they could plant some things themselves, but mainly they would have to live off of roots. In effect, they were condemned to be there, almost like a death sentence, since they would all be bitten to pieces by mosquitoes. They knew many would get malaria, and some might die. All we could do was wish them luck, and we were off.

Tiger Valley

In conversation with the Kachins who were paddling with me, I found out some disturbing information. According to them, there were no villages at all along the track where I was headed, even though the map showed a whole bunch. Apparently, all the people that used to live there had recently picked up and moved. I questioned them more, and they said, "We don't know too much about it, but word is, they left on account of tigers." The tigers had apparently gotten so bold and numerous that everyone was forced to evacuate. I thought to myself that the tigers must have been pretty bad. Most of the Kachins I knew were stalwart folks; they used old muzzleloaders, loaded them with whatever they could find, and would go after just about anything. But these two had given me just enough information to start me worrying.

We continued down river until we got to the trail. I bid my two Kachin friends goodbye and thanks. They headed back to Dalu, and I struck out by myself. I managed to catch up with my men in short order. Right away, Dow Grones told me he had also heard some rumblings about a tiger situation. He said the Kachins were complaining about one particular valley along the track. We kept walking anyway, but we could tell that all of the Kachins were wary about the trip. The territory we were walking through was mostly flat or slightly hilly, dense jungle. The area they were worried about looked to be seventy-five or eighty miles away, and as we approached it, the mountains got higher.

Within range of the place in question, our men became extremely reluctant to go on, so I got them all together to find out what they actually knew. The story they told was that tigers in that valley had begun coming into the villages, taking the livestock and sometimes people as their prey. The villagers had tried to defend themselves, but the tigers kept coming. Finally, the whole valley had been abandoned. Our men had also heard that a Japanese column had come through the area from the other direction, maybe a month or so before. The Japanese had been warned that the valley was inhabited by spirit tigers, were-tigers, you might call them, tigers that were magic and couldn't be killed. In spite of warnings, they had gone on, but with serious consequences.

I asked how wide the valley was, and they said, "It's big, pretty close to forty miles or so from one side to the other." For us there was no way around it, so after some thought, I said, "If we get up very early in the morning and go like blazes until late at night, if we walk twelve or fifteen hours, we can get across the valley; we can make it in one day." With a lot of convincing, they reluctantly agreed to the plan. So we kept going until we got near the rim of the valley. I could see by the map that they were right, it was very deep, and about a forty-mile hike, at least that was my guess, because the trail had a lot of turns and switchbacks. But there definitely was a trail marked.

Where we stopped for the night, there was a good view of the gorge. Just a short piece away from us, a stone outcrop stuck out from the bottom of the valley. It looked to be an old volcanic core, black, ghostly, and gigantic. It wasn't like a mountain, more like a spire, dark and jagged, with trees sticking out of it here and there. The Kachins said, "That's where the magic tigers live. That's where they come from." I could see how people would think it was mysterious and ominous; it looked ominous to me, too. We stopped where we were and camped just short of the rim of the canyon.

It was a huge canyon. We think of canyons in terms of the American West, where things are rocky and open, like the Grand Canyon. It's not that way in Burma. This canyon was covered with vegetation, very dense forest, even though it was incredibly steep. When traveling on a trail in such dense jungle, it's like moving through a tunnel. That night, anticipating the next day's journey through that tunnel, I'd never seen an outfit so upset. The feeling of unease was everywhere.

Some soldiers told me more about what they had heard of the Japanese expedition. Apparently, the soldiers had made camp in the bottom of the valley beside the river. Tigers, when they're hunting, make a kind of coughing sound that confuses their prey. It's hard to tell which direction the sound is coming from. Deer and other prey panic when they hear that noise and sometimes run right into the tigers while trying to get away. The Kachins said that during the night, the Japanese began to hear the coughing of several tigers on the hunt. They built up their fires, but they kept hearing that coughing close by. And it was a considerable force of Japanese, not just a handful of people. Furthermore, they had a whole bunch of Kachin coolies with them who had been pressed into service. They built fires all around them as the night went on, but the coughing continued.

Finally, late in the night, a huge tiger bounded into the circle of firelight where they had made camp. The story went that the tiger pounced into the circle, grabbed one of the Kachins by the middle of his back just like a dog would grab a rat, picked him up, bounded out of the firelight, and disappeared. The Japanese went crazy. They started firing off into the bushes with machine guns and everything else, and then, in the middle of the night, they packed up and left. They got out of there.

The night we spent on the canyon rim was the dangdest thing. We generally had a rule against fires at night when Japanese might be nearby. But that night, everybody built fires and crammed in around them. There were around 150 of us at the time. Usually, we'd put guards out on the trails. Instead, that night they all gathered tight together. Tigers, *sharaw*, they were worried about them, even up there on the rim. Nobody slept. I hung my new hammock up between two trees. Kachins were all jammed in so close to each other that two men slept right under the hammock. It was quiet, but I'm pretty sure most of the men were wide awake.

At about three o'clock in the morning, I rounded everybody up. We packed up and started out in the dark, heading down into the valley. Usually, people made noise on the trail, talking and chattering and rattling stuff, but that morning, I didn't hear a thing. They were walking as hard as they could go, with single-minded purpose. I would hear the occasional clink of a canteen, but mostly everybody moved silently. The sun came out, but the foliage was so dense down there that light hardly got through the trees. However, we could see enough to walk, and walk fast.

The trail was muddy, and we began noticing the biggest tiger footprints I'd ever seen. I mean, they were like full sized plates, giant paw prints right in the trail. I was up at the front of the column, and the prints looked fresh to me, some of them going the same direction we were and some coming the other way. When I saw those prints, I walked even faster. I always lived with the fear of Japanese attacking us, but this was an oddly more powerful and primitive fear, the fear of being hunted by a beast. It raised the hair on the back of my neck.

We got to the bottom of the valley before noon. It was a long way, but we had moved with remarkable speed. On a normal day, somebody would want to stop every now and then. This time nobody wanted to stop. We finally came out into a clear space, a long, muddy slope going down to the water. There was a banyan tree on the other side of the creek, pretty high up on the bank. Somebody had taken the time to carve a message on that tree in English and in Burmese—I don't know who had done it. It said, "TIGER. Don't camp here." It gives me the chills even now to think about it.

Well, I'm telling you, we went down to that creek, and nobody stopped to get a drink of water or anything. All 150 of us were walking as fast as we could go. When we got to the other side, I made everyone stop for a few moments. I said, "Let's look around and see if what they had to say about that Japanese camp is true." So we went over and found where they had camped. There was evidence of huge fires at the camp. We found empty cartridge cases all over the place where they'd been shooting, and we found the usual debris left by the Japanese. They often ate fish which came dried in paper packages, and those packages were lying all around. We scouted out through the woods, and in short order, we found the dead Kachin. He was just bones with a little meat left, but he was a Kachin all right because his turban was still there. Bones were scattered all around. The tiger had grabbed him and taken him off and eaten him. We did not need any more convincing.

Without a word, we formed up again right quick and took off. We didn't stop walking, not once on the way up that steep canyon. It may have been my imagination, but as dusk approached, I thought I could hear tigers coughing, but we kept our heads down and walked. We kept going until about 10:00 p.m., when we finally crested the other side in the pitch dark.

When we got well beyond the edge of the canyon, everybody just stopped. We didn't make camp; we didn't build a fire; we didn't do anything. Everybody was completely exhausted. We all crowded in and bedded down on the ground. Fortunately, it didn't rain. If they had something to eat left over from the night before, folks ate, but we didn't formally fix anything. We stayed there until dawn the next day, then we went on up the hill further to put a few more miles between us and the tigers.

I'd like to go back someday, not into the valley, just to take a look from a distance at that terrifying spire. It may not be as big as I remember, but it sure was impressive and looked like a place where spirit tigers might hide out. I got to where I halfway believed all the magical things the Kachins told me anyway. And when I experienced a few more mysteries up on top of the mountain called Undung Bum, I didn't doubt them anymore.

A Sad Greeting

The day after we came out of Tiger Valley, we found ourselves on the slopes of Undung Bum. At that point, Dow Grones and his crowd left us. They took off down the valley of the Uru Hka to the southwest, and I took my people, and we headed uphill. We needed to find a place that had food. As a rule, we could only carry enough food to last a week or maybe ten days because hand grenades, guns, the base plates for mortars, and ammunition were all very heavy. I mentioned earlier that most people had left the area, so we were depending on a rumor, and that's all it was, just a rumor, that there was a Naga village near the top of Undung Bum. The Nagas we knew of lived many miles to the west. These people were way out of their territory, if indeed they were there. The map didn't show anyone in that particular area at all.

At dawn, we set out. A scout walked ahead of us as we began climbing the slopes of the mountain. I was not far back down the line when he came running back with a terrified look on his face. He said, "Come look! Come look!" So I went with him, and right in the middle of the trail was a trap that had been sprung by a gigantic sambar deer. The deer was hanging motionless a good ways up in the air. The trap consisted of a sapling, a pretty thick one, that had been bent down with a loop, rigged so that when something stepped in that loop, it sprung the trigger, and the sapling straightened up. The tree was big enough and strong enough to pick that deer up by the one leg. He'd obviously been up there for a long time, since he was about half rotten, and it must have taken him some time to die, a grim thought.

The scout knew immediately that this meant something bad. People around there didn't leave traps unchecked, not one single day. But this deer had been left up there long enough to rot. The first thing that came to his mind was, "The Japanese must have taken the village." So we proceeded with great caution, leaving the deer suspended in the air. At least we knew somebody had been on top of the mountain, so the myth of the village was probably a reality. As we approached, we saw a hut in a clearing, or *gee*, they call it, a hillside field, not plowed, just cleared. Folks there often didn't plow, they just "sweetened," I think anthropologists call it, where they'd burn fields, then plant seeds, pull weeds, and hope they had a crop. It was springtime, and there was usually somebody in the paddy huts, most often children and women. Men cleared the fields and burned them, but from that point forward, the women and children did most of the weeding and watching. There was always a problem with monkeys and parrots and elephants and other animals, so folks were stationed there to drive them off. In a hut out in the middle of the field, they'd often run vines off in different directions, like ropes. Down at the end of each vine, they'd put a clapper made of a bamboo stalk. They'd usually just use one that was already growing there and then split it. The rope was attached to half of it, so if they jerked the rope, it popped back and made a noise. Children sat there and jerked on the ropes to keep the animals away. Sometimes they hung streamer-like objects on the vines, pieces of bark that hung down to frighten the birds. That's the setup we saw when we came to this field.

We crept up to the edge and looked. Sure enough, there was smoke coming through the roof of the little hut. But nobody was outside. I started toward the hut with three or four Kachins following me. All of a sudden, just like clowns jumping out of an automobile at the circus, people started pouring out of that hut, running in every direction. We hollered that we weren't going to hurt them, but they kept running. We finally chased down a boy who was about ten years old. That stopped the exodus. Several of the women came back, and we managed to communicate with them and convince them we meant no harm.

Our first question was, "Are there Japanese in the village?" And their answer was, "No, no Japanese." The next question was, "What's wrong? Something's wrong because we found that deer back there." Their reply was, "*Ana kerah.*" That meant "bad disease." I can still remember the feeling of horror when I heard those words. We found out right away that the disease they were talking about was smallpox, and we became very afraid because none of my men had ever been vaccinated. Well, I had been, and the few Americans with me, but none of the Kachins had. And here we were, walking into a village with smallpox! We managed to find out that there had been about a hundred people in the village, and some forty of them had died already.

One of the women and the boy came with us toward the village. When we got near, I walked on up by myself and found everyone there was essentially immobilized. People were dying. I met the headman, whose name was Let Hko Him, the only one in the village who had been vaccinated. He had a great big mark on his arm from the vaccine he had gotten long ago from the British, so he hadn't caught the disease. Talking to him, I came to the conclusion that the greatest death toll was among children and younger folks. The old people, if they got it, didn't die. Their faces were all covered with sores, but it was the younger people who died—such a great tragedy.

Quickly, I got our radioman to send a message back to headquarters to send smallpox vaccination materials for all of my men and a whole bunch of extras. I figured we'd vaccinate all of the villagers, whatever their condition. I didn't know if it would do any good, but we'd try. Fairly soon, an L5 flew down and free dropped, all wrapped up and padded, enough vaccinations for all of my men and a lot more.

So we vaccinated all the people in the village regardless of whether they were sick and all of my men. We also vaccinated me and the other American soldiers, even though we'd been vaccinated before. Each little vial came with a needle to make a scratch on the arm. We broke the little vial and put a drop or two of the stuff on the scratch. After that, nobody died, and none of my men got smallpox. I'm not sure we did any good by vaccinating the villagers, since they'd already been exposed, but all who were alive when we got there lived.

The *Myrhtoi* of Undung Bum

We camped on the ridge near the top of the mountain, about a mile north of the Naga village. We didn't want the men to stay in the village with the smallpox. Our campsite was up a steep climb at about seven thousand feet. It was not a big campsite, just a few shelters near a small creek. I put up a lean-to for myself between two big trees—the typical two forked sticks with one pole across and a lot of little poles on one side with some leaves covering them. That type of shelter requires no lashing; it just stands up by itself. That's what I built to sleep under at Undung Bum.

With us at that time was a man by the name of Labang La, who claimed to be what they call a *myrhtoi*. A *myrhtoi* is a kind of priest and prophet that claims he can foretell the future and do all sorts of magic things. Labang La didn't have a uniform, but I had used him as a spy, and he was one of us. I sent him to get information, and after we got camp set up, he came to tell me he had sent two Naga boys over to a nearby Kachin village to check it out. As the crow flies, Lamong Ga, the Kachin village, was only about three or four miles east of our Naga village, but to get there required going down into a very deep canyon and up the other side. Lamong Ga village was right on the supply line of the Japanese regimental headquarters, which was in a nearby place called Tawmaw, so the *myrhtoi* figured the folks in the village were bound to know something.

The next night, we heard a big hullabaloo back in the Naga village. A bunch of folks came running up the trail towards us. They brought the two boys with them that had been sent to Lamong Ga, and the boys were all beat up. Their faces were swelled up; their eyes were blackened; they had obviously been hurt pretty badly. We finally got the story out of them with the help of the headman, Let Hko Him. The boys had gone to the Kachin village. But they were noticed. The headman of Lamong Ga village, it turns out, was a Japanese sympathizer. He got the Japanese from Tawmaw to come down and interrogate those two boys, and they really laid into them. The boys said that after they had been kicked around for quite a while, they finally told their captors that there were about three or four thousand Americans on top of Undung Bum, and they thought that the Japanese halfway believed them. The Japanese took the news back to Tawmaw. Then Lamong Zau Htawng, the headman of the Kachin village, had the boys tied up and put a guard on them. During the night, some villagers sneaked over and cut them loose, and they escaped. Although they had a lot of bruises, they were able to make it back. When they got home, Let Hko Him brought them straight to us. We questioned them, tried to find out everything we could. But they were pretty sick from the beating, so we sent them home after a short while.

I turned to Labang La, the *myrhtoi*, and said, "All right, you sent those Nagas over there. Now the Japanese undoubtedly know where we are. They're probably confused about numbers; nevertheless, they know where we are. You're a *myrhtoi*, why don't you foretell the future, tell us what's going to happen next, so we'll know how to react." Without blinking an eye, he said, "Yes, sir, I will." He said, "Excuse me. I need to go get something." Labang La went into the bushes and rustled around. Practically the whole outfit heard what was going on, and they were all standing around waiting by the fire when he returned. He came back with two leaves. I don't know the exact type, but they resembled monkey grass where the veins run lengthwise. He squatted down by the fire and began to chant. He closed his eyes and rocked back and forth on his heels. He took the leaves, which were each about a foot long, and split them between the veins, so he had something like a cat o'nine tails with seven, eight, or nine, I forget how many little strings hanging down. All the time his eyes were closed, he stroked those leaves and pulled on them and sang in a high nasal voice. He seemed to make up the song as he went and used some phrases that I'm sure were magic. People crowded around him in the dark to watch.

Finally, he stopped. Without opening his eyes, he took two of the strands and tied them together in a knot. He opened his hand up and pulled the strings out, and he messed around with them a little bit, looking at the pattern. Then he looked up at me. The whole crowd hung on his every word. He said, "Tomorrow around sunset, two men will come up the trail. I don't know whether they'll be Japanese or not, but they'll have on Japanese uniforms, and they'll be armed. You must put a guard on the trail to capture these men. Do not kill them. Capture them." He said, "If you kill them, the Japanese will be up here quickly. On the other hand, if you catch them, the Japanese will not come." Everybody drank in everything he said. I responded, "Thank you very much. We'll go ahead and put the guard out immediately. We don't want to take any chances." So we put a guard of about twelve men on the trail where the two men were supposed to come and some more on the other trails from whatever direction, and we waited.

Late the next day, I said to Labang La, "The sun's going down. What's the situation?" And without hesitating, he said to me, "They've got them." I said, "You mean they've already caught them?" "Yes." Well, by George, within a few minutes, here came the whole crowd walking up the hill with the two prisoners. The men that they caught had been armed, both of them. One was a tall fellow; he was a Burman, and the other was a Kachin. Both had on Japanese uniforms with little kepi hats, and both had Japanese rifles. They were in the service of the Japanese; there wasn't any question about it.

The Burman was really recalcitrant. He wasn't saying anything. But the Kachin was younger, and he sang like a bird. He answered every question we asked him. The Burman was real smart. If you said, "Are you with the Japanese?" he'd fire back at you, "I don't have to tell you anything." We were sitting up in my hut between the two big trees during the interrogation. I tried for a while but finally gave up questioning him. I told Mahka La to take the prisoners down and give them something to eat, both of them, but to tie the Burman up. We assigned a guard to the Kachin, but I didn't think it was necessary to tie him up. He'd been completely cooperative.

I went on about my business up at my shelter. The radioman and I were trying to compose a message to headquarters to let them know what was going on. Encoding and sending a message was a slow procedure. While we were busy with that, we heard a ruckus. Down the hill a piece, there was a fire going and a lot of loud talking. I tried to listen. There was some very loud cussing, and I recognized Mahka La's voice. I was about to go down and see what was going on when I heard this bloodcurdling scream.

I ran down the slope to the camp, and there in the firelight was Mahka La. He had been questioning this Burman, and the man had talked back to him. Mahka La, with one sweeping stroke of his sword, had cut the man's ear off, cut his ear plumb off. He was saying, "And I'm going to eat the rest of you," and he was eating that ear. He chewed it up and was eating it. I was so completely shocked, it was like being slapped. Mahka La had blood all over his mouth. He was chewing on this man's ear right in front of him, and it had turned the Burman practically to jelly. The man was groveling on the ground and making all sorts of funny noises, begging for his life. I quickly made the determination to keep cool, so I made some light remark like, "Does it taste good?" With that, I managed to get Mahka La off of the idea that he could chop the fellow to pieces, and I broke up the meeting for the night. The man's wound had pretty much quit bleeding by then, and I said, "We've got all we need out of this guy. Let's tie him up good. We'll talk to him some more tomorrow."

Well, they didn't tie him up good enough, and during the night, the Burman got away. He escaped, and I don't know to this good day where he went or how he got away. The rope was still there—there was blood on it—and he was gone. It wasn't the first time that sort of thing had happened. You cannot tie a man up with a rope with his hands in front of him. If you tie him up tight enough to where he can't get away, you're probably going to kill him; it will cut the circulation off, and he'll be awful sick, if not dead. If you tie him up in a humane manner, he'll get out. He may pull nearly all the skin off his hands, but he'll get out. If the post in a house was not too big, we would sometimes tie a man's hands around behind it, and he usually wouldn't get away. But some men got away even then, and even out of handcuffs. We'd find the handcuffs in the morning empty, still closed. So this time, we lost our prize prisoner, after having gotten very little out of him except his ear. In spite of his escaping, however, the Japanese didn't come after us.

After the *myrhtoi* predicted so perfectly what was going to happen with the spies, I always listened to him. Labang La told me he had, I forget what he called them exactly, powers or ways to accomplish things. For one, he said, "People in this part of the world believe that a person can be two places at one time." He said, "I can do that." There wasn't any way I could check him on that. I said, "That would be very useful. I may call on you to transplant yourself down the way, when I need to get some information." This man, Labang La, I would say he was middle-aged. He was getting gray-headed. He'd been at it a long time.

Even though the *myrhtoi* had told me that the Japanese wouldn't come, I decided we'd better move. It seemed unlikely that the escapee could get back to the Japanese quickly since we had put guards on all the trails, but he'd probably get there eventually, so we picked up and moved some distance further from the village. The night after we moved, there was a terrible thunderstorm. Since we had left in a hurry, we didn't have much protection from the rain. The storm raged and blew, and we could hear branches falling and see lightning flashing almost constantly. It was a real whipper-do of a storm. The next morning, we saw some limbs scattered around, but nobody was bothered except to get wet, which was not unusual for us. Then I looked up the trail, and here came Let Hko Him, the headman of the Naga village. I greeted him, and he said, "Would you please come with me?" I said yes because I was curious. In silence, we walked until we got to our previous camp ground. He still hadn't said anything except, "Come with me." As we went up the hill toward my old lean-to, he pointed to it. A neighboring tree, a huge tree as big around as a beer barrel, had fallen during the night and come down right square between the two trees where I had built my lean-to. The tree had landed right on my shelter. And I mean, it was smashed flat—squat to the ground. If I had still been there, why, I would have been as flat as a pancake and pretty messy.

I stood there and stared at it. I forget what I said or did. But I think Let Hko Him and the folks in his village thought I was magic myself, because of all that had happened; nobody had died from smallpox after I had gotten there, and then this tree had fallen on the place where I'd slept just the night before and would have slept again if we hadn't moved. They thought I had a charmed life and could practically do no wrong in the village of Undung Bum.

The Runner

Nevertheless, we had to do something, not just wait for the Japanese, so I approached my advisors, my *salang ni*. I can't emphasize enough how important they were to me. They knew the country and the people and could talk the different lingos. Before we did anything, even when we got to where we were blowing up bridges and setting up ambushes, I'd go over plans and get suggestions from them. So, I got them together and said, "What about this man Lamong Zau Htawng, the headman of Lamong Ga? The one who beat those boys. What do you think?" And Let Hko Him and the rest of them agreed that we ought to put him out of business. Even some of Lamong Zau Htawng's own villagers obviously disagreed with him since they had helped those boys get away.

So I took some twelve men. I picked the biggest ones I had and said, "Let's go over to Lamong Ga and see if we can't capture Lamong Zau Htawng and interrogate him." Just before dark, we started out. We went down the same trail where we had apprehended the two spies. It was about four or five miles to the village but easy to see in the moonlight. The sky there was so clear, it just looked like you could reach up and touch the stars. Most of the time, in fact, the sky was unpolluted, except in the early springtime, when they set all the fields on fire.

Every man carried whatever gun he had, and we headed down through the big canyon. A couple of local Nagas came along who were familiar with the village. They didn't like Lamong Zau Htawng either. It took us some time to get there. We finally climbed out the other side of the canyon. Walking toward the village, we were getting along fine until we began to get close, and then dogs started to bark. We should have known it was going to happen, there were always mangy-looking dogs around the villages. In fact, one reason people kept them was to give warning. Guinea hens served the same purpose. They always hollered.

We sped up after that. We knew which house he was in, and we divided into two groups. I took one group and went to the front door, and the others went around back. When those dogs began to bark, the people in the house fed the fire to get some more light. By the time we got there, it was burning brightly. We walked up to the front door, and in as loud a voice as I could muster, I hollered for Lamong Zau Htawng to come out with his hands up. The door opened just for an instant. From the firelight inside, we could see someone standing in the door peering out. He shut the door quickly. We could hear people running and jumping. Then all of a sudden, the back door flung open, and he came tearing out.

Usually, there was a porch in the back, but his house had a door right at the edge, and he came out of that door like a shot out of a gun. Everybody was hollering, "Stop, halt," whatever. But Lamong Zau Htawng ran like a deer. He had a rifle in his hand, and he came out shooting and running like the dickens. Everybody opened fire at him. The last shot was fired just before he hit the bushes.

We could see that one bullet splintered the stock of his rifle, busted it up. Way later, I learned that another bullet apparently hit him in the abdomen, but he survived. Even with that wound, he just ran like the devil and got into the bushes and away. We chased him for a while, but nobody could catch him. Even though our attempt failed, we met with folks in the village and thanked the people who had helped the Naga boys.

Chemistry 101—Gunpowder

There were so many people who helped us along the way. There was a village even closer to Tawmaw. They left to get away from the Japanese, but their headman stayed with us for a while as one of my advisors on Undung Bum. He was very useful. He also happened to have the worst cleft lip I'd ever seen. From his nose down, where the lip joins, his didn't join, and he had a couple of teeth that stuck straight out. He was a different-looking character. Even so, he was a respected village headman. He was older—I'd say between sixty and seventy, somewhere in there. He did so much for us along the way with supplies and information, that I felt like maybe I should help him out.

A hospital had been established back in Ledo. It was a well-equipped hospital with doctors from Johns Hopkins, I believe. So, I sent a coded wire and described the man's condition. "You've got this wonderful hospital; there's bound to be a plastic surgeon in the group. Would they be interested in helping this fellow out? He's done a lot for us." They came back immediately and said, "We've got the top plastic surgeon in the whole United States here, and he would be tickled to death to do it. Send this guy on over." I thought I was going to get to do something really good for the man. I presented him with the idea, and he thanked me and said, "I need to think about it." I said, "Let me know soon; they're ready for you, and we can fly you there." By this time, we had a little airstrip way down the hill that Grones and I had cooperated in setting up. The old man came back to me the next day, and he thanked me, but said, "I've looked this way all my life, and people know me with my teeth sticking out and my funny-looking lip. I believe I'd just better run the course like I am." I practically burst into tears, but I understood how he felt.

When I could, I tried to help folks that helped us. Usually, the best I could do was give them something. I gave Let Hko Him, the headman of the Naga village, a Springfield Model 1863 muzzle-loading rifle, still in the cosmoline. Our command had some of those old guns, surplus property, left over from the War Between the States! I gave him a boxful of caps and a few bullets and told him, "You've got to make your own gunpowder." Some of the Nagas were so primitive that they didn't fool with guns. But these particular folks did. In fact, many Nagas, Kachins, and other groups I ran into out there knew how to manufacture their own gunpowder.

The sanitary facilities in the villages were very meager. The primary place to urinate was right in the house. The house stood up off the ground, with enough room for pigs and cattle to get underneath. If you needed to urinate, even if the room was full of people, you just went over to this certain hole in the floor and accompanying notch in the wall. Each person wore a skirt, a *labu* they called it, men and women. All they had to do was slip that thing up, and they would urinate through the hole onto the ground below. For number 2, they went off in the woods somewhere, and they found a log or something to climb to keep the hogs and the dogs from literally rooting at them.

To make gunpowder, every so often, they would dig up the dirt beneath the hole where the urine had been dropping, and they would put that dirt in a basket. Then they would pour the boiling water through the dirt, dissolve the urates that were in it, and catch the water in another container under the basket. They took that water and boiled it down to concentrate it and were left with practically the same thing as saltpeter. Then they would add charcoal, which they pounded up into a powder. The third element needed in gunpowder is sulfur. In some places they mined sulfur near the surface of the ground, but most of them got it from China, where there were a good deal of sulfur springs. Caravans would come through those hills loaded with salt and sulfur, and they would trade and get materials, including those necessary for gunpowder. They'd mix the concoction up in the proper proportions; the condensed urine extract, the powdered charcoal, and the sulfur, and the product served well as an explosive. They used the homemade gunpowder in muzzle-loaders, mostly flintlocks and matchlocks.

Maung Tu and the Elephants

Up on Undung Bum, we were not far from the Japanese regimental head-quarters at Tawmaw. For resupply, the Japanese were using animal transport, mostly elephants and bullocks, on the trail that came up from the railroad at Mogaung. We commenced a series of raids on that trail, intercepting the cara-vans as they came up. The bullocks would come in great numbers with just one or two men to control the bunch of them. Each animal wore a wooden bell to locate it, and they were all trained to follow the leader. You'd see them coming along the trails, loaded down. As for the elephants, they had drivers, *buzi* they called them in Burmese, and great big saddle packs. The saddles were made out of mostly rattan with some padding between the elephant and the cargo. At night, the drivers would unload the elephants, put rattan loops around their front feet to hobble them, and let them out in the jungle to feed, but the cattle weren't let loose since they might get lost or eaten by tigers.

Generally speaking, it was not difficult for us to eliminate or drive off guards. They weren't expecting anything in the beginning, and by the time they were prepared, we had taken a whole bunch of both elephants and cattle. We took them and went back up to our camp on Undung Bum. There was a boy called Maung Tu on one of the elephants, who had come up with the Japanese. We hired him and the whole crowd that was with him, so we had elephants, drivers, and all. The drivers were mixed, but mostly Burmans who had been impressed into service by the Japanese. We paid them in silver rupees, so they didn't mind coming with us. Maung Tu stayed with us from the spring on up until September of 1944. I think the only clothing he owned was an old pair of shorts that had come off of some British soldier. He was a young fellow, and those shorts reached way below his knees. He had no shirt on ever, and he wore what used to be a Gurkha's hat, broad-brimmed hat, the kind with a band on the outside and a sweat band on the inside. The bands were long gone; there was no cord; this irregular thing just sat on his head. I don't know where he came from, but he was a Burman. He was a good fellow, and we made Maung Tu the head of our elephant train.

Among elephants, it's mainly the males that give you trouble. But one particular female called "Big Mama" was pretty cantankerous. One time when we were loading her up, she snorted and roared and reared up and charged through the crowd. She hit this house, a Kachin house, and literally knocked it down, plowed right on through it, and ran off. Maung Tu went sailing after her. Here was this youngster—he couldn't possibly have been over sixteen years old and maybe five feet tall. He grabbed somebody's spear as he went. The local people often carried spears that had a blade on one end and a spike on the other; they could throw them or fight with them like bayonets. So Maung Tu tore out after the elephant with this spear. Big Mama had carried her pack saddle off with her, loaded with rice.

After an hour or so, why, Maung Tu came back riding on the elephant, and she was bleeding all over the ground, and the rice was pretty much gone. Maung Tu had stuck her right in the trunk with the spear, and blood was coming out of that wound in jets. He stopped. The elephant knelt down, and he got off. He got a rag from somebody and managed to bind up that wound. Then Maung Tu went right ahead and loaded Big Mama's pack saddle with more rice, mounted, and rode off. He wasn't scared of her one bit. Here was this small boy who went running after a crazy elephant, and he caught her, and then I don't know exactly what happened, but he poked her in the nose, and she obeyed him.

Another time Big Mama ran off. We had sent the bullock train ahead with a separate group, and they were coming back to pick up more stuff. Elephants do not like bullocks for some reason or another. Well, Big Mama was at the head of the line with Maung Tu on her back. Around the bend came this herd, whereupon Big Mama trumpeted and roared and went charging right through all the bullocks, scattering them every which way. She tore off in the woods, went under a low limb, and knocked Maung Tu off. I think he saw the limb coming and half jumped off; it probably would have killed him if he had hit it head on. Well, he came running back and asked me if he could go after her. I told him, "Go ahead if you think you can find her." So he left, but we kept on going. This time he didn't return for about four days, but he did come back with her. Her pack saddle was damaged, but other than that, she was fine.

Our elephants were invaluable. We used them to carry supplies and to clear drop grounds. I had an axe, but when it came to cutting down trees, Kachins could do better with a knife than I could with that axe. They would tackle a tree as big around as a whiskey barrel with one of those knives. Generally, they'd stand on uneven ground and cut wherever it was most convenient. They didn't try to get the maximum log out of it; they simply got the tree down. Then we'd move the elephants in, and they'd finish the job.

The bullock trains were mainly run by Chinese traders, caravan people, and in peacetime they carried stuff all the way from China over into Burma. The Japanese had requisitioned them, so we just took over from the Japanese, but we paid them well. We accumulated, I think the final number was forty-six elephants, complete with drivers, and a bullock train of around a hundred bullocks with men to tend them.

We began using elephants and bullocks in earnest. Up to that point, our transport had been 100 percent human beings. We'd pick up coolies in one village, and they'd carry us to the next, and we'd pay that crowd and recruit another. Most of them were women. They made the best coolies. They rarely complained. In fact, mostly they were cheery, singing all the time. When it was raining cats and dogs, and we were slipping and sliding, they were much better at staying upright, and they'd laugh at us.

Leaving Undung Bum

When we finally left Undung Bum, we had quite a celebration there with the Nagas. There was feasting and dancing. Our *salang ni* decided that, before we headed out, we should make a big offering to the spirits. The Nagas sacrificed a buffalo. They pulled his head across an X shaped structure and chopped it off with a huge knife. The man made it almost all the way through the buffalo's neck in one blow, and blood went every which way. Then they butchered the buffalo and examined the entrails to foretell the future. I'm not an expert zoologist, but the *myrhtois* examined what looked to me like the liver and the pancreas. They deliberated, pronounced that we should leave on a certain day, and prescribed the route that we should take, and everything worked out all right.

Often, both Nagas and Kachins sacrificed chickens, pigs, or dogs. Most sacrifices were associated with feasts and dances. They'd pull the tongue of a chicken out by the roots. The tongue looked like an arrowhead with two long tendons going back with hooks on the ends, where they extended back into his neck. And they'd tell you what was going to happen by the way the tongue looked. In other animals, they'd examine various other organs. I never did really find out exactly what they noticed about the parts, but they would turn them over and over and over again. I don't know that their methods were secret, but I never heard tell what they were. The *myrhtois* and *jaiwas* spoke a different language when they were performing religious practices. They chanted, and nobody there could understand them except other magic folks. It was a sort of fraternity; reminded me of Latin in the old Roman Catholic Church. Every animist village would have those poles with the skulls of sacrificed animals outside, but for a big animal like a buffalo, the head would be kept inside the chief's house hanging up on the wall. The sacrificed head was for the *nats* and spirits. Then folks would eat the rest of the animal. So when they killed a buffalo, nothing went to waste. They looked at the entrails, but then they cooked them all up and ate them as well.

On top of Undung Bum, these Nagas blew trumpets to announce the celebration. The trumpets sounded like tubas or French horns. You may have seen similar ones, like those in Tibet, big long things, longer than a man is tall, with big bells on the ends. The reed pipes that the Nagas used squawked like bagpipes, the horns they blew like trumpets, with their lips, embouchure. Another instrument they had was a sort of jaw harp made out of bamboo, and they twanged it across the mouth. And, of course, they had drums and gongs.

Jade Mines

After the celebration, we left Undung Bum and headed south. Some of the young Naga men joined our forces. There weren't many of them—only about a half a dozen—since a lot of the young men had died from smallpox. We set out toward the Uyu River with all of our gear and new recruits. When we went to cross it, the river was in spate; it was about a quarter of a mile wide and a muddy torrent. We crossed it in a boat operated by some Shans. The Hkamti Shans over there used to inhabit the whole of northern Burma but were driven south by the migration of Kachins and other tribes who had moved from up around Tibet some hundreds of years before. But the vestiges of those Hkamti tribes were still around.

The river would have been a formidable barrier without the ferry. It was a big boat—I'm guessing fifty feet long—and we loaded a whole ton of men and gear in it. Just two Shans moved that boat. Another on the back manned a steering sweep. But the two men with poles walked along catwalks on either side of the boat and pushed that whole thing full of twenty-five to thirty men, all their gear and everything else. They'd go to the front of the boat, ram their pole into the bottom, and then walk toward the back of the boat on those catwalks. Those boatmen had magnificent physiques. They wore very little, just small rags tied around like shorts. They were so strong and well developed from doing that work all their lives, that they could literally propel the boat with their feet and legs. As they walked to the end of the catwalk, they'd jerk the pole up, run to the front of the boat, and slam the pole down into the water again. In the meantime, the boat would usually come to a halt in the swift current, but they'd get reset before it began to go backwards.

We got all the men across, but the elephants would not cross the river. Maung Tu would lead those big bull elephants into the water, but they'd get halfway across and go under to where nothing was sticking up but the tops of their heads and their trunks, and they would just turn around and trumpet a little bit and go back to the bank in a big hurry. So we had to leave them there. We didn't even try to get the bullocks across. They would have drowned. They had to stay there and wait for a week or ten days before the river went down. Then they were able to follow us. Meantime, we kept going south towards a place called Hwehka.

Hwehka was in a jade mine area. I had not known what jade even looked like before going to Burma. I thought it must be green. But I learned more about it while I was there since we camped right in the middle of an abandoned mine. The area looked like a glacial moraine, a great jumble of rocks and boulders of different sizes that obviously had come from somewhere else, moved there either by water or ice. The ground was covered with them, all with rounded shapes, no jaggedy edges for the most part. Some were as big as a football, some the size of a chair, and some as big as a piano. They were dark gray, blackish gray on the outside, but if you could find one that was broken open, inside it was mainly white, but might have streaks of color in it, and that's what was valuable. Most of the jade we saw was white. But they also had a lot of what they called "mutton fat," a kind of brown jade. The most highly prized was green, all the way from dark to light, light green.

People weren't trading because of the war, but I was told they would trade for those rocks almost sight unseen. They would take a wheel or a stone and grind a little bit of the surface off so they could tell, just a strip not as big as your hand, exposed in a rock that might be as big around as a chest-of-drawers.

And then they would bid on that rock in a kind of auction. Everybody had an idea of what was down inside of the rock, although I'm sure that some were better than others at picking the best ones.

There was a lot of old rusty equipment there. One Kachin with us was a blacksmith. He found a rock drill, all covered with rust, and told me, "I can make you a sword out of this. It'll be a whole lot better than these swords made of soft iron." To use one of their iron knives, you had to be really good. If you were the least bit off, you were liable to bend the knife, and after several swings, you'd end up with what looked like a piece of scrap iron. But that rock drill was hard steel, and he made me a good knife. I carried that knife for the rest of the war. I've still got it now. And that fellow made it for me right there. He just built him a fire, hammered away at that drill and came up with a damn good knife.

A real Hkahku (headwater area) Kachin knife was worn over your shoulder. It had one sharp edge all the way out. The blade was narrow at the handle and wide at the tip. In addition to their unusual shape, their knives were interesting because they were made to be right- or left-handed. A right-handed knife had the bevel to the right side and the flat side to the left. They would generally just pick up a stone with the proper surface on it, and they'd whet the knife, always on that beveled side. It really worked well. If you were cutting something like bamboo, which has a real hard almost glass-like surface on it, with a two-beveled Western knife, lots of times the knife would bounce off. But with that one straight edge, a Kachin knife was a lot more likely to sink in and make a real cut.

Once, while we were scouting around the area of the jade mines, we turned the corner in the trail, and there was a huge elephant in spitting distance, right in the middle of the trail. When we got a good look at him, we noticed he was hobbled. He was a tame elephant that the Japanese had evidently lost. We kept the elephant's attention while a small boy slipped in under the elephant, grabbed the tag end of the rope, and got the hobble off. Maung Tu managed to get on the elephant's back, so we added another elephant to the train. We used those elephants for the whole rest of the summer, hauling supplies and stealing stuff from the Japanese storehouses situated near the railroad.

All the while, we kept going south. We went past a place called Lonton, a Shan village, located at the bank of Lake Indawgyi. *Indaw* means "lake," and *gyi* means "grand" or "huge." It was a beautiful lake about twenty-five miles long, about seven miles wide at the widest point, and shaped like a pear. The big end of it was down toward the south, and the narrower end was up at the north. It was obviously on a fault of some kind, because cliffs all down the east side were real steep, but the bank was long and sloping on the west. It was a magnificent lake.

We had to walk through water there since it was flooding. Half the time, we were up to our waists at the lake's edge. There for the first time, we encountered what they called the "buffalo leech," which would attack in the water. You'd be wading waist deep, and this thing would come at you like a swimming snake. It was upsetting to see one head for you, to say the least. He'd dive under before he got to you, but you knew he was down there somewhere, busy trying to work his way in under your clothes. We decided to stop near the lake, pretty close to the railroad, so we went up to the village of Nadawng, right on top of a knot on the ridge above the west side of the lake.

The Magic Crocodile

We stayed up on the hill at the Kachin village of Nadawng for about a week or ten days in August of 1944. Down in the long valley below was Indawgyi Lake and the Shan village of Lonton. Around the campfire one night, the headman of Nadawng told me the legend of how the magnificent lake formed. I tried to learn as much as I could wherever I went, legends and all, so I was happy to listen. He launched into the ancient tale, "Many, many years ago, the river ran through this valley, and there was a good-sized town near where Lonton sits, but on the river bank, since there was no lake." He explained that the folks in that town had a pretty bad reputation for stealing and not being respectful.

He went on, "The people there did a lot of fishing, and one time a fisherman went way upstream from the village in his boat. While paddling around checking out his traps, he came across a nest composed of sticks and straw, and in that nest was a giant egg." The headman formed his arms in a circle, touching together the tips of his fingers, as if putting his arms around the imagined egg, indicating its enormous size. "The fisherman was fascinated with that big egg. It was really heavy, but he had a fishing net in his canoe, so he rolled the egg onto the net and managed to drag it into his canoe." The storyteller continued,

> He paddled back down river, put ashore, and hailed everybody in the village, "Come, look what I've found. I've got this egg, this giant egg." So they all came down to take a look. Nobody, not even the oldest person in the village, had any notion of what it was. Somebody finally thought about an old man who lived out from the village. He was not of the same tribe and not at all popular with the people who lived there. He lived up on the side of the hill with his two small grandchildren, who had lost their parents some time ago. They said, "What about the old man up there on the hill? He might have some idea about this egg. He's been here since way before any of us were born." So they brought the old man

down to the village. When he was shown the egg, he practically went into a state of shock. He said, "Oh, my God, you've found the egg of the crocodile who is the god of this river. It is magic. You must take it back." They said, "What are you talking about, old man?" He repeated, "I'm telling you, take it back. Wherever you got it from, take it back. It is an egg of the magic crocodile, and when she gets back to the nest, there's going to be the devil to pay. I'm warning you." They said, "Old man, you're crazy. Whoever heard of a magic crocodile and all this fantasy about her egg? Whose ever egg this is, why, it looks to us like it's good enough to eat." So they drove him off. He went back up the hill still saying, "I'm warning you. You'd better take it back." When he reached the hut where his two grandchildren were waiting, he began to weep. He was distraught because they had stolen the egg of the magic crocodile.

In the meantime, the villagers decided to have a celebration. They had found this egg and made up their minds to eat it. It was so huge they didn't have any pot big enough to hold it, so they gathered up a whole bunch of pots and prepared the fire. They broke the egg open gently and began to pour the contents out into the containers that they had. Then they started cooking it. Everybody put pots full of egg on fires all over the village. And a strange thing began happening. As they cooked, the egg expanded, and they required even more pots to contain the egg. They had to call all over the village for more pots and more pots. They even went up to the old man and demanded his pots, but he wouldn't give them up. He said, "I warned you not to mess with that egg. Something awful is going to happen." And they said, "Oh, old man, you're just nuts. We're going to dine like kings on that egg." The egg got bigger and bigger, and they filled up every conceivable vessel in the whole village with the one egg. When they filled up everything, why, it stopped expanding. Then they started eating. They ate and ate. And they had plenty of local rice liquor to drink. They celebrated into the night, having a big time, beating drums and dancing, enjoying their good fortune in having found this delicious egg.

In the meantime, the old man sat up on top of the hill, grieving. He could hear all the noise, the music, the drums beating. Finally, everything became quiet. All of the revelers were asleep. Then he felt the ground tremble. The earth began to shake, and he heard a rumble like thunder in the distance. His grandchildren asked what was happening, and he told them the magic crocodile had discovered that her egg was gone and was thrashing her tail in anger. As they listened, the rumble became louder and louder.

He could see down to the village from where he was. As the tremors got stronger and stronger, the whole earth began to crack open. A huge chasm formed right in the village and spit out dust as it gaped wider and wider. The walls of houses collapsed as they fell into the cleft. People ran in every direction to try to get away, but the ground just crumbled underneath them and swallowed them. In front of the old man's eyes, the whole village disappeared into the abyss, a cloud of dust lingering above it. Then the old man and the two children realized with horror that the widening chasm was headed in their direction. He grabbed the two children and his bamboo staff, and they commenced running farther up the hill. They kept running and running and running. Right behind them, the earth kept falling away and disappearing into the bottomless hole.

Finally, the old man just plumb gave out. He turned around, and, with all his might, he stabbed his staff into the ground. In the face of the dust and roaring noise, he knelt down, and he prayed to the magic crocodile. He said, "We've done no wrong. We warned the village that they stole your egg and that if they did anything bad with it, the consequences would be something awful. Please do not swallow us up." And lo and behold, the ground fell away right up to where his staff was planted, and then it stopped. The thundering noise ceased. Gasping for breath, he and his grandchildren knelt there and waited to be consumed by the earth. The chasm had swallowed up his house along with everything else but stopped at the spot where he had planted the staff in the ground. After the three had rested, they went on up to another hill and made camp. That campsite where he and his two grandchildren stopped is a village today. It calls itself by the name which means "the place where the cataclysm stopped," and that huge hole in the ground became Indawgyi Lake.

And the Nadawng headman told me, "The old man stuck the little end of the bamboo staff into the ground." Branches that normally grow on bamboo point upwards, but according to the headman, "Today there's still a clump of bamboo in that very spot. Unlike anywhere else, the branches coming off of that bamboo point downward." Later on, I had a chance to go by there in a canoe myself, and it did seem like the bamboo grew with branches pointing downward. That's the story of how that lake came about. By that time, so many things had happened that I couldn't understand, that the story seemed to make sense. Maybe an earthquake caused the lake to form; it's obviously on a fault line in the mountains. Anyhow, the magic crocodile got her revenge on the people who ate her egg.

Funny thing is, as far as I know, there are no crocodiles in that part of Burma now. On the other side of the mountains, in India, there are beaucoups of crocodiles, big crocodiles. I don't know about the area closer to the coast, but there weren't any in upland Burma that I heard of. Anyway, it was an interesting story to hear him tell it. And he believed it. To him it was just like the Bible. He was telling me a fact.

I must say I adopted a lot of the customs of the people over there. I may have mentioned this before. I learned pretty early that they made sacrifices to the *nats*, these spirits, demons, whatever you want to call them. There are supposed to be thirty-seven principal *nats*. I've got a book about them, but there are thousands of other *nats*. Every feature of the landscape has got its own *nat*. A spirit might be a noticeable rock, a creek, a valley. So, on the trail, if we crossed a creek, for example, I'd notice that each Kachin would pull a twig off of a tree, a flower or an acorn or something to make a symbolic gift, a small sacrifice to the *nat*, the spirit of that creek. And I got to where I did the same thing.

Target of Opportunity

An awful thing happened there on Indawgyi Lake during the war. The Air Corps had a habit of hitting what they called "targets of opportunity." If an aircraft hadn't dropped its bombs before returning to base, the crew was supposed to get rid of them. This, I'm sure, was for safety. I guess they didn't want anyone landing with a thousand-pound bomb hanging on a plane. So, crews were directed to drop them on things that looked like they should be bombed, so-called "targets of opportunity." In this case, the beautiful pagoda on Indawgyi Lake often became such a target.

The lake is incredibly deep on the east side, the cliff side, but shallower on the opposite bank. The people told us that they had taken out rocks in boats to make an island upon which they built this amazing pagoda. It must have been a good hundred feet high. Beautiful thing, all covered in gold leaf. It gleamed in the sunlight and at night in the moonlight, it was just gorgeous. It stood about a half mile from shore at the widest part of the lake. They had made a causeway to it, built up to a specific level, so for three quarters of the year it was underwater, but in the months of March and early April, the end of the dry season, it was open. At that time, they had a big festival, and people would come from all over the country to get on their knees and crawl out to the pagoda, where they would meditate or contemplate or whatever they do there.

We didn't get to see the pilgrimage. The causeway was covered with water when we were there, and it may have been canceled by the war anyway. It wouldn't have been safe to go out there, particularly because the US Air Force used it as a target of opportunity. Pilots would dive on that pagoda firing their machine guns full blast. They did it while we were there looking at them, so I know firsthand that it happened, and that it was us. And they dropped bombs. I saw it with my own eyes. Fortunately, they never hit it with a bomb as far as I know. The bombs just hit the water, making big geysers when they exploded. But they did shoot it. There were pockmarks where it had been hit by .50 caliber machine gun fire. When our planes came down and shot up this sacred object that these people venerated, I was horrified. It was very hard to explain to the folks there, especially since I didn't understand it myself.

The Meanest Man in Burma

While we were at Nadawng, they brought in a Kachin from the village who was completely unconscious; his lower belly was all swelled up and rock hard. The story we got was that he had been unable to urinate for several days. It looked like he was going to die unless we did something. He was breathing heavily and out cold. It occurred to me that in the radio kit there were some pieces of wire with insulation on them. I thought I might be able to take a pair of pliers, and pull the metal out, leaving a narrow tube like the catheters I'd seen Doc use. It was far-fetched, but I worked away at it, and finally, with a shout of triumph, I pulled the wire out of that insulation.

The piece of tubing was a little over a foot long. I got some ghee or mustard oil, whichever it was that we had, and greased the tube up. Then I sat on the man's thighs. Somebody else held him down in case he moved. I carefully inserted the tube and managed to keep feeding it in. It was not easy to do, but I screwed it around and worked it in a ways, and all of a sudden this blood and pus and everything you can imagine came streaming out of the make-shift catheter. It took a little while to empty his bladder, because the caliber of the tube was small. At that time, we had some sulfa medicine. Not too long after we got the fluid out, the fellow began to come out of his coma, and we were able to give him pills for the infection. He got all right. The people there, Kachins, Nagas, Shans, they all had amazing recovery ability. Doc Abdul had commented on that. He said, "You've just got to give them a little help, and they'll get well." They would get big sores or infected lacerations, but just give them sulfanilamide, half a normal dose or a quarter of a dose, and they'd pull out of it.

I figured this fellow had some venereal disease, maybe gonorrhea that had blocked him up. The Kachin custom at the time, as I understood it, was that before marriage, people were pretty free to mess around. But after they got married, they stuck with their one person. So, it was not unusual for the head-man of the village to offer the services of his unmarried daughters. This caused problems every once in a while. It required tact to refuse without offending, but I couldn't see any of that going on without it having drastic effects on our ability to get things done. After the incident in Nadawng, I tried even harder to keep to the rule, but it posed some difficulty since the Kachins had their custom. *Jinghpaw tung* they called it.

The headmen at several villages offered us the opportunity. Some of my men got word of the fact that I had turned them down and were pretty unhappy. One reason I got the nickname of "The Meanest Man in Burma," was that I was strict on that subject, but there were other reasons that the name stuck. I had to march the men without mercy sometimes. Even though people were exhausted, there were times we just had to keep going; there was really no choice from my perspective.

Ting Bawm a.k.a. Ringting

The main line supplying the Japanese was a meter gauge railroad track running north and south. It extended from Rangoon up to Myitkyina. From our position at Nadawng, in late August of '44, we began blowing up that railroad at intervals. First, just the track and then some bridges. There were a number of small bridges near us, and we dropped two or three of them to the ground. At that time, we had some Kachins with us who had been trained to use explosives back at Nazira, the OSS headquarters in Assam. When my group was walking to Dalu, those folks joined them. A Kachin named Ting Bawm was in charge, and he became one of my right-hand men and a friend. He came from a place called Pinma, about two hundred miles northeast of Myitkyina. It's way up there—I mean really in the boondocks. When he was a boy, he had gone to school in Myitkyina at the Baptist mission school, a boarding school, and he could read and write Jinghpaw. While he was there, he met a Kachin girl named Konsin. Kachin marriages were arranged, and it was against the rules to marry within your own group, but Ting Bawm violated the rules. He married Konsin and for that reason became somewhat of an outcast. He went down to the valley around Sumprabum and Putao and ran into a recruiter for OSS 101. In late '42, he was sent over to India and was taught about demolitions.

Everybody that was trained by Detachment 101 back at Nazira was given an alias, so he became Ringting. That's what he was called all through the war; I didn't know his real name until it was all over. At the very last he just said, "My real name is Ting Bawm." The ten or eleven men who were with Ting Bawm had names like Husky and Sammy and Bobby and Billy; names given to them at random, the theory being that if the wrong folks knew their real names, someone might try to harm their families. My old friend N'gumla also worked with Ting Bawm's group. He had not been in Nazira, but he knew how to operate a BAR, or Browning Automatic Rifle, and was a good soldier.

Ting Bawm's standard procedure was to scout out a bridge in daylight, see how many piers were under it, figure out the best place to plant the charges, and so forth. Later, he would take in his whole platoon. The BAR men would get in position on each end of the bridge; then the people with the explosives would move in and plant them. His group used mostly Composition C, which looked like putty and was pliable, and they had a big roll of what they called Primacord to tie explosives together. To blow up a big, long span, they would plaster charges onto the sides of beams, tie them together with Primacord, and stick caps into the charges. They frequently used staggered charges to cause a shearing effect and cut a beam in two. They'd light one end of the fuse and run like blazes. And they had other equipment. They had a pressure device to put under a rail so a locomotive would trip it. If they wanted the engine to go on across it, they could put it on a timer, and the blast would go off back under the train. They had another device that sat on top of the rail and detonated right when the engine wheel smashed it. Nothing was electronic. Everything was very elementary.

Ting Bawm's platoon would come back from a mission with the hairiest tales you can imagine. They couldn't get the match to light, and the Japanese were bearing down on them, all that kind of stuff. I remember one particular job that they took me to see. They had blown up a train traveling at a very rapid rate, using a charge with a pressure device, and managed to completely overturn the locomotive and the first few cars. We were lucky to have Ting Bawm and his team. They had never seen action before they joined us, but they knew how to do it. We told them, "Just get out on the railroad track and blow up whatever you can." And they accomplished some spectacular work.

In every case though, after they blew up a spot, the Japanese would be right back in there. We could almost hear them, banging around, building a bridge back up. Their engineers would crib up something like a log cabin underneath the bridge, where the piers had blown. They would gradually jack it up, stick another set of timbers under it, jack that up, and get it back to level. They didn't have cranes or anything like that, but they were really good at the field expedient.

Trip to Nazira

We moved down from Nadawng south toward a place called Hkadu. There was no trail after the village called Woi Gahtawng, so we cut through the jungle. The elephants really helped get us through. When we got near Hkadu, we made camp right on the cliff above the railroad, where it came through a long valley. On top of that cliff, we decided to set up our base of operations. While we were there, I received orders to go to the headquarters of OSS at Nazira for a meeting.

During the spring and summer of '44, a terrible battle had been going on to the west, in Naga land of India. General William Slim, commander of the

British 14th Army, had moved the IV Corps to set up headquarters at Imphal. There was a station on the supply road at a place called Kohima. The Japanese 15th Army launched a full-scale operation against the British. They headed up into the Naga Hills with maybe 100,000 troops. In the spring of '44, those troops charged across the Chindwin River, and attacked. The British brought in troops from all over. The battle lasted until the middle of the summer, and the British, Gurkhas, and Indians, right then, at Kohima and Imphal, broke the back of the Japanese Army in Burma.

All of that action had started while we were at Undung Bum. After those battles, the troops began driving the Japanese back across Burma. Because they were south of us, if we kept going the way we were going, we would have been in the way. So, following orders, I walked back to Indawgyi Lake from Hkadu by myself. I had a piece of panel, my rifle, and some supplies. It took me a couple of days. I came back through the village of Woi Gahtawng. I remember it particularly because of an experience I had there.

The women in the villages would get up before the men and pound rice. They stored their rice with the husks on it, in granaries up off the ground to keep rats out. The women would climb up there to get the rice. They had mortars made out of sections of logs, a foot and a half or two feet in diameter, hollowed out down to a depth of maybe a foot and a half. Their pestles were about five feet long and shaped like dumbbells, with a small gripping section in the middle and two big ends. They'd pour rice into the mortar. Then they would start pounding the rice with the pestle. Most of the time there would be two women working together, and you'd hear them early in the morning pounding, thunk, thunk, thunk, thunk at a steady pace. Then they'd start singing in high, clear voices. In the dark before dawn, I remember lying there listening to them sing. It sounded like paradise. When we used women as coolies, they'd carry heavy loads, and even when it was raining and everyone was slipping and sliding in the mud, they'd sing then, too. They seemed the happiest people. I wish I'd had something to record that early morning music at Woi Gahtawng.

I visited with the headman that day, a man named Woi Wa. While we sat in his house and talked, all of a sudden this "boom" sounded. Somebody was shooting outside. "Bam," it went off again, and "pow," several more shots. Old Woi Wa, he never budged, he just kept right on talking as though it didn't amount to anything. So I thought, well, if he's not worried, I shouldn't be either. After this went on awhile, I finally asked as nonchalantly as I could, "Who is that shooting?" He said, "Oh, that's old So-and-so. He's got something against all white people, especially the British. He hates them, and he knows you're one of them, so he's emphasizing his displeasure by shooting in the air." So I just sat there and continued my talk with Woi Wa.

They were sending a float plane to pick me up. At the appointed time, I walked south of Lonton to an uninhabited part of the lake, hid, and waited. Sure enough, here came the plane. I put my panel out where they could see it and put a bunch of green stuff on the fire to make smoke. The man who picked me up was in an L1 plane. It was early in the morning, there was not a breath of air, and the lake was smooth as glass He taxied over towards me, but he couldn't get as close in as he wanted. It was hard to maneuver in there. I took my rifle and everything with me and managed to thrash around in the water and get up to his plane. It was twenty-five or thirty yards out, not very far, but I had to swim, which was difficult with clothes, shoes, and equipment. He climbed down out of the cockpit and helped me get up on the float. We got into the cockpit and got going, but he couldn't take off. The water was so smooth, he couldn't break the surface tension. After trying for a while, he finally ended up going around and around in a circle, making his own waves. That broke the tension enough, and we were able to take off. The plane had wheels on it that stuck down through the bottom of the floats, so we landed at Nazira on the ground.

Even though I'd been in the OSS for a while, I'd never been to headquarters until then. We had a conference there for a couple of days. Since the Americans were now in Myitkyina, and the British were coming across from the west, headquarters decided it was time for us to move east of the Irrawaddy River and further south. It was pretty obvious that the Japanese would try to move south to get away. They had come into Burma with something like 325,000 men, but they were down to about 100,000 by this time. The British and Americans finally had them outnumbered. The plan was for me to go back to my outfit for a few weeks. Then I was to go to Myitkyina, take off from there, and jump in further to the southeast.

After I had gotten my new assignment, we all got together—Bill Cummings, Peers, and I—and they pinned a medal on me for my performance at Sharaw Ga. That was the time I told you, with the citation about refusing to be evacuated after being wounded. It was the bronze star, with no wise cracks this time.

"Civilization"

After I got the medal, they gave me leave to go to Calcutta for about three days before heading back. It was the only time I had any leave to speak of, late summer of '44, and it was a disaster. A fellow named Red Maddox and I went together by train to Calcutta from Nazira. Red was an Irishman, or at least half Irish, and his real name was Patrick J. Maddox. He was in the British Army, one of the Territorials assigned to the OSS. He could speak Burmese and worked for a lumber company in Burma before the war, so he knew what was going on. We had both been called out to discuss the new plans, then Peers decided to give us a break before our next assignments. We had no written orders, just verbal instruction from Peers, "Go down to Calcutta, look around and see the world again."

Well, in 101, why, there wasn't much spit and polish. As a matter of fact, the situation we were in, there was no spit and polish whatsoever. We just wore whatever we could find. I had a khaki shirt, a pair of khaki pants, and an overseas-type cap that I got from somewhere, and two sets of captain's bars, one on my cap, and the other one on me. So I had close to a proper uniform, but Red didn't. He had on an American shirt and some Limey britches and a kind of a tropical helmet, a mixed bag. When we arrived, we got off the train and went straight to the Grand Hotel. After we registered, he said, "There's a uniform place right down the street. Let's get me outfitted." I said, "I'll lend you a set of my captain's bars in the meantime." So he put those on his hat. I had mine on my collar but none on my hat, so now I wasn't technically in uniform either. Well, we walked out of the hotel, and we turned left, and we had hardly walked twenty-five steps before we encountered two American MPs. And those fellows there in the big city; they were sticklers for a proper uniform. They stopped us and said, "You're not in proper uniform, and we're going to have to take you to the provost marshal."

When they brought us in, there was a second lieutenant behind the counter, and he demanded an explanation. He said, "Let's see your orders." "Sorry, we don't have any orders." We tried to tell him we were from OSS 101. He'd never heard of OSS 101. "Well, what's your serial number?" Well, I knew my serial number, so I told him mine, and I was trying to keep talking so they wouldn't ask Red his serial number. I knew if he quoted his, why, we'd probably be stuck sure enough since he was from the Territorials. In spite of my efforts, the fellow asked, "And how about yours? What's your serial number?" And Red said something like, "538," and I thought to myself, nobody since George Washington has had a number that low. Then the whole story had to come out. "My name is Peter K. Lutken, and this man, this is Patrick J. Maddox, and he's actually from the British Army and he's been reassigned . . . ," and you could tell the fellow was thinking, yeah, and my name is Santa Claus. Anyhow, we couldn't talk them out of anything, so they took us to a provost marshal in the upper stories of some building, and we had to undergo the third degree. We told the man, "Why don't you call up the OSS 101 office here in town? Colonel Coffey is there, and he'll vouch for us."

We probably should have checked in with him first instead of the hotel, but we were right there after getting off of the train. So they called up Col. Coffey at the OSS 101 headquarters in Calcutta. This marshal gave him our names and what we had told him. We heard the voice on the other end of the phone say, "Never heard of either one of them." Then the marshal said, "I've got no alternative. We're going to have to keep you here until I can get some explanation." So we were ushered down to the hoosegow and had to stay there overnight.

Next day, we were taken back up to the office. Colonel Coffey was there with the marshal. He had gotten a hold of Peers back up at Nazira. We saluted when we came in. They told us to sit down. Coffey was a little bit embarrassed because he had not checked up to find out who we were. I think Peers had gotten angry with him. Instead of enjoying a vacation, we had enjoyed an incarceration. The upshot of it was that they turned us loose, and Coffey said, "Next time, for God's sake, check in with us before you go to see anybody else."

After that, Red and I both decided we'd better get the hell out of there and back to the jungle where we belonged! But before we got away, I forget just how it happened, we went to see some friend of Red's, an Englishman who was getting ready to marry a Tibetan girl. It was spur of the moment. The church was nearby, and we stood as witnesses while this British soldier married his Tibetan girl. She was all dressed up in her Tibetan outfit, and she was beautiful; I wish I had pictures. Her outfit was even more elaborate than the Kachin outfits, but very much like them, with silver and heavy embroidery, dark colors, blue and red. I can't remember their names, I don't remember anything else much, just that we stood there, signed our name to the marriage certificate as witnesses, and that was that. Afterwards, Red caught the first train out of Calcutta to someplace in Assam where he knew somebody connected with his company, and I headed back toward Burma as fast as I could.

A Close Encounter

While I was gone, Edgar Buck, the fellow who'd been in on the swim party, had led several raids to pick up Japanese supplies. As the expression goes, he acted like fire wouldn't burn him. Our group was still at Hkadu, up on top of a canyon, with steep slopes down to the railroad, not exactly a good place to get drops. So, for all intents and purposes, the men were living off the country. The Japanese had some granaries nearby where they stored rice. These were not guarded for the most part, so Buck would take a few men and elephants, go right down to the granaries, load the elephant's pack saddles with rice, and go back up the hill.

Ting Bawm and his group also continued blowing bridges in my absence. They had recently blown up a train and wanted to show it to me after I returned.

The whole demolition group went with Ting Bawm and me to see the remains of the train. We had to sneak up on it since wrecked trains were usually guarded well. We managed to get down to the meter gauge track, which threaded through the thick jungle. There was not much maintenance, so the bushes and the trees grew very close into the track.

The men thought they remembered just where they had blown up the train, but when we got down there, they couldn't find it. The track was pretty straight for a long distance. We stopped, looked up and down the tracks, but couldn't see anything. So we decided to dispatch two men along the track each way to go some distance and then come back and tell us if they found the site. We waited and we waited, and the sun climbed up into the sky, and eventually we began to get careless.

We walked out on the track and looked up and down to see if we could see our folks coming. We were standing there, all of us right in the open, I was talking to Ting Bawm, when all of a sudden, he looked over my shoulder and shouted, "*Khap Mu!*" It was crazy; instead of shooting, he yelled, "*Khap Mu!*" which means "Shoot!" I whirled around to see what he was looking at, and there was a Japanese soldier, no further away than the length of a picnic table, just right there at us, coming out of the bushes. As I turned, I shot reflexively, just pointblank. The soldier fell like he'd been hit with a poleax. He collapsed forward, almost onto the track, and died instantly. We jumped on him right quick, rolled him over, and began checking his pockets. He had a map case with some insignia on it, so we took that.

While we were at it, the woods opened up with gunfire. Apparently, there was a large Japanese encampment very close by. We couldn't see them; they were firing from behind the bushes. Right quick, we all jumped down in the ditch on the backside of the track and fired back in their direction. When they began throwing hand grenades at us, I decided we'd better leave, so I gave the magic words. Over the din of gunfire and grenades, I hollered what was probably my most common order, "*Aye, manang ni, prong mat wamu!*" which meant, "Oh, friends, let's get out of here!" We all immediately turned around and lit out through the jungle. We ran pretty fast, but the jungle was thick. In heavy cover like that, when you get fifty yards away, why, you might as well settle down and walk. We eventually did, but kept up a good clip, putting some distance between us. Even so, they kept on shooting for a good fifteen minutes after we left.

The men that we had sent scouting heard all this rumpus and figured out what was happening, so they cut diagonally through the jungle, met us on up the trail, and we all proceeded back up to Hkadu. We didn't get to see that train, but we did come down the next day to a different spot to see one pretty-good-sized bridge that they had dropped into the river. They had done a good job on it.

Nurse Naomi

As per the orders I had received on my trip to Nazira, I prepared to go to my new location. I said goodbye to my fellow Kachins. They were to pack up and come to the airfield at a place called Inkangahtawng sometime after me. A few of them would be transferred later, but I was to go first to set things up. I walked back to Indawgyi Lake by myself and got a canoe from that same Shan village, Lonton. I had found out earlier, when I was back at the village of Nadawng, that there was a nurse named Naomi living not too far from where I was headed. She had been one of Seagrave's first nurses but left some years before and was staying with her husband and family at a village nearby. So when I was at Nadawng, I sent word to her that if she would like to rejoin Seagrave, I could arrange it. She jumped at the chance and sent word back that she would come anytime. Her children by this time were big enough that other kin folks could take care of them.

We arranged to meet at an abandoned village at the upper end of the lake. So I got in a dugout canoe by myself, and I paddled. It was twenty miles up there. I paddled all night and some of the day and finally got to the other end of the lake. The British, early on, had evacuated one whole brigade from that lake with a Sunderland flying boat, a great big, seagoing, four-engine cargo plane. It was intended for the ocean, but they brought that thing in there and evacuated the brigade from a long-range penetration. The brigade had camped at the place where I ended up, and they had left one big mess, but they were long gone by this time.

The afternoon I arrived, I began to get fever and chills. Naomi showed up, and I told her, "It's good you're a nurse; I'm not feeling too good." She made me lie down. She told me later that my temperature got up above 106 at one point. I was out of my head, not making any sense. She covered me up with some old parachutes left there by the British. On the floor of an abandoned hut, she poured water over me for at least two nights and a day before I finally came out of it. I figured it was not malaria because I'd had malaria, and I knew what it was like. She thought it might have been something they called tick typhus.

When I did come out of it, we got in the canoe. The lake water is really beautiful, clear as a bell, and deep. The Indawgyi has streams coming into the southern end and a river going out the northern end. The north river is called the Indaw Chong. I was just woozy as I could be, but I managed to paddle us all the way along that river to Kamaing. We left the canoe there with the villagers and walked up to Inkangahtawng. We flew out in a light plane, an L5 that took the two of us to Myitkyina, where she met up with Seagrave. Shortly thereafter,

Seagrave moved to Bhamo and then further south with the Chinese. I didn't ever see Naomi again, but I'll never forget her kindness.

Parachuting 101

At Myitkyina, I spent a few days getting ready for the new assignment to parachute behind enemy lines. The OSS had a station there, so I got maps of the area and did some figuring. By that time, Mahka La made it to Myitkyina. Ting Bawm had headed up north for a while to see his wife and children and planned to find us later. Mahka La and I were joined by an Indian by the name of Paul, who was to be our radio operator. They issued us a radio, just two boards with a tube, a couple of condensers, a few wires, some dials, a generator and a code book.

Our appointed jump day was some day in late October or early November of 1944. We were introduced to a sergeant whose name, I think, was Katowski. He took us into this warehouse and said, "Here, pick out your parachute." The OSS people who jumped were each given one parachute. Paratroopers normally had a reserve chute, but we did not have the luxury. Sergeant Katowski, gave us about thirty seconds worth of instructions. We all three listened intently. None of us had ever jumped before. Paul had been in an airplane—they had hauled him over from India—but Mahka La had never even been in an airplane.

The instructions were pretty simple. Something like, "You've got a chute, it's on your back, and there's a cord attached to the plane, a static line that pulls open the chute. You just step off of the edge of the plane." There was no door, just an open place. The sergeant said, "When you step off, fold your arms and hold your chin down so your head won't snap. As soon as the chute opens, reach up and grab the two risers. Like on a swing in grade school, you can stop yourself swinging by pulling against the motion. You don't want to hit the ground sideways." Then he told us, "Once you land, grab and pull the bottom lines so that you spill the air out of the parachute. If you don't do that, the wind may drag you."

After that intense lesson, we got on the plane early the next morning. I don't remember whether we had any breakfast or not. I don't think we did. It was cold; I do remember that. We left about 4 a.m., and it took a couple of hours to get where we were going. We had picked out a mountain just south of Sinlumkaba, which had been a hill station under the British. Everybody still talked about what a nice place Sinlumkaba was. There was a mountain range there, forty or fifty miles southeast of the big town of Bhamo. One reason we picked that place was that Mahka La was from that neck of the woods, just south of where we were jumping, a village called Namhkai. The plan was to jump in and move down to Namhkai where he knew people and maybe pick up some folks to help us. Mahka La felt sure that they would have some arms, since a few of them had been soldiers in the first Burma campaign.

The pilot circled around to find a good spot on a hillside. It was before dawn and still pretty dark. All of our gear was packed in one big basket with its own parachute. We dropped the equipment and watched where it landed. It didn't float far. Then I jumped, I should say, stepped out of the door, like the sergeant said. I managed to stop myself from swinging pretty quickly, landed on all fours, and slipped a ways down the slope on my knees. It took a few seconds, but I remembered the rest of my instructions, so I grabbed the lines, pulled, and the air tumbled out of the chute. Amazingly, the two others also made it without major injuries. Pretty good for our brief training session. I went back and got that parachute, by the way, after all the fighting was over. I found where I'd buried it, underneath a paddy hut, and brought it home.

We found a couple of local Kachins to help us carry our extra stuff, the radio and a bunch of rations. We had also been given two homing pigeons. In the course of that day, I sat down with Paul, the radio operator, to encode a message, which he put in little capsules on the pigeons' legs. It just said, "Arrived okay at approximately so-and-so grid on the map, and we're moving out as rapidly as possible to the south." I never did get to check if the pigeons made it back, but I suppose they did. We were about seventy-five miles from Myitkyina, where the pigeoneers were. It was funny to me, the fellows who handled the pigeons were great big men, real physical specimens, well over six feet tall and two hundred pounds, cooing and billing with their pigeons. In contrast, the men who had to go out and fight with the Japanese were often the scrawniest looking characters you ever saw. After we sent the pigeons aloft, off we went.

A New Addition

First, we headed toward Namhkai, Mahka La's hometown. I say town, it was just a small village. Fortunately, we had sent word to the people before we arrived. As we approached, a boy came running out to warn us that a Japanese patrol was coming through the village right then, so we found a convenient ditch, hid, and waited. We peered through the bushes and watched the patrol pass by, but we didn't mess with them; we didn't want them to know we were there. After they left, we went in and recruited some additions to our little group, making about a dozen of us all told.

From there, we encountered the road that runs from Bhamo to Namhkam. It was a blacktop, one-lane road that wound around through the hills, built by the British years before, to maintain a telegraph line. I think the line went all the way to the China border near the town of Muse. As we approached the road, we heard a noise coming from the direction of Bhamo, a bunch of horses, clipclop, clipclop, on the blacktop. We hid again and watched, and I'd say at least a hundred Japanese came by on horseback. It took them quite a while to pass. They were not in a hurry, just ambling along. I don't know whether they were a cavalry outfit or what, but they were on horseback. After they passed by, we went down the steep bank to the road. We had to slide to get there. At the road, one of our lighter fellows shinned up the steel pole and cut the telegraph line. There were two wires with insulators; he cut them both and slipped back down. Then we crossed the road. On the other side was a big clearing. We ran up the slope so we wouldn't be exposed too long but were careful to leave no trace.

We then proceeded to another Kachin village but stayed in a paddy house, not the village itself. I remember that night well, it was in early November, a cold clear night with no wind at all, and I heard the music of a flute. The Kachins' idea of courtship involved music, they didn't believe much in smooching. A lot of courting went on when the young people worked in the fields. Every so often you would hear music on a quiet night. This particular time it must have come from over a mile away in another paddy house. I'll never forget that beautiful sound on that still, cold night. There was no moon; stars were everywhere.

Some of the villagers came out later and talked to us. They told us that they had a man called Percy with them who had jumped in by parachute a while back, along with several others. The Japanese had ambushed the crowd and killed all except Percy. The Kachins had kept him hidden since then. They wanted to know if we'd like to take him with us. We told them to bring him on up. It turned out he was another radio operator from OSS 101, an Anglo-Burman with the code name Percy. And, man, he was the happiest fellow you ever saw. He had no idea how he was going to get out of there until we showed up. His .45 pistol was all he had in the way of weapons. With him, we had two radiomen, and he continued on with us for quite a while.

A Messenger and a Miracle

We moved on down toward the Shweli River, which forms the border between Burma and China for a short distance, then cuts across the Shan Plateau, and eventually runs into the Irrawaddy. As we approached the Shweli, our radio went bad. We were unable to get any communication at all. We could receive, but we couldn't send. Our radiomen knew how to do the key and operate the thing, but neither one had much technical knowledge of the workings of the radio. We needed a fixit man. We had to communicate, or we wouldn't be able to accomplish anything. The only thing to do was to send somebody back to friendly territory and request that they send us someone who could fix a radio.

As I look back it, it was a one-in-a-million chance to successfully send a message by someone on foot and then to have an airplane find us in the jungle and get a fixit man to us. We had to encode the message so that if the messenger got caught, the enemy wouldn't know what was going on. Mahka La persuaded a trustworthy Kachin from a nearby village to undertake the trip. Percy and Paul encrypted the message, and we gave it to this fellow and paid him money in advance, silver rupees. We figured it would take the man about eight days to get there and then some time to round up somebody who could fix radios, so we had to look ahead as to where we might be. We weren't in a good place and didn't want to stay there, so we plotted out on the map, then put our estimated coordinates in the message and told headquarters that we'd be within a short distance of that point, wherever we could find an open spot.

We sent the man off with our fingers crossed and then headed south. The messenger got to Bhamo, or near Bhamo, where fighting was going on. Thankfully, he was a resourceful man. He found some Americans and gave them the message. In the meantime, we headed to the place where we said we would be, got there a day or two ahead of time, and found a small clearing accessible to an airplane. It was all full of stumps and logs, but it was the best we could do. By then, we had accumulated a few more men, I guess about fifteen to seventeen, all armed with various and sundry weapons. Some of them had old Chinese Mausers. Many years earlier, the Chinese had used Germans to train their troops, so the Chinese still had a bunch of Mausers from that time. Some of our men had gotten them off of dead Chinese or traded for them. Others had Lee Enfields, British rifles, and a few had old muskets. They were all armed with something.

The day of the drop, we got up long before light. We lit the fires, and waited in the cold, gray dawn. It reminded me of an old picture show where a bedraggled army is under seige and somebody says, "Dinna ya hear it?" as the bagpipes of the reinforcements gradually become audible in the distance. We began to hear the faint but welcome sound of a C-47. Bless Pat, somebody had gotten our message! We put leaves on the fire and made a huge ton of smoke. Some of these fellows, most of them, really, had never even seen an airplane close up, much less seen somebody jump out of one. The excitement was at a fever pitch. First thing the plane did was drop a package, a basketwork box made out of canvas and bamboo. The parachute opened up and came swinging down. Then the plane circled around once more, and this time we saw a man jump when the plane was real close to the ground. I don't suppose it was more than 150 feet up.

Out the door came this gangling fellow in his green fatigues. The chute opened; he swung around a few times and then drifted off down the hill where we couldn't see him. Everybody was screaming and hollering and running over to make sure he was all right. As we breasted the brow of the hill, we could see him down there, on all fours, patting the ground. We approached him at a dead run, and he looked up at us. Even from a distance, I could tell he was squinting. When I got to him, first thing he said to me was, "I jumped with my glasses on, and I've lost them." Well, it was a damn-fool stunt to jump with glasses on, and he knew it. But he was all excited; it was the first time he'd ever jumped. He moaned, "I've got to have my glasses. I can't see squat without those glasses."

We had probably fifteen men at the site. I said, "Okay, he came down this way, and his glasses probably came off of him when the chute first jerked open." We tried to figure out the trajectory. The plane was going maybe seventy-five or eighty miles an hour. The glasses wouldn't fall straight down, so we made a guess as to where they might be from the direction the plane was going. Then we spread everybody out on the hillside and said, "Look at every inch of the surface." We set folks about six feet apart and proceeded down the hill in a skirmish line, all of us on the ground, patting it, parting the grass, trying to find those glasses. Finally, a great shout broke out and somebody yelled, "Htam sai," "I found it!" Everybody cheered.

The radioman's name was Curtis Schultz, Curt Schultz. As I got to know him, I found out he was a limited serviceman. What you and I could see at twenty feet, he couldn't even see at two feet, or however it works, he was nearly blind. He was also limited because he had heart trouble. But they were going to try to get somebody out there to us, no matter what, so they sent him. And he turned out to be damn near a genius as far as the radio was concerned. He kept it going all the time, rain, shine, or whatever. And, of course, he had two other operators to help him out, and lots of tools since they had included another whole set and a new radio. So Schultz became a key part of our group and stayed with me until they shipped us out. After that, I kept up with him until he died. That was not long ago, maybe two years or so. Schultz was a great fellow and in spite of his heart, tough as nails.

Our Job

The main purpose of our mission at this point was to gather information for the Chinese, who were heading our way. The information we gathered went to Detachment 101 headquarters, which was at Nazira in India, but they sent it back to NCAC headquarters. In general, we needed to know where the Japanese were, what they were up to, the strength of their units, what they were armed with, every detail we could find. Some of that information we got from direct observation. For example, at campsites, the Japanese left certain characteristic trash, dried fish rations, and most of it came in paper packages that were real oily, so we knew they'd been there. We even found evidence of their diet where they'd been going to the bathroom. And of course, there were the telltale signs of cartridge cases if there had been any action, and footprints. They wore shoes that had a special place for the big toe, like a sandal; it left a definite print that was unmistakably Japanese, 100 percent sure.

Our main source of information, though, was from villagers along the way. We'd send men to villages along the line to find where Japanese establishments were and whether they were command or quartermaster posts or first aid stations or regular outfits. The men gathering the information would always come in right at dusk. I'd end up talking with them around the fire, or sometimes in the dark if we were worried about being spotted. I had to extract all the information that I could get. The men were not all that sophisticated, I suppose is the word, so I had to use vocabulary that they'd understand. For example, for artillery, I used the word *yamdok*, a primitive word for a cannon. I'd ask them whether the gun had wheels on it, two wheels or four wheels, or how big was the barrel or whether the enemy had tanks. I'd try to get a description of what kind of radio they had, what did the machine look like, did they have wire strung up in trees? I even carried a little book, which I still have, with pictures of Japanese insignias. If an informant had seen an officer, I'd pull out that booklet. "Is this what he had on his shoulder? Did it look like this?" And the fellow might point to one of the pictures.

This questioning went on far into the night virtually every night, I hardly got any sleep. We'd send men out in the morning, and they might be gone two or three days. We paid some of them in opium. Those opium *wallas* were anxious to get a hold of that substance. *Walla* is actually a Hindi word. It just means a fellow. Kachin for an addict is *gani lu amasha*. It just means "he uses opium." I suppose in modern terms, I would probably be called a drug dealer. We knew a lot of the men were double agents and got paid off by the Japanese too, and we kept that in mind. But we figured we got the best of the deal because we kept moving. And we almost always used Kachins. We were convinced that the Kachins were mostly on our side.

Crossing the Shweli

Besides ordering us to gather information, Peers had said, "See if you can recruit a battalion and cause some trouble. And keep moving south." So we kept moving south. I decided that there was so much traffic around the Shweli River that if we divided into two smaller groups, we would stand a better chance of getting across. By that time, Ting Bawm had hiked in and made it back to us. I put him in command of the second bunch. The whole group numbered about seventeen or eighteen, so about eight or nine went with him. We planned to cross the Schweli River at places about fifteen or twenty miles apart and then meet at a place further south that I picked out on the map, a village called Ho It, on the side of a mountain called Pangnang Bum.

I picked out Ho It because it was isolated, and the name Ho It implied that it was Chinese (close to the border there were a few Chinese villages around). If so, it would probably be neutral. We were moving into a territory heavily populated with Palaungs, and the Palaungs were Buddhists who generally favored the Japanese. Furthermore, they were so strict they wouldn't even kill a louse, and their villages were full of lice and fleas and rats and everything else. So, I just picked the village Ho It off the map, and it was lucky that I did.

I took my bunch, and we hid out on the bank of the Shweli River, up in a draw. We actually had to wait a couple of days while groups of Japanese went by. We could easily see them. They went by day, so we eventually crossed at night. We made a raft and took two trips to cross. It was the dry season, and the water was swift, but not like in the rains. After the crossing, we had to travel a little distance on the same trail that the Japanese were using. I got the men to cut branches. It was a dusty road, and we dragged those branches behind us to try to eliminate our footprints. With seven or eight men all dragging brush behind them, it messed everything up. After that, we managed to get on a trail going south with no problems, and we eventually made it to Ho It. Ting Bawm's group planned to cross the river to the west of us, but they failed to show up at Ho It. For a while, it was a mystery what had happened to them.

Other Men's Gods

We had figured right, Ho It was a Chinese village. They were quite different from the Kachin and Palaung villages, where the houses were on stilts. The Chinese built houses right square on the ground with dirt floors and no windows at all, no light inside except from fires. The walls were made of a mud/wattle arrangement which provided good protection against the weather. In the bamboo dwellings of the Kachins, the breezes wafted right on through. The Chinese preferred to keep warm.

We made it to the village and, in short order, managed to meet the old headman, the *laoban* they called him. He could speak Jinghpaw, so I asked him about the situation. He told me that the Japanese and some Kachins and Palaungs under Japanese command regularly patrolled the area. Nevertheless, we were tired and accepted his invitation to spend the night at the village. He provided us with a good Chinese supper at his house. In conversation, we learned that the principal occupation of the people of his village was running caravans. They herded horses and mules up into China and back down into Burma.

As I was getting undressed to go to bed, actually to sleep on the dirt floor, an event occurred in which I learned a valuable lesson. The fire was in a boxlike arrangement in the middle of the floor. The inside of the house was black and smoky, very dark. Up on the wall was a structure like a mantelpiece, which I had not even noticed when I came in, and there were a few items sitting on it. I couldn't tell what they were in the dark. When I got ready to lie down, I pulled my britches off, rolled them up, and just seeking a place to put them out of the way, I stuck them up on that shelf. Immediately after I had done that, the old *laoban* began wildly jabbering in Chinese. Obviously, he was extremely upset about something. He was almost screaming, and I could barely get a word in. I finally managed to get him to explain. He told me, "You have put your pants on my altar!" Well, I reached up right quick and pulled my trousers down off of that shelf. In my ignorance, I had put my pants on the altar dedicated to his ancestors, a sacred place. I knew I was in hot water, so I apologized at great length and repeatedly told him that I was just an ignorant white man, that I didn't understand the ways of the noble Chinese. He finally began to smile again. Thankfully I was able to communicate well enough to get him to realize I meant no disrespect. After that, we did not post a guard; we just went to bed. We were tired; we'd been walking for Lord knows how long, ten days at least, maybe more than that.

Death in the Night

We were rudely awakened about midnight or close to it. The villagers let us know that an enemy patrol had showed up in the dark and decided to stay in a house right down the hill. The two men wore Japanese uniforms and carried Japanese arms, but they were Kachins who worked for the Japanese. Apparently, they had been there many times before and had earned a reputation for kicking the villagers around and taking whatever they wanted. Since they were armed, they had always gotten away with it. The villagers gave us a brief description of the two men and their location. They were in one of the larger houses with several rooms and doors at front and back.

My inclination was to try to capture them. They might be able to give us information. So we got our men together quietly. We had to bide our time until the enemy went to bed. We waited and waited and waited. Every once in a while, a woman or sometimes a child would come out and give us an update. We finally got the word that the two men seemed to be asleep, so we divided up into our two groups. I took one group to the front of the house, and Mahka La took the other to the back.

On a signal, we entered slowly and carefully, but before I got through the front room, I heard a great rumpus in the back. It was chaos. By the time I rushed through and got the fight stopped, the two men were beaten to death, or well on the way to it. A knock-down-drag-out fight had broken out, and my men had killed both of them. There we were with two corpses on our hands. By that time, the whole village was awake. The *laoban* said, "We must bury them right away and get rid of all signs of them." He led us all up the side of the mountain to a gully about a quarter mile from the village. Folks brought their hoes with them. Those were the tools that they mostly used over there. They didn't have any shovels, just hoes. So, with the whole village working, in jig time, they dug a pretty deep hole. We dragged those two men into the hole, covered them up with dirt, and put some brush on top. Then we went back to bed.

Pangnang Bum

The next morning, I had a long conversation with the *laoban*, mainly about his horses. I found out that his village, along with another village or two in the vicinity, was engaged in the same caravan business. I hoped that if we did succeed in organizing a battalion, his folks could furnish our supply train with their horses. I also told him that we wanted a place to hide up on the mountain Pangnang Bum for a while. So he took us up the side of the mountain to a ridge with a pretty good view of things. We were up about seven thousand feet, where the jungle thinned out. It was cold up at that altitude since it was up in November or December by that time. At the place he picked out for us, on top of a ridge, there was a big crabapple tree. We set up camp underneath that tree, and for quite a while, we practically lived off of crabapples. We tried to build as few fires as possible, but we built fires there during the daylight and roasted those crabapples in the fire. We just put them in the coals. They were on the verge of being rotten, but cooked that way, they were really good. And there were thousands of them. That was our main sustenance while we stayed on that hillside.

We asked the old *laoban* to be our watchman along the trail by his village. It was the regular trail that the caravans used traveling back and forth to China. So he became our lookout. There was a small Kachin village nearby, but the most important Kachins in the area were down at a larger village called Manton, about twenty or twenty-five miles to the southwest. Through our discussions with local folks, we found out the names of three well-respected and influential fellows who lived in that village; Dashi Yaw, Hbau Yam Gam, and Nhkum Zau Seng. We sent a man over to Manton to invite them to come and talk with us. They came in a big hurry. I sat down with them and made a clean breast of everything we planned to do. They knew the Japanese were close by. Their regimental headquarters was in a place called Namtu. At that time, we were two hundred miles behind enemy lines, in a strategic place, put there to cause havoc. So I gave the three a big sales talk about how the war had been going so far, how Kachins had helped us, and I told them we'd like to recruit a whole battalion of Kachins.

I said, "If we set as our goal to get one able-bodied Kachin per household in the area, how many do you think we could recruit? Could we raise a thousand?" The three men talked among themselves. They counted on their fingers, mentioning names of villages and people. It took them quite a while to come to a conclusion. They finally turned around to me and said, "We can raise a thousand," and they sounded pretty confident that they could.

Talk

The key to everything we accomplished was talk. Whenever we came to a village, we talked to people to find out the lay of the land, where the tracks were, where folks came from, and where they went in the ordinary course of their lives. If we were planning to go to a particular village, we'd find out all we could beforehand, the name of the headman, who else was important, and what they did. I made notes as we went. The main thing I have to say about intelligence is, you've *got* to know the language. You can work through interpreters, but it's not the same. Since I was able to talk to Dashi Yaw, Hbau Yam Gam, and Nhkum Zau Seng, we were able to recruit the battalion. In Iraq and Afghanistan and such places, it seems we don't have many people who know the languages, and I haven't heard of concerted attempts for us to learn. You can't rely on that gun all the time. You can't become friends, you can't really understand folks, you can't learn from them, if you can't talk to them. I don't know what current military priorities are, but having soldiers learn the local language ought to be one of the most important things they do.

My Jinghpaw was never perfect. Kachins often laughed at the way I said things with my southern drawl, but they were patient and happy to help. And I listened. In every village that we went through, every paddy field, I'd stop a minute if I could and chat with folks. People knew about me, an American fellow who was speaking Jinghpaw, and they would greet me knowing that I was trying to learn. I hardly spoke any English in the field except with the radioman, since all the messages were in English. The key to my job was communicating with Kachins.

We sat under the crabapple tree and planned our operation at that first meeting. We decided to have the recruits gather in a few weeks' time, December the 31st, New Year's Eve, 1944. The three men then headed straight back to Manton to start recruiting. It had to be done by word of mouth and secretly. They personally had to recruit folks or send trusted individuals. If the recruits had any arms, they were to bring them. It almost went without saying that they would at least have swords. We were to provide them with uniforms and other weapons and organize them into a battalion. The recruiters were to keep their eyes out especially for any old soldiers who had performed service in the Burma Rifles. There were some Kachins and Gurkhas in the area who had.

The recruits were to show up December the 31st, not one day earlier. That night we would organize, and the next morning, we'd arrange a drop to provide them with their supplies. We wanted to commence operations as quickly as possible but also as secretly as possible. We told them to come to the top of the mountain, not the village. It was a twin-peaked mountain, so we picked the easternmost peak. In the meantime, we moved away from the crabapple tree and went on up to the top of the mountain ourselves, found a clear spot for our drop ground, and camped not far from that.

I made arrangements for the drop with headquarters. I radioed, "I know it's a bad time, January the 1st, but it's a distinctive day, and people know about it, and that's what we want. The men will get here on New Year's Eve, and we'll get organized the next day." So, having faith in Nhkum Zau Seng and his two cohorts, we ordered equipment for a thousand men. We pretty much asked for whatever we thought we could get. The heaviest weapon we ordered was the 60 millimeter mortar. Browning automatic rifles or Bren guns, we'd take either one, and new M1 rifles. There was a gun called a UD gun from United Defense Corporation, a good submachine gun, 9 millimeter with 20 shot magazines, lighter and better looking than the awkward Thompsons. We requested some of them as well as M3 submachine guns (they called them "grease guns" and that's what they looked like). They were .45 caliber. All told, I had eight different kinds of ammunition on order, not because I planned it, that's just the way it worked out.

While we were there on the mountain, we built a stockade, a compound made out of poles. We put guards out on the trails, and if any civilians came up, we put them in the compound. They had to stay there as long as we were there, so that information about us wouldn't get back to the Japanese. Fortunately, it wasn't a well-traveled spot, but there were trails that came up and down, so we had some detainees. We didn't intend to hurt them. They just had to stay there until we left.

Recruits Arrive

Starting early in the morning, December 31st, eager recruits came pouring in from everywhere. Over a thousand men arrived by the time it got dark that first day. Nhkum Zau Seng, Dashi Yaw, and Hbau Yam Gam knew most of them, so we set up a registration system with those three to write down all the names. We separated the men into companies—A, B, C, and D. It was hectic, to say the least, with folks standing in long lines to get registered. Some had experience in the Burma Rifles where they had ranks of the British Indian Army; a *jemadar* was in charge of a platoon, the equivalent of a second lieutenant; a *havildar* was like a sergeant; a *subedar* like a captain; a *naik*, a corporal; a *lance naik*, a private first class. We would interview them and say, "Were you ever in the Burma Army?" "Yes, I was." "What was your rank?" "I was a *naik*." "Okay. We'll make you a *havildar*." We gave anyone with experience a promotion right there on the spot, and Nhkum Zau Seng, Dashi Yaw, and Hbau Yam Gam sized up the rest as to who might be able to do what. They knew a lot of folks personally. By daylight, we had separated everyone into companies and platoons, but we were still breaking them out into squads for a few days after that, and there was a lot of shifting around.

As I remember, it was around that time that Tubu Gam showed up. Everybody knew him. I say everybody; all the people in that region knew Tubu Gam. He was a Kachin but wore a Japanese uniform when he arrived. Some time ago, he had been a *jemadar* in the British Burma Rifles and a pipe major. He had marched in front of the band. After the British left, he served for a while under the Japanese. He brought a whole company of Kachins with him, dressed in Japanese uniforms, and they marched right in amongst us. He announced, "I picked the wrong side, and I want to change. I want to join your battalion." He told us the Japanese had recruited him at the beginning of the war, but he had some bad experiences with them and changed his mind. After a long discussion, we decided to take the whole crowd of them, but we were careful to keep them separate from the others. Of course, we made them take off their Japanese uniforms but let them continue to use their Japanese weapons. That was one reason we believed his story; his company brought a whole lot of arms and ammunition with them and gave them to us.

In the meantime, we prepared for the drop. We built three fires with a lot of greenery piled up to make a big smoke, with my panel right between them, "P" for Pete. We stationed the companies at different places around the field and told them to stay out of the way when the drop started. Then we waited for daylight. This being the cold season, the paddies were all filled with fog. From where we were, it looked like a sea of cotton wool over the whole countryside with the mountain peaks sticking up out of it. We were on one of the taller peaks. The Japanese were down in the valleys somewhere, under that blanket of fog. They might hear us, but they couldn't see us.

The Big Drop

Before sunrise on that New Year's Day 1945, the recruits on the mountainside heard the sound of the approaching fleet of airplanes. There were six planes, C-47's, all in formation. This was one time, thank God, that OSS 101 really did their job and came through with the goods. We could hear the planes a long time before we saw them. I can still hear that low drone in my mind. When they first came into view, a great cheer rose up from the men. They couldn't believe what was happening. It was like a miracle. A lot of them had never seen an airplane close up. And of course, these were close. They were dropping from just a couple of hundred feet. Most of the food was free dropped, but anything that was breakable had parachutes. Each one of those planes could carry about six thousand pounds of goods. That meant a lot of parachutes. The whole mountainside was covered with them. It looked surreal. At the signal from us, everybody went out on the drop field and picked things up and carried the supplies to the location where we had a temporary quartermaster established. Mahka La was in charge of that. He was an old soldier himself, so he knew one end of a gun from the other. Nevertheless, he had a huge job trying to keep track of everything we got.

I just can't describe the excitement that was generated that day. The men were whooping and hollering. It was like Christmas. They were issued uniforms, and were putting them on right out there on the field, old wool uniforms, American surplus property left over from World War I. Of course, all the uniforms were too big. I guess maybe a few of them managed to find something that fit, but mostly their sleeves were all rolled up and their britches rolled up. We did get some good shoes, British ammunition boots with heel plates, toe plates, and hobnails. But the Kachins never really wore them beyond that day. They'd tie the laces and hang them around their necks. When we'd come to a village on the march, they'd stop on the outskirts and put their shoes on. They wore them just to show off. When they got to the other side, they took them off and continued on, barefooted. We issued some tennis shoes later on that were made in China that they sometimes wore, but mostly they went barefooted.

Asking for More

After the initial excitement wore off, I realized I needed someone to instruct people on the basics of M1 rifles. Mahka La and a few others knew a lot about firearms, but none of them had any experience with the M1. The old soldiers knew the Lee Enfield rifles backwards and forwards. But these new ones were semiautomatic rifles that could really put the bullets out. So, we needed an instructor. Ting Bawm knew the M1; he had been taught by the OSS back in India, but he wasn't back yet. If you recall, I had left him when we split to cross the river. The story I finally got was that he crossed the river with his group of about nine or ten but then made an unlucky choice. Turned out the Kachin village he picked to stay the night was home to a company that the Japanese had commissioned. When Ting Bawm and his men got up in the morning and started out the door to take care of things, a group opened fire on them. The enemy caught his men pretty much with their britches at half mast and killed them. And as far as we know, all were lost except Ting Bawm. He got away, but he was hit right across the face with a bullet. Split his cheek open. He fled into the jungle and stayed in the vicinity for a while, trying to locate any of his men that might have survived, but he never found a one. He didn't know whether we made it either, and he wondered what he was going to do if he ended up down at Ho It all by himself. So, he chose to go all the way back up to Sinlumkaba.

They radioed me that he had made it back up there and asked what to do with him. I told them, "Send him to me. And by the way, I need somebody who can help me teach these new fellows marksmanship, how to handle a rifle, how to keep it clean, and all that kind of stuff." So, at the next drop, they sent a sergeant by the name of Eckhart along with Ting Bawm. The plane showed up at our same drop ground, flying very low. The weather was bad, and the air was really rough that day. Eckhart had jumped before, but Ting Bawm had not. We watched Eckart jump and land on his back with a resounding thump, but he was fine. Then we looked up and saw Ting Bawm. Two men were literally throwing him out the door of the plane. We couldn't see where he landed. He ended up on down the hillside, scratched up but okay. It had been so rough in the plane that he'd been vomiting all over the place. So, when it came time for him to jump, they just picked him up and threw him. He was pretty weak when we got to him, but he recovered quickly.

We had set up a rifle range about a hundred yards long as part of our prepara-
tions. I put Eckhart to work immediately. Sergeant Eckhart was a thirty-year-old
man. He'd been in the army most of his life. I told him specifically, "Sergeant,
hardly any of these people can read and write. They don't know numbers either.
Just start them off with the battle sight. I don't want you to confuse them with
talk about windage or elevation; that's not important in jungle fights, anyway.
Keep things simple and straightforward. These guys can hunt. They're great shots.
They're used to muzzle loaders, and none of this adjusting business is familiar
to them. The important thing is that they know how to work the rifle, how to
load and unload it, how to put it on safe, how to keep it clean, the elementary
stuff. And I want you to get that knowledge to them in a hurry because we're
going to be shooting at somebody here in the next few days." So right away, he
took one company down to where we had established our rifle range.

I appointed Ting Bawm head of what we called the I&R platoon—information
and reconnaissance. He was to instruct men in demolitions, handling explosives
and that sort of thing. Bren guns were the heaviest automatic weapons that
we had, and the old Burma Rifles soldiers were familiar with them, so we had
several people to instruct that, and a few of the old soldiers knew something
about mortars. For the first three or four days, lots of instruction was going
on, and I went roaming around checking to be sure everybody was doing what
they were supposed to do.

When I went to check up on Eckhart, he was lecturing the men through
an interpreter. And there he was, going through an elaborate explanation of
the sight, how to set the windage on it, and all that sort of stuff. I got mad. I
told him, "Look, if you can't do what I want you to do, I'm going to have to get
somebody else. I know you must have your routine, but I made clear what I
want these folks to learn." Well, he gave me so much trouble back that I finally
told him, "I'm sorry, but I want you to leave tomorrow morning. I'll give you
a couple of fellas to go with you, and you can walk out." So he left. That's the
last I ever saw of Sgt. Eckhart. I learned that he did make it back, and I feel
sure that he gave them a report that I was crazy. No telling what he told them.
Anyhow, Eckhart was bullheaded and didn't want to take orders from some
greenhorn like me, so he had to go. Fortunately, Ting Bawm was there, and he
took over with the instruction and did a great job.

Next time I communicated with headquarters, I requested an American
leader for each company. By this time, I'd become a major. They sent Chuck
Roberts, who was a captain, and lieutenants Gordon Totten, Al McCargar, and
Wesley Richardson. We also got two other folks for quartermaster positions. One
of them was named Tate, and the other was a man from Texas, in the vicinity
of San Antonio. I can't remember his name offhand. He was an old cowboy, a

valuable man because he could handle horses. In the meantime, I had negotiated with the *laoban* of Ho It to get me 250 horses for a supply train. In the initial supply drop, we got rope for a picket line. With 250 horses, that meant a lot of rope. We also got some smaller rope for use as halters and got some food for the horses. *Busa* was the chopped hay, and it came in bales. *Gram*, they called the grain. Mainly, though, the horses lived off the country, grazing when we stopped. So mixed in with all these new recruits, we had horses too. They were a bunch of hammer-headed nags, all 250 of them, but those Chinese really knew how to handle them. They were their horses, of course. And the *laoban* brought a whole bunch of his caravan men with him.

I got a camera at one of the drops and a bunch of film. From there on out, I began to take most of the pictures that are in the scrapbook. And that's not nearly all the pictures that I took. The rest of them I sent to headquarters at various times, but I never got them back. They're probably in the archives somewhere. If I ever got to look in the archives, I could probably recognize some of my own stuff. They had a big photo section. Most of the shots were taken right around headquarters, but there were a few field pictures, and I took some of those.

Combat Chaos

After some very basic training, we were ready to start on our mission. There was a Japanese cantonment near a village called Maung Tat, just down the hill from us. We had obtained information about the precise location, so I dispatched Al McCargar, B Company, for the first encounter. I gave Al maps and told him, "Our scouts say the village is next to a large group of paddy fields. There's a big clump of bamboo out in the middle of those fields. That's where the Japanese are. If you take your mortars and set them up to hit that bamboo clump, the soldiers might run out into the fields, and you could kill a few of them."

He decided to attack at night, since we had mortar shells that would illuminate the countryside. I forget the name of the particular mortar shell, it's the kind that bursts up in the air and has a parachute and a flare, so it floats slowly to the ground and lights up a big area. So Al went down, set up his mortars, and got his men in position within range of the bamboo clump. McCargar had the mortars set up behind him, to shoot over his men and light up the area around the bamboo clump. Turns out, the mortar shell with the parachute is heavier than a regular shell, so it requires a bigger charge. His men didn't know that. At the signal, they fired their mortars, but the flares ended up floating down directly *behind* him, instead of over the Japanese. Here they came, slowly drifting down,

silhouetting him and his whole outfit. He managed to correct the situation, but
by that time the Japanese were firing madly at him and his men, whose position
was perfectly lit up by their own mortars. Needless to say, it was not a successful
operation. But everybody sure learned a lesson about mortar shells. McCargar
came back and reported on the fiasco. Fortunately, no one got hit. He did a good
job getting the men out okay, and after a while, he was able to laugh about it.

Namtu

While we were at Pangnang Bum, I was anxious to get somebody into the town
of Namtu to find out what was going on at the Japanese regimental headquarters.
Namtu was a big mining area. The Chinese had mined that valley for hundreds
of years, using primitive techniques, small tunnels driven way back into the
mountains. The British came there in about 1912 and put in a shaft that was
something like a thousand feet deep and built a smelter to refine the ore. They
produced lead and zinc and silver and gold for the Burma Corporation, one
of the biggest businesses in Burma. It traded on the London Stock Exchange.
There were great difficulties with this particular mine on account of water,
and they had hired Herbert Hoover as an engineer at one time, to design the
drainage and pumping system. The mine was a big enterprise.

There was a golf course there, a nice golf course. Wherever they went, the
British made sure they had all the amenities, polo grounds, golf courses, you
name it. They even had a clubhouse on the course. When the Japanese came
in and took over, they began to operate the mine. We heard that they were
established on the golf course, in the clubhouse.

The population in the surrounding countryside was primarily Kachin,
most of the Chinese had run away. It was only about a hundred miles back
to China along the Burma Road. When the Chinese left, the Japanese forced
the Kachins to work in the mines. Their supervisors were mostly Indians who
had been brought over by the British. They'd been unable to get back to India,
so the Japanese kept them and kept the mines in operation for quite a while.
By the time we got down there, though, the mine and the smelter had ceased
operations, since our Air Force had been bombing the area.

The main mine was 17 miles from Namtu at a place called Bawdwin, up in the
mountains. The railroad up to it was a masterpiece of engineering. It climbed
3,000 feet in those 17 miles, and had innumerable tunnels and one famous
grade where it spiraled around and came over itself, climbing up all the time.
From our Air Corps's point of view, the smelter was a big target, and they put
it out of business pretty quick, but the mine was a different proposition. They

weren't able to do much damage. It's just my opinion, but I think they wasted a lot of time on a harmless target. I don't believe the mine was able to supply the armed forces of Japan with much of anything useful.

But we needed to find out what was going on down there. So we tried to get folks into Namtu to scout it out. We made several attempts. In fact, almost daily we sent somebody down there, but with no luck. I finally found a fellow who knew something about it. I don't remember his name. He had a friend, and the two agreed to go to Namtu and try to get information. But they had some conditions. They said, "That whole area is guarded by the Japanese. They've got checkpoints on every road, every path coming in and out of the town. As Kachins, we're suspect. On the other hand, Shans and Chinese can get in or out, no problem." Kachins and Shans are easy to tell apart because they each dress in a distinctive manner. The Shans and sometimes Chinese wear big, voluminous pants instead of the skirts that Burmese, Kachins, and the Palaungs wear. The men said, "We need some Shan clothes. We can speak Shan, so we have no trouble there, and we can get some chickens to sell in town."

As I explained before, we kept folks at a stockade we had built and then released them when we left. There were some Shans there, so I told the two men to go down to the stockade and borrow some clothes. So they went, and came back before they left looking just like Shans in the proper attire. They got down to Namtu very quickly and came back with all kinds of information, even the name of the Japanese commanding officer. They found out that the Japanese had some artillery and the numbers of units. I patted them on the back and congratulated them and sent in messages by radio with the information that they supplied. I sent them on several other missions after that, and they kept using the Shan clothes that they had gotten out of the stockade as their disguise. They seemed to work well as a team.

Fog of War

After we got that information, for our second strike, we decided to hit the Japanese right at the mine in Bawdwin. I sent Richardson's group, D Company. I picked them partly because B'rang Nu, a Kachin *subedar*, was his second in command. B'rang Nu was a real soldier, with combat experience. He'd fought alongside the British against the Japanese early on. Years later, when I visited Burma, I met members of his family and actually attended the funeral of his mother, who happened to have died shortly before I arrived.

I put the strongest man with Wesley Richardson, because Richardson was a young fellow, a greenhorn. Also, I sent a good interpreter with him, a Karen named Judson, who spoke English well. So D Company went there and encountered the Japanese in an area cluttered with old mine tunnels. The Japanese had constructed fortifications in and around the mine. During the confusion of the firefight, Richardson and his interpreter got separated from the rest of the company. I don't know the particulars, but B'rang Nu continued the battle, did some damage to the enemy, and returned with his company intact. They suffered no casualties, but it was a mixed bag. Richardson was mortified. I didn't fault him for it. One thing about battles anywhere, but especially in the jungle, is that they can be chaotic and confusing. Sometimes you succeed, and sometimes you don't, and this time was not exactly what I would call a success. Anyhow, since we had hit a one-two punch at them, the Japanese knew for sure that we were up there somewhere and that we intended to make trouble.

We constantly sent back information to headquarters. One thing we mentioned was that a village to the southwest of us, a Palaung village, was the site of a Japanese outpost. We didn't ask them to bomb it, or even give an exact location, but I guess the Air Corps was always looking for targets, so they proceeded to bomb that village, or what they thought was that village. We were on the other side of the mountain and couldn't see what they were up to. We could hear it, though. As it turned out, they bombed the wrong village. They bombed a nearby Kachin village; one of the villages from which we had obtained a number of recruits. So all of a sudden, an irate contingent of Kachins showed up wanting to know, "Why in the Sam Hill did you bomb us? We just sent you the best men in town to be your soldiers, and the next thing you know, we get bombed." Fortunately, everybody had fled before any bombs hit. But the Americans had bombed it heavily, just a little-bitty Kachin village.

I tried to explain, "I'm just as sorry as I can be. They made a mistake, and if they've hurt anybody, we want to compensate for that somehow." Luckily, they didn't hit anything, really. They just blew some holes in the ground. But the villagers also told us, "There is one bomb right in the middle of our village that scooped out a hole about fifteen feet deep. It bounded up out of the ground, down through the village, and ended up right near the headman's house, without exploding. What do we do about this bomb?" I asked, "How big is it?" They indicated with their arms what I figured must have been about a five-hundred or one-thousand-pound bomb.

Curt Schultz, the radio man, had received a little demolitions training. He always wanted to get in on some action, so he said to me, "Let me go down and see if I can blow it up. It's probably a thousand pounder. You can't move something like that; the only solution is to clear everybody away from it and blow it up right where it is." So I said, "Okay. Percy and Paul can make radio contact while you're gone. Take what you need." We had gotten plenty of

Composition C in our drop, so we issued him a good supply of explosives, and he struck out to do the job.

I guess it was the second day before we heard any noise from over there. Maybe it was longer than that, I've forgotten, but he got there. He made two attempts to blow up the bomb. We heard both of them. After the first went off, I said, "That doesn't sound big enough for a one-thousand-pound bomb." A while later we heard another explosion, about as loud as the first one. A couple of days later, Schultz made his way back. He'd used up all his explosives in two shots. He said, "I couldn't blow the dadgum thing up. It's still sitting there. I blew the fuse off of it, so it's got no way to go off accidentally, but why the whole thing didn't go, I don't know. Maybe it was a dud to start with, or maybe something got screwed up when it hit the ground."

We had to send a crew there to get the bomb out. Fortunately, the village was located on a slope, and our men were able to prize the bomb loose and roll it down the hill. They said, "After we started it rolling, it went out of control. We just had to let it go." It bounded down the hillside like it was alive and finally ended up way down in a steep draw by a creek. What a mess. Here we'd gotten recruits from that place, and then not too long afterwards, our folks bombed their home. War is horrible when things go as intended, but so much worse when mistakes happen.

Ying Siang

In the meantime, there was a steady trickle of people coming up the hill, and we continued to put them in the stockade. I interviewed each one of the detainees at length to find out all the information I could because they had often come from somewhere near the Japanese. One of the folks who showed up was Chinese. He had a pith helmet on but no gear with him and was on foot. From our conversation, I found out he had been in the office of the Burma Corporation at Namtu. He was an engineer, principally concerned with making plans for development of the area. He was a real draftsman. Later, I learned he could print amazingly well. It looked like steel engraving, he was so good at it. He spoke English, as well as Palaung, Shan, Jinghpaw, and Lisu. He was an invaluable fellow.

I said, "I can use you, if you would like to come with us. We're fixing to go on down into the Shan states and need an interpreter." So he joined us. His primary responsibility was to talk to the Palaungs and Shans. I was not sure exactly why he was up there, but I had a gut feeling that he was all right. His name was Ying Siang. He had a wife and several children, and his family was still in Namtu. They weren't really safe down there since bombing was still going on; nevertheless, he decided to go with us.

Around that time, a cook boy came to me one day and said, "*Duwa*, there are two dead men down the hillside. You'd better come see." He had been foraging for firewood and had run across two naked bodies in a state of advanced decomposition, with their throats cut from ear to ear. I went down there to take a look. They had been dead for quite a while, and they were definitely naked; otherwise, it was hard to tell much about them. I told the cook boy, "We don't want anybody to know about this until I find out what happened." I didn't want to start a panic, so I got some of the kitchen staff to bury them. My initial efforts to find out about them led nowhere.

To skip ahead, a couple of months later, long after my Shan outfitted spies had left us, Ying Siang asked me, when we were alone, "Do you remember when you hired me to go with you?" And I said yes. He said, "Well, I was looking for my brother." After he got to our stockade, he did his own investigating and found out about the Kachin agents who had gone to Namtu dressed as Shans. He finally figured out that my Kachin agents had murdered his brother along with a Shan man just to take their clothes. It had never occurred to me that they would do such a thing, and it was a real shock when he told me. Apparently, the agents had gone to the compound, taken two folks, walked them down the hill, stripped them of their clothes, and killed them. They must have stripped them before they killed them, because they didn't get blood all over the clothes. I was never sure, but that would have explained why the decomposing bodies were completely nude. The suspects had long since left us, so there wasn't anything we could do.

Even after learning of this horrible occurrence, Ying Siang continued with us to the end of the campaign. And after that, the two of us maintained our friendship over the years. I always admired him for the fact that he served faithfully, in spite of his brother's fate. He moved to Hong Kong after the war, and I kept in contact and actually visited him and his family once. He died not too long ago.

Tiger! Tiger!

During those days at Pangnang Bum, we'd turn the horses and mules loose to forage. Then at night we'd round them up, all 250 of them. Unfortunately, although we tried hard, there would almost always be one or two that wandered too far away. Tigers soon found out and began killing them. They'd get one almost every night. I've talked before about the noise that tigers make when they're hunting, that coughing sound, well, we heard that sound often. When a mule or a horse is attacked, they make a noise as well. You could hear the frantic noise of a dying mule even a mile or two away.

There was one big old mule that had a broad arrow burned on its rump, which meant that it had been the property of the king. We found it dead, not too far from the camp, maybe a half mile down the side of the mountain. A tiger had been eating on it. When tigers killed something like that, they would come back and feed on it two or three nights in a row. This mule was lying on a slope, and up above it, a big rock projected out of the side of the mountain. The slope otherwise was solid jungle. I thought to myself, I'll come here and sit and wait overnight and, by God, I'll kill that tiger. We can't let him keep eating our animals.

So that night, I took my trusty rifle, and just at sunset, I went down by myself and sat on the rock. It was only about thirty yards from the mule. I thought the tiger would come back, and I would have a clear shot at him. I forget where the moon was that night, but it was dark because fog settled over the top of the dang mountain as soon as the sun went down. I quickly realized I had made a big mistake, I could hardly see my hand in front of my face, much less a tiger. I couldn't get back up to camp. It was a half a mile away, and there was no trail, no nothing. It'd be crazy clamoring up the side of the mountain in the dark. So I sat there all night long. It was cold as the devil, and I was shivering. If the tiger had come, I certainly wouldn't have seen him. I felt like tiger bait myself, awake and fearful all night. Finally, at the break of dawn, I got the hell out of there and didn't come back until good daylight.

I was still determined to kill the tiger, though. I'm sorry I felt that way, I respect tigers, but it was wartime, and we needed the mules. So, I came back with a small detail and two hand grenades and pull devices. We tied one tripwire to the mule's hip bone, which was sticking out where the tiger had been chewing on it, and another to the mule's head. The first night nothing happened. The second night, there was a big boom, so we went to check. Both grenades had gone off, but no tiger was to be seen. The Kachins are great trackers, though, and they searched the surrounding jungle and finally spotted some blood, followed the trail, and found that tiger. That's the tiger skin hanging up on the wall here. They skinned him and gave me the skin.

The same day, the Kachins set another trap using an old muzzle-loading percussion cap gun. They set it on an animal trail nearby, with the gun pointing about tiger high off the ground. It went off the same night, and they brought in a tiger, obviously a younger one, who had probably also been eating the mule. We didn't have a problem after that.

Fearful Symmetry

I walked to a nearby village one day, taking a couple of men along with me. We came back just about dark. It was January, during the *chota* monsoon and cold, there'd been a storm up there that day. Weather over there is a whole lot more predictable than it is here. Everyone knows it's not going to rain in November. It never rains in November. And October, about the last half of October is almost as certain not to rain. But then around the year's end, it rains again.

So, it was raining and cold as the devil, there was even some ice. When we got back to camp, we were worn out and frozen. I was looking forward to getting into my lean-to. It was a small shelter, and I was the only one in it. It was still light enough to see when I ducked down into the little hut. I looked up as I went in, and I was staring a tiger in the face. I didn't think, I just reacted. I scrambled back out of that hut in a big fat hurry, practically knocked it down trying to get out. Then peels of laughter came out from all around. Everybody had been waiting for me to come back, hiding to see what I would do, and I didn't disappoint them. I came out of there in a panic. They all giggled, hooted, and hollered for quite a while.

Then they explained to me that they had skinned that small tiger without cutting the hide at all. They made an incision around the lips, and then just peeled his skin back, rolled it off of him whole. They left the paws on, and the tail. Then they turned the whole thing back right side out, stuffed him full of straw, and set him up there in the back of my hut. In the half light of evening, it was the most realistic thing I'd ever seen. It scared the pants off of me. I thought there was a damn tiger in my shelter. So, they had a big joke at my expense. I laughed, too, after I pulled myself together.

Leaving Pangnang Bum

Before we left Pangnang Bum, we had a big *manao*, celebrating the inauguration of the 7th Battalion. I've got a couple of pictures of the festivities. They built an arbor, with a table where they served a feast, and they had the *manao* dance. A *jaiwa*, a chanter, sang for us. He was an impressive fellow. He beat time to his music with a clicker. He also had an instrument he played, a jaw harp made out of bamboo, "Dum, dum, dum, dum." Then he would recite and then make music again. He must have been thinking up the next verses while he twangled on his harp. He went on like that for maybe an hour, singing the praises of the 7th Battalion. He would sing in a high, nasal voice, very unnatural sounding. And he'd rock back and forth constantly, with his eyes closed. Everybody listened intently. There wasn't a sound except him. I have a copy of another such ballad, but not that one. The *jaiwa* was the main part the program. Later, people got up and made speeches.

On the way to the *manao*, I got just sick as a dog. I had fever and chills and vomited. It was obviously malaria. I had several recurrences of malaria. In fact, I had recurrences of malaria after I returned home from the war. When I got to the celebration, I was able to participate and get up and say my piece, but I was not feeling very good. After my speech, they gave me a name. They dubbed me Ka'ang Zhao Lai, which roughly translated means "He who has been through it all, from beginning to end," and they gave me a sword, which I still have.

On the Trail

We were in communication with headquarters on a regular schedule. Greenwich Mean Time, that's what we went by, GMT, and it was way off of local time, about a six-hour difference. Schultz was in charge of the radio set-up. We had Kachin boys turn the generator. In recruiting, we had trouble with requirements for age. Of course, no one had any documentation. The one rule I made was that in order to fight, the recruit had to be able to take an M1 or Lee Enfield rifle by the small of the stock and hold it straight out until I slowly counted to ten. If they were strong enough to do that, why, they were okay to be a soldier. There was really no way to tell their age, so that rule was the best I could come up with. And we adhered to it. But we often had a slew of boys, early teens, that showed up wanting to be with us. When we put them to the test, they'd occasionally break into tears when they couldn't do it. We sometimes let them come with us as cook boys or messengers or for odd jobs like turning the generator, but they were not allowed to engage in combat unless they could pass the test.

By radio, we let the folks at headquarters know we were headed south with our 1,000 men, and 250 horses and mules, minus the few we lost to the tigers. I suppose it was mid-January of '45 by that time. The plan was to go around Bawdwin, south to a place called Hungwe. As we headed out, we dispatched one platoon towards Namtu. They were to go fairly close to the Japanese and then circle back to us further down the line. They were from B Company, McCargar's outfit. The *jemedar* was an old soldier who had been with the Burma Rifles. He was a big, tall Kachin. He and his group were to go to the vicinity of Namtu and see what they could find out along the road that leads south from there to the town of Hsipaw. I'll get back to their story later.

On the way south to Hungwe, we got a drop at a small village. As I mentioned before, they had sent me a little thirty-five-millimeter camera, a dadgum good camera, and film in a tropical pack, an aluminum can all sealed up with wax, so water couldn't get in. So I took some pictures at this drop. The village itself was up high on a ridge. The drop area was a field to the side of the village. It happened that the villagers at that spot were in bad shape. They were Palaungs, but the Japanese hadn't been too kind to them and had requisitioned most of their rice, essentially leaving the villagers to starve.

No matter how carefully rice was packed, when they free dropped it, some of the sacks busted when they hit. As usual, several broke open this time. You may have heard about gleaners, poor people that come into fields after everybody's left to pick up what they can. Well, these villagers became gleaners. After we'd gathered our supplies, we told them, "Have at it," and they swarmed out onto that field. They picked up every grain of rice they could find, and they got a lot of food out of it. It was full of dirt and rocks, but it was food. They were in bad shape, and every little bit helped.

Casualties of War

We had some wounded men by this time. As we marched along, we would send patrols fanning out to nearby villages, and had incurred several casualties. None had been killed at that point, but seven had been wounded. Well, we had lost one man earlier on Pangnang Bum, an accidental death. One of the types of guns we got in the drop at Pangnang Bum was an M3 submachine gun, they call it a "grease gun." It had a pure blowback breach, meaning it never locked. When you pulled the trigger, this heavy breach block moved forward with a permanent little kit sticking out on the face of it to hit the primer. When the charge went off, the breach block went backwards, and the bullet went frontwards, then back and forth as long as you pulled on the trigger. We had sent some soldiers to check around a neighboring mountain called Marit Bum. *Marit* means "to pine." There's a song, "I pine for you, you pine for me." [Sings in Kachin]. The name really means that the sight of the mountain fills you with nostalgia. And it's a spectacular mountain. While they were camped there, a soldier was cleaning the M3 gun that he'd just recently learned how to operate. He was on one side of the fire, and there were several people on the other side. He lowered the breach block, intending to unload his gun, but must have turned loose of it right at the last. There was no bullet in the chamber, but he had left the magazine in the gun, which was a big mistake. The mechanism carried the bullet up into the chamber and fired.

It hit the man right across the fire from him and killed him dead as a wedge. That caused a big stir because the Kachins have specific rules. If you kill somebody, it doesn't make any difference whether it's an accident or it's on purpose, it automatically sets in motion what they call Jinghpaw *tung*, Jinghpaw rules or customs. It can set a feud going, an automatic feud between the two tribes. Now, everybody knew that the man didn't mean to do it, but they thought he had to follow their rules. I talked to them, but they were still worried. I said, "This is different. This is a wartime situation, and you ought to make an exception. You can't hold this man and his whole tribe responsible for this." I finally got Nhkum Zau Seng, one of my trio, to take my point of view, and he managed to talk them out of it, but it wasn't easy. Around that time, I made up a set of "Ka'ang Zhao Lai's Rules of Warfare." I think I still have a copy of it somewhere. It followed standard US Army rules, but with some necessary differences since we had no prison. Nhkum Zau Seng typed it up on a typewriter, and he typed copies for the commander of each company. There were rules on burglary—going to sleep at your post, desertion, murder, or whatever. We had punishment that ranged all the way from reprimand to firing squad.

One of the wounds sustained near Hungwe was an accidental self-inflicted wound sustained by Paul, the radio operator. Along the way, we would take ten-minute breaks every once in a while. My usual procedure was to holler, "Halt," and the message would be passed on down. I had a watch, a wristwatch, that I carried in my pocket. I got to where I could take a nap and just wake up in around ten minutes. At one of the stops, I was woken early from my nap by a shot. Here came Paul holding his injured hand, running up to me. He had been fooling with his pistol and shot himself right through his left middle finger. A .45 has a pretty big bullet, just short of half an inch in diameter. It had gone through his finger at about the second joint and made a star-shaped hole on one side, not really a hole, more like lines. The other side looked much more irregular. The bullet had gone through bone and all. Looked to me like it should have blown his whole finger off, but it didn't. So he came running up, sat down, and wailed, "Cut it off. Cut it off!" I said, "No. We're going to put a splint on it and preserve what's there." So I got a stick and some gauze out of the first aid kit.

As I was putting the splint on his finger, he said, "There's something wrong with my leg." He had puttees on, the British wool-wrap leggings. Paul's puttee, in fact the whole bottom half of his trouser leg, was soaked with blood. We undid the legging, took his shoe and sock off, pulled up his britches and found that the bullet had gone right into the fatty part of his calf. He had been sitting down when the gun went off. The bullet had gone through his finger and then into the top part of his calf, but he was so worried about his finger, he didn't even notice the calf wound.

I could feel the bullet all the way down just behind his ankle bone. It was under the skin, and his shoe was filled with blood. He couldn't walk, so we set to work, building a sedan chair for him out of bamboo. It had two big, long poles with a chair in between, and could be carried by either two men or four. It looked like something for a sultan. We carried him on to Hungwe. The other people who had been wounded were all able to walk but also needed hospital attention.

An Eventful Landing

We needed an airfield to evacuate the wounded. We found a field for drops that looked like the deck of an aircraft carrier, up on top of a ridge. It would have been ideal, but it wasn't long enough for airplanes. There were certain specifications for airfields; they had to be at least 750 feet long and about 100 feet wide, with both ends clear for an unobstructed approach, and the surface needed to be straight and level. We were eventually able to locate a relatively straight section at the bottom of a canyon, at a paddy field. The field had a few dikes across it that we knocked down, but it still had some problems. The canyon was steep on both sides, and at the upper end was a sheer wall, so there was only one approach. You had to land facing that wall, turn around, and take off the other way, regardless of which way the wind might be blowing. Furthermore, about midway into the strip there was about a twenty-degree bend, a dogleg. We radioed in and said, "We've found an area that we think might work."

Before we'd even gotten a message back, an airplane showed up, and Vince Trifletti was in it. He was a funny, happy-go-lucky pilot with the emphasis on lucky. He showed up in the best airplane they had for that kind of problem, an L1, the same kind of plane that had picked me up at Indawgyi. But this one had only wheels, no floats. Vince flew in, checked the field out, and decided to land. Unfortunately, he was a little high, so when he hit the bend in the strip, he went off the side into a muddy place. The plane stopped with its nose stuck down in the mud and its tail in the air. Fortunately, Vince had cut his engine off when he saw he wasn't going to make it and climbed out intact.

The whole village of Hungwe came down to help. We threw a rope across the tail of the plane and pulled it down. Then we literally picked the plane up and set it back up on the runway, the almost runway. Trifletti said, "I don't think I can take off unless you cut down those two trees at the end," which we did with dispatch. Then we had ourselves an airfield. And we shipped Paul out to Nazira, where they had a hospital, along with the rest of the walking wounded. Planes came in and out of that strip several times. The men who flew those planes did some remarkable things on the strips we made, hardly any of which met their specifications.

A Trial

At Hungwe, we were sending out patrols in all directions and had a steady stream of agents bringing in reports. As usual, I was up late at night questioning them. We were in a good position, not far from the Bawdwin mines where the Japanese were, but our main problem was that this area was mostly inhabited by Palaungs and Shans, not Kachins. While we were there, an awful occurrence took place. One of our recruits raped a Palaung woman. Her father objected when he found out what was going on in his own house. A violent argument ensued, and the soldier killed both of them, shot the Palaung girl and her father. The news came to me rapidly. There were several witnesses in the house where it all took place.

This soldier was a known bad fellow and a drunk. The Kachins immediately dissociated themselves from him. They said, "He's a half breed; he isn't a real Kachin." He was a half Shan, I think it was. Anyhow, the incident brought everything to a stop. The headman of the village was understandably furious. I talked to Nhkum Zau Seng and my other Kachin advisors. Nhkum Zau Seng's official title was battalion adjutant. He kept all the records. We had already written up our rules and the articles of war, so we had that to go by, but this was complicated because it involved not only civilians, but Palaung civilians. The Kachins and Palaungs often didn't get along too well.

I told Nhkum Zau Seng, "There needs to be an investigation and trial. We need a court martial. I'll appoint you and Dashi Yaw and Hbau Yam Gam to conduct this, and you three will be the judges. You do what you think is right. You know this country, and you know these people, including the accused. So please get cracking and go ahead and do it today." So they conducted a trial in a local house. I didn't sit in on it at all, on purpose. I didn't want the Kachins to think I was railroading things, since Palaungs were involved. I told our American personnel, "Stay out of it. It is best that it be a judgment of peers."

They tried him and condemned him to death by firing squad, whereupon that same afternoon they took him out on a hillside, stood him up and executed him. I had ordered that no American be present at the execution, but this sergeant from San Antonio, my cowboy friend, snuck up and watched the goings on from a distance. I found out he'd been there, and I upbraided him, "Don't do that again. They've got the rules, and they know what they are." The offender was duly buried, and that was the end of that. As the Kachins saw it, he was not under the regular Jinghpaw *tung* because he was not a Jinghpaw. For them, the fact that he was a half breed figured into the situation. Otherwise, we might have had to go through a lot more rigmarole than we did, because of things concerning custom and relations with other tribes.

Moving Down the Road

When Vince Trifletti came in another time to the dog-leg airfield, he brought a major with him whose name was Hamm. I've forgotten his first name. I think he'd been sent by headquarters to check on me. By that time, Eckhart had gotten back to headquarters and probably reported that Lutken had gone mad, gone native, didn't even talk English. Major Hamm was a nice fellow. I have his picture among the group, but in just a couple of days, he went back to headquarters with whatever report he was going to make. I have no idea what he said, but as far as I know, nothing bad came of it. We continued on south, went through many little villages, really covering some ground, marching hard all day, every day.

It was in February '45, the peak of the dry season. And in the dry season, the whole countryside over there was always on fire. The villagers cleared their fields, stacked the trees up in piles, and then set fire to the fields and burned them off before they planted. I'm not so sure it makes sense, but in south Mississippi in dry season, it was just as smoky as the Shan states. The fires caused us problems, though, because most of our fellows were barefooted. With the whole countryside on fire, why, there were hot coals all over the ground. And even though their feet were pretty tough, on hot coals they got burned. So they were hop-skipping around a good deal of the time, and there was a lot of smoke. But we were at a high altitude, the climate was pretty mild, and there were no leeches except in the real wet places down in the river valleys. The mosquitoes were year round, though. And those little flies, dim dim flies, they like high altitudes.

Our spies determined that near where we were headed, at a village called Mangai, a Palaung village, there was an outpost of maybe a hundred Japanese. Down the hill from Mangai to the east, the trail continued to Namtu, the Japanese base. That same road extended west, through Mangai and on to a village called Longtawk, where it intersected with our trail, then further west to Namhsan, another Japanese outpost. So, our trail went right between the two outposts at Mangai and Namhsan that were on a road to the Japanese base at Namtu.

We decided to go all the way from Hungwe to Longtawk in one day. We got a very early start, but the whole column was around two miles long, and as we moved, the line stretched out longer and longer. We'd take short rests to get caught up, but 1,000 men and 250 horses take up a lot of space. Furthermore, we were getting into territory where the jungle was not as dense, and there were open spots on the trail. So, we set out in the smoky morning, and walked as hard as we could. We sent an advance party to check out the junction at Longtawk, where the road that crossed our trail went to Namhsan west of us and Mangai and to the east. We were worried the Japanese might come over from either outpost, so I dispatched a group ahead to post a guard at the intersection and not to leave until the last mule had gotten across. It was a well-traveled track, but nobody was on it. We passed villages on the way which were close by, though, and I'm sure people knew we were there, and they were probably not sympathetic to us. We were lucky, though, and arrived at Longtawk right at sundown.

The Japanese were bound to know, or would find out very quickly, that we had passed the junction, and they'd know it both at Namhsan and Mangai. They'd see our footprints or hear about us from villagers. We couldn't hide our whole damn crowd. So I elected to attack Mangai the next morning.

The men were worn out from hard marching all day long. For me to ask them to keep going for another ten miles or so in the dark was a lot. I took only D Company, Richardson and his folks, and left everybody else at Longtawk. The headman of Longtawk told us there was a trail that led through a canyon about a thousand feet down, then back up the other side to Mangai. To get there, we were going to have to walk all night long and go like the dickens. He also told us that the Japanese were on the east side of the village at Mangai, which was on a sharp ridge.

Attack on an Outpost

We went almost *kunkuman*. We didn't carry anything except weapons and ammunition, including a bazooka: it wasn't designed for jungle warfare, but it could still blow things up. We had only used it a few times. Once at the Bawdwin mines, our fellows did a pretty good job of firing it into the tunnels in the hillside. The bazooka was made to penetrate the armor plate of tanks, so it didn't scatter shrapnel in all directions the way an ordinary explosive shell would. Nevertheless, for shooting into a tunnel, it was effective. So we had that bazooka and a sixty-millimeter mortar.

There was a waxing gibbous moon, so for the first part of the night, we had good light. But the terrain was steep, and we struggled getting down into the canyon and up the other side. When we made it up to the ridge, it was a little past midnight. At that time, the moon was beginning to set. Then it really got dark. The trail was right on top of a narrow, hog-back ridge, very steep on both sides. We had the one company, but it wasn't full strength, I'd say about 150 men in three platoons. According to our information, there were approximately 100 Japanese, enough for a substantial resistance, but we were counting on surprise. We didn't intend to capture or hold anything. As awful as it sounds, we just hoped to kill as many of the enemy as we could and then get out, get back to Longtawk and continue our journey south.

As we made our way, there was no conversation, just quiet, with the occasional clink of canteens. I was a quarter of the way back in the column, which strung out pretty far. Wesley Richardson was on the tail end, to keep the rear up to speed. As we were clinking along, all of a sudden, there was a great rumpus up front with lots of shouts and the noise of something crashing through the bushes. The whole front end of the column panicked and began running back down the trail toward me, but nobody was shooting. I managed to grab a hold of one Kachin running and said, "*Palo y? Palo y?*" "What is it? What is it?" And he said, "*Ja'in! Ja'in!*" meaning Japanese. He tore loose from me and kept running.

All the men came streaming past, and I couldn't stop them. As the last one came running by, I laid down in the grass. The trees were not too dense there, just scraggly pine trees, so I had a good view up onto the trail. In the starlight, I lay there for a while wondering what in the Sam Hill I was going to do since my fearless soldiers had run away. Directly, I heard somebody coming at a slower pace. I hid in the grass as this figure walked toward me. When he got near, I could tell by his hat, a big, Gurkha-style hat with a brim, that he was one of us. When I recognized him, I called him by name, and he jumped. He was the officer, the *jemadar*. I asked him, "What in the devil is going on?" He said, "You won't believe this, but the point man ran into a water buffalo." A great big water buffalo smack-dab in the middle of the trail. It immediately charged into the bushes, and the scout panicked. He didn't really know what it was, this big, bulky thing crashing around, so he turned and ran into the next guy, then that man ran, and eventually the whole damn front end of the column ran, except for the *jemadar*. He said, "I tried to stop them, but I couldn't." The water buffalo hadn't gone very far before it stopped, so he was able to determine the cause of the panic. Here we were on the way to attack Mangai and we'd been routed by a water buffalo.

We had some signals that we had taught the men, whistles imitating a bird, so the two of us walked down the trail and called and began to find the men one at a time. They were all chagrinned. They had realized on their own that they had run away from some unknown thing. When no shots were fired, and nothing happened, they finally slowed down. Everything was perfectly quiet, nothing going on except our whistling. It took us well over an hour to get them rounded up. They were pretty ashamed of themselves, but we got them back on the track, all of them. Then we marched on down to a great big banyan tree. I made them all sit down and made a speech, "You men have lived around water buffalo all your life. You've ridden on their backs. You've herded them with sticks. I can't think of anybody who's more familiar with water buffalo than you are, and yet you ran in panic when one of them made a big noise. You're not acting like soldiers. But you've got a chance to redeem your reputation. This is what happens from here on out. I want you men to just kick hell out of the Japanese when we get to Mangai. Remember what you're supposed to do. Let's form up right quick. We've got to get going." By that time, it was beginning to hint at daylight. But we were close, so we continued on.

Shortly, we came to the brow of the ridge and looked down on the village. It was a typical village of that part of the world. The Palaung houses look just like Kachin houses, on stilts with long, thatched roofs that reach almost to the ground. We had a good view of the village and could see the knot of a hill past it where the Japanese were. In the wintertime there, like here, the leaves are off of the deciduous trees, so we could see pretty well.

We had originally planned to set up the mortar above the village and fire it at the Japanese camp as the signal to start the attack. We planned that one platoon would go straight down the trail, I would take one platoon and go around the right flank, and the third platoon would go around the left, north of the track. But when we got there, the north side was so dadgum steep that it was obvious we were not going to be able to go there. So we decided to send two platoons down the main track and mine around the flank.

We got the mortar set up for a clear shot. I told Richardson, "When I give the signal, you pound the hell out of the Japanese camp. Just shoot up all your ammunition as fast as you can." We had carried about twenty-five rounds for that mortar. So he got ready, but about that time, not more than seventy-five yards in front of us on the track, two Japanese soldiers walked out of the trees, slinging their rifles over their shoulders. They were coming out of a campsite right close by. We had been talking, not loud, but without knowing they were there. But here they came. The patrol that was supposed to go down the track was already in position, ready for Richardson to start mortaring. Instead, here came two Japanese, so the patrol opened fire immediately. They killed those two right off the bat.

That started the whole thing. The Japanese at the nearby campsite came out like they were coming out of a hornet's nest, barreling out onto the track. There probably were close to a dozen in that particular spot, serving as an outpost to defend against people like us. Too bad for them, because our folks were there in a bunch and mopped up on them very quickly. Those that we didn't hit turned and ran down the trail toward the main Japanese camp. I quickly gave the high sign to Richardson, and he opened up full blast with the mortar toward the main camp. Immediately, I took my platoon, and we banked off to the right. The others charged straight down the trail, firing the bazooka. My group raced as fast as we could, but we were slipping and sliding on pine needles and grasping trees as we tried to make time on the downside of the steep ridge.

Why it happened I don't know, but all of a sudden, some houses in the village caught fire, first one, then a couple more. I don't think the mortar hit the village, I really don't understand to this good day how it caught fire. Anyway, it did, and it was just like *Gotterdammerung*, with towering flames and smoke in black billows rolling up into the sky. All the houses in the village didn't catch, but those two or three were completely consumed. I hoped whoever was in them got out. Folks were certainly awake by that time and scattering like quail.

Our men on the main trail continued on through, firing at the Japanese who were running right ahead of them. More Japanese come fogging out of the main camp, running down the trail beyond them. It took my platoon about twenty minutes running as fast as we could to get to the Japanese camp from our flank. The houses were still burning in the village, but by the time we got there, the Japanese shelters were empty. They had all bugged out. Richardson had shot all his ammunition and followed behind the first group. We all met at the Japanese camp. We counted, and, including those in the initial assault, sixteen Japanese had been killed. There was a lot of blood around, indicating others had been hurt, but they were all gone. We sent part of a platoon in pursuit down the trail to try to catch up with them.

In anticipation of our attack, I had sent Ting Bawm with his I&R platoon down a parallel trail to a village called Bangtong over on another ridge. I'd told him to go down that trail and get close to the river, hoping he could block the Japanese if they were to retreat to the bridge on the road to Namtu. Turned out, his bunch got excited when they heard all the uproar going on. Noise echoes up in those mountains, so they began shooting. I think they were just firing into the air. I never did get a satisfactory explanation. His story to me was, "You people were shooting, and we just couldn't keep from it. We wanted to make a racket too." Anyway, he did cut across the canyon and try to get to the bridge but failed to beat the Japanese to it. When Ting Bawm got there, the Japanese began firing at him from across the river. They had made it to the other side. That was pretty much the end of the operation.

As I said, the count was sixteen, including the men that came out of the woods at the first. They were still right there in the trail where they had fallen. They didn't even get to fire a shot. We ourselves had only one man wounded, shot right through the knee joint. He was in terrible pain. The Kachins have a great resistance to pain, but he was obviously hurting pretty bad, so we rigged up a stretcher to carry him. We also tried to search the woods for villagers, to tell them to come on back. Most of the houses were still intact. However, we weren't able to contact the headman of that village until the following day, and we had to explain a lot since we were at least indirectly responsible for those houses having burned down. Luckily, the paddy fields in the valley below were unharmed, and none of the villagers were seriously injured.

The *Sawbwa* of Dongpei

We went on back to Longtawk and decided to stay for a while. At the same time, we maintained a guard in Mangai, the village we had attacked, and sent patrols out in other directions. From the folks in Longtawk, we got word that the *sawbwa* of Dongpei State was under house arrest by the Japanese. He was apparently in a cave near Namhsan, with a Japanese guard on him, not far to the west of us. The American Air Corps had bombed and burned the *sawbwa*'s palace. They seemed to pick out big, obvious things to hit. His palace was made of stone and brick, but there was enough wood in it that it burned. When I finally saw it, it had no roof, but the masonry walls were still standing. There was a long front lawn, with houses on either side. Obviously, it had been quite a palace.

The story we got was that the *sawbwa*, a Palaung, had six wives living in separate houses. Marriages of that type were political. He governed a lot of different tribes, and the wives were representative of those tribes, a Kachin wife, a Palaung wife, a Pa'O wife, a Lisu wife, and so on. His sons and daughters were then connected to the various tribes. We dispatched a detail to investigate. They reported back that the Japanese had a small guard on the *sawbwa*, only two people, but the *sawbwa* himself had a large entourage. We understood from the headman of Longtawk that the *sawbwa* wanted to escape. With that in mind, we sent a patrol up the road towards Namhsan to get him.

Namhsan was a big tea center. They grew green tea. The hillsides were covered with tea bushes. They didn't cultivate them like the British did in Assam on those plantations with hundreds of acres planted so close that they looked like carpets. In Namhsan, there were just small plots planted by villagers, maybe an acre here or there. But there were a lot of them. And the people processed the tea themselves and packed it in bamboo tubes. They'd take a joint of bamboo and pack green tea leaves in it and cover it up with a leaf and then take a piece of bamboo fiber and wrap it around to tie the leaf down. That tea was for sale everywhere around Namhsan.

I didn't send any Americans on the detail to extract the *sawbwa*, only Kachins. When they reached the palace, they successfully ran off the guards, shot at them, but I don't think they killed them. Then they brought back seventy-three people, including all of the *sawbwa*'s wives, sons, daughters, kinfolks, hangers-on, servants, the whole entourage. I've got some pictures of that. The *sawbwa* was a jolly fellow, kind of plump and well dressed. Of course, he came out on foot, just like everybody else.

He didn't stay with us long. I told him, "On the strip back at Hungwe, we're having a plane come in to carry out a wounded man, and we'll be glad to get two of you out, but we can't take all seventy-three people. The rest will have to walk. Our armies are moving through the area. I'll inform them that your crowd is coming, so they'll be expecting them." He said, "I'll take one of my wives." And for my money, I think he took the best looking one, his number 1 wife.

Sad Stories

The *sawbwa* had a brother by the name of Sao Hkun Tha. Hkun Tha was well educated; he'd been to college at the university in Rangoon. He could speak English as well as anybody, and with a proper English accent. Hkun Tha had been a captain in the Burma Rifles, he had a King's Commission, they called it, and had military experience. Before he left, I asked the *sawbwa*, "To help with our relations with the Palaungs, I'd like for your brother to go with us." He said, "It's certainly all right with me. Talk to him." So, I did, and he agreed to come and help us out with the Palaungs. He did well, but we still ran into some difficult situations. Palaung territory was not like Kachin territory where we were in friendly hands.

During that time, we had a good soldier with us, a *havildar*. Out on a patrol once, he ran across a bunch of horses. It turned out that the horses belonged to some Palaungs in the neighborhood. Well, he and his patrol decided to take two of them. He was making off with them when the owner showed up. The owner protested, "These are my horses." Then the *havildar* asserted his authority, I guess you'd say. In the ensuing argument, the *havildar* killed the owner and came back with the horses. That was that. I forget how I found out about it, but I did, and I called him in to talk about it. I asked him point blank, "Did you steal these horses?" He said, "Well, yes, I took them." I said, "Did you shoot the owner?" "Yes, I shot and killed him." I lost my temper at that point. I said, "Now, look, we're in Palaung country and we're trying to get along with the Palaungs as best we can, and now you've shot one of them. This is going to make things very difficult for us. We've got rules around here. I'm not saying you murdered the man, or even that it's your fault. I don't know what happened, but I'm going to have to put you under arrest while we figure this out."

I put him under guard in a lean-to, but as I told you before, you can't tie a man up with rope. He can get loose. So, in the middle of the night, I heard all this rumpus, and the guard came running up to me and said, "The *havildar* has escaped. I don't know how he got away, but he took my gun with him." We sounded the alarm, and the whole dadgum camp headed out to look for him. We figured he couldn't have gotten very far. We had pickets out on all the trails. He knew that, so he was bound to have taken to the jungle.

During the course of the search, we heard a single shot, just one shot. We went in the direction of the noise and found him dead. He had committed suicide, stuck the rifle in his mouth and pulled the trigger, shot himself right through the top of the head. That's been on my conscience ever since. I always tell myself that I truly had no idea that what I said to him would have that result. And I didn't say it in front of anybody else. It was just him and me. But it still haunts me.

That wasn't the only suicide that occurred during my years in Burma. Way back at Pebu, a Chinese sentry blew his own brains out. But that was in the Chinese Army, I had nothing to do with it. Thinking back, there was another sad incident while we were still at Pangnang Bum involving a Gurkha. His patrol ran into a bunch of Japanese, just encountered them on the trail, by accident. He was the point man. They began firing, and he returned fire. Then all by himself, he just charged them, ran right into them, firing at them as he went, and they killed him. No one ever did explain why he did it. I guess he felt like it was his duty to get rid of them, and it worked. The Japanese turned around and went the other way.

Tragedy

The following events require some background information about the mines. Early in the course of the war, after the Chinese miners fled, the Japanese decided to round up Kachins and put them to work in the mines. They conscripted the Kachins from the countryside around Namtu, and sent them down hundreds of feet underground to chip away at rock. The Kachins were superstitious people anyway, and did not appreciate being forced underground. A number of them got killed on the job. Although the Japanese were the ones who forced them, they had a bitter grudge against the Indian foremen as well, since the Indians were their immediate supervisors. When the Americans began bombing the place in earnest, the mines pretty much stopped operation. The Indians fled out into the countryside and established themselves in camps to wait things out. They built palisades around their camps; they were afraid of the local Kachins because of the hatred between them.

Way back when we were about to leave Pangnang Bum, I mentioned before that we had sent a big, tall Kachin *jemadar* with a patrol to explore around

Namtu including the area around those mines. The patrol came back and reported to us several times. They scouted around a whole slew of villages to the southwest of Namtu, and brought back a lot of valuable information, which was much appreciated.

After we'd moved on down from that area, a Sikh named Ramji showed up, introduced himself and said that he represented a refugee camp of Indians, Gurkhas, Nepalese and Sikhs who had been connected with the Bawdwin Mine. He said, "We would like to volunteer to help you." Many of them had previous military experience, so I thanked him, and told him I would check with my people.

The Kachins usually got along all right with the Gurkhas, and with the Indians, just not those who had been involved with the mines. However, none of my *salang ni* strongly objected to the group having their own company, so I said, "Well, bring them around, and we'll set them up in their own company." Partly thanks to Tabu Gam and his group, we had quite a number of Japanese arms, so we brought the Indian and Gurkha company with us and armed them with Japanese weapons.

One night, after they had been with us a while, Ramji and I were talking. He said he had something important to tell me in private. I said, "Well, nobody's here. Go ahead." So he related an incident that involved the *jemadar*, the scout, and the platoon that I had sent on the flanking expedition around Namtu. One of the places they had stopped was a refugee camp of Indians who had been supervisors in the mines. As I mentioned, the local Kachins had a deep grudge against those people. The Kachins in that platoon were well armed and the Indians didn't have many weapons. So the Kachins broke their way through the palisades and killed maybe as many as twenty men. My mouth went dry as I said, "Thank you for giving me this information. We'll have to take some action. I don't know what it will be yet. I'll have to investigate."

I called in the *jemadar* shortly thereafter. He didn't deny anything. I said, "I just got the word that Indian people were killed by your platoon," and he said, "That's right." And I said, "Why did you do that?" Then he gave me the long story about being mistreated, and the deaths of his own friends and relatives. He said, "Those people are our enemies." I said, "I'm sorry. You're a good soldier and you've generally done a good job, but that was wrong. Those people are with us. They're on our side." It was a sticky situation, I knew other Kachins would be sympathetic toward his actions. Also, I suppose my recent disaster of an attempt to enforce justice was in the back of my mind. I told him, "I want you and your group to pack up your stuff and go back home. You are discharged. You've served well in many ways, but that was wrong, and I can't use you from here on." It was difficult for the *jemadar* to understand. To him, the people he and his men killed were enemies, as much as the Japanese, maybe more so on a personal level.

To skip ahead and finish telling of this debacle, when I got back to Bhamo, after all of my expeditions were over, I was called to appear before Brigadier Bowerman. He was the British Civil Officer in charge of Upper Burma, and he said he wanted to discuss the incident. He had spent many years in Burma with the Kachins. He knew all about the territory, and the mines, and he could speak Jinghpaw. He handed me a report which had been sent to him by Ramji, who, by the way, had done well after he'd joined us. We called his company the "Headquarters Company," and they served admirably through the campaign.

I read the report and said as far as I knew, it was true. I told him, yes, I had sent these men on a long-range penetration with certain things to do, but killing those supervisors was certainly not one of them. From the Kachins' point of view, they had been badly mistreated, forced into slave labor underground, and lost friends and members of their own families in the mines. So when they got the opportunity, they took a diversion from their assigned duty and eliminated the men that they thought had been responsible for the abuse. I told him that I had found out about the killings long after the fact. When I did, I had dismissed those involved, but I had to keep going. Even Ramji realized the powder keg this might have been if brought out into the open, which was why he so wisely told me about it in private.

Brigadier Bowerman and I had a long talk in both English and Jinghpaw. Fortunately, he understood about the chaos of war, the problem with the mines, and the difficulties of handling a thousand armed men. We parted friends. He said, "There will be no charges brought," and told me he would contact Ramji and apologize for this "unfortunate and tragic circumstance of war." Thankfully, Brigadier Bowerman recognized a fact which we don't always recognize in the United States; in wartime, the control that the commanding officer has over his troops is somewhat limited, especially when they are remote and in danger. All sorts of bad things happen, often tragically, to civilians.

That episode was the worst shock I had in the war. After everything was over, I remember hearing that they put the Japanese General Yamashita on trial because his troops had killed a bunch of folks in Manila. As I recall the story, when the Japanese were losing, the allies were routing them pretty severely. The Japanese then went amuck in Manila and killed a bunch of civilians. The charge was brought against Yamashita for the crime. His American attorneys apparently worked hard to successfully prove that there was no evidence that he had ordered any such thing, and that this was done by his troops at a time when it was not possible to control them from remote headquarters. All the same, they hanged Mr. Yamashita by the neck until he was dead. When I read that, I thought to myself, there but for the grace of God, go I. If I hadn't had the good fortune to be evaluated by a man who knew the country and knew the people and the situation, I might have been blamed for something that I had no idea had even happened until much after the fact.

The Kachins saw themselves at war with enemies who were mostly, but not exactly the same enemies as ours. When they open up the windows and let everything out in peacetime, it doesn't look good, but the man on the spot is faced with difficult conditions. At that point, I was convinced that the war against Japan was going to last a long time, and I needed the full support of the Kachins. And they were, as a rule, faithful, honest, steady, excellent soldiers, some of the best people I have ever known.

McCarger at Namhsan

I will emphasize again that all information is imperfect and out of date; by the time you get it, things have usually changed. Al McCargar was a great soldier, and I think very highly of him. While we were at Longtawk, I sent him on a mission to attack the garrison at Namhsan. We'd been told the Japanese were there and thought it was a good opportunity to surprise them, do some damage, then depart on our journey south. We were not trying to take anybody's property or hold any ground. Our method was basic: hit and run, kick them in the teeth, leave, then kick somebody else.

So off McCargar went, riding on a horse. He was an old rodeo cowboy from California originally, although when he joined up, he had been living in Maine, of all places. He lit out on this assignment with his company and a map, and he didn't come back for about a week. When he did come back he was really angry, and had ridden hard over rocky territory. The horse's feet were ruined. They had to take the the horse out and shoot him. When I asked McCargar what happened, he said, "I did what you told me. We approached the garrison at Namhsan, formed up as skirmishes, and charged. When we got up the hill, there was nobody there. Apparently, they had left two or three days ago, just abandoned the place and moved on to parts unknown."

He was mad at me because I had given him inaccurate information. I explained, "Al, do you think I did that on purpose? You've been around here long enough. You should know that all information is unreliable. The mistake you made was in not getting your folks to scout things out before y'all charged a position occupied by nobody!" Then I told him my own story of the march to the lone mountain at Karachi. He calmed down. We laughed about it after a while, except for the poor horse. Later, I'd sometimes rib him about the *Charge of McCargar's Brigade*, the charge up the hill toward nobody. Al and I remained good friends and kept in touch long after the war.

A Gift

At Longtawk, we were smack in the middle of territory where everything was on fire for agricultural purposes. The woods and the mountains were filled with smoke. We got a drop at Longtawk, and the smoke was so dense, we could hardly see the airplane until it got right down on us. It was a miracle that the pilot even found us. At that time, I sent Totten and C Company to a small village occupied by the Japanese. Totten actually had some success, and drove them out. Apparently, the Japanese had been pretty rough on the people there. Treatment of local people by the Japanese varied widely, as did the treatment of prisoners. Anyhow, they treated these particular villagers badly, so the villagers were grateful to us.

The headman of the village showed up at my headquarters in Longtawk afterwards, Hkam Sai was his name, and he brought me a beautiful sword. When someone gave me something, I always tried to give them something back, and the main items of trade we had were parachutes. The fabric was a real prize for the women, and so was the parachute cord. There were about 8 or 9 cords to a parachute and each cord was about 10 or 12 feet long. Women would unravel the cord to get the thread. I have no idea how much thread, probably several miles could be obtained from one parachute. We also gave folks needles, buttons and occasionally some regular cotton thread, so I gave this fellow some.

Parachute material was valuable out there in the jungle. I used it myself. The pack I carried through the second half of my stint, I made out of an ammunition bag, the kind used in drops. That first pack I'd made out of the rice sack was too little, so I got this ammunition sack and used webbing and thread from a parachute to make straps and a flap top. The pack was about four feet by about fifteen or eighteen inches square. It was so big and floppy that when I got up in the morning, I could just dump everything in it and sling it on my back. I came to the conclusion early on, that a low center of gravity makes for a good pack. Those packs that tower way up high, they're not very good. When you go through the jungle, you get hung up and have trouble keeping your balance.

Air "Support"

As we moved on south, the British were rapidly driving the Japanese across Burma. The Japanese were exhausted, and we began running into them as they retreated. Although we didn't realize it at the time, the end was coming. In March of 1945, they were on the run, the ragged remnants of a huge army of 325,000 men. According to their own statistics, the Japanese left about 185,000 known dead in Burma and lord knows how many wounded and missing on top of that. I reckon nobody will ever know what the death toll really was.

We moved further along to Hunang and then to Pangkaw, generally headed toward the big valley where the main road meandered from Mandalay east to Lashio and then clear up to the China border. There's a huge gorge in that valley, where the railroad, road, and river all run through it together. Not too far to our west was one of the highest railroad bridges in the world, the Gokteik Viaduct. I think it's still there. We eventually made it to the rim of the gorge and scouted for a place to cross.

There were a lot of Japanese all up and down the valley. Just to the southwest of us was a railroad bridge with a significant number of them guarding it. We finally picked a spot to cross near a village called Hong Hing. There was a Japanese garrison close by, so I came up with the idea of using air support to distract them while we crossed. Headquarters had told us that good air support was available at the time. They said they had a wing of bombers and fighters that could dive bomb whatever we wanted.

We arranged a certain day, and planned to send Chuck Roberts and his company to plant a panel on the road. It was a blacktop road, but it wasn't in good shape because nobody had maintained it since the war began. The plan was to put a panel there in the shape of an arrow, pointing toward the Japanese garrison. After the bombing started and the Japanese were otherwise occupied, we hoped to cross about another five hundred or six hundred yards to the west.

We camped up on the high ground north of the crossing at a place called Namyun. Chuck and his company left way before daylight. We took off pretty soon after since there were a lot of us, and we headed down the steep hill to the river. Mules and men got strung out a couple of miles along the trail. Right on schedule, up came two P47s. They had great big stubby-looking radial engines, two thousand horsepower, twenty-four cylinders, and I don't know how many fifty-caliber machine guns and bombs. They spotted our panel right away. It was easy to find, and Chuck had it pointing right toward the Japanese. Unfortunately, we thought we'd left plenty of room for the planes to go beyond us before they started their dive, but we hadn't, and they came down right over us, a good three hundred yards in front of the panel.

I was about halfway back in the line, when the planes let loose practically over my head with all those machine guns going full tilt. They were aimed at the Japanese, but came roaring down very low and started shooting right when they got over us. They kept it up until they were close to the target, then they pulled up with engines roaring. Our mules and horses went wild at the noise. The two P47s used up all their ammunition and dropped all their bombs in about three passes. And those bombs were huge. They must have been thousand pounders; the earth shook when they hit. The result was absolute pandemonium. Most of the mules took to the bushes. We were running everywhere trying to catch them. If the Japanese had struck us at that moment, we would have been routed for sure. It was comforting to know that the planes were on our side, but this particular time, they mainly succeeded in scaring our own animals away. We were rounding up mules until dark.

When we finally got organized, we headed straight for a village called Namon. We set up defenses on all sides and stayed there for a couple of weeks. From Namon, we sent patrols out, as usual. They informed us that the Japanese were using a road south from the town of Kyaukme, so we decided to put a roadblock there. Chuck Roberts with A Company set up that block. I sent Al McCargar with B Company to the east, over in the vicinity of the village of Pangsong to established another block. We dispatched those two operations from Namon, and the first to run into trouble was Chuck Roberts on the road south from Kyaukme.

A Fork in the Road

My principal radioman, Curt Schultz, had bad eyesight, but he was always wanting to be in on some operation. You may recall, we sent him to blow up the dud bomb back in Mawng Ping village near Ho It. Well, this time, he wanted to be in on a roadblock. So I sent him with Chuck Roberts, who set up on a road leading south from the town of Kyaukme, near a village called Nongsing. Curt got in position overlooking the path with his UD gun. The first night, a Japanese contingent came down the road on foot. There was heavy cloud cover; it was pitch black dark, no moon, no stars. Schultz's eyesight was bad in the daylight, but in the dark, he might as well have been blind. He later told me that when the skirmish started, "People all around me began firing, but I couldn't see a dadgum thing." The only illumination was from the muzzle flashes on both sides. Schultz tried his best to fire in the proper direction, but it was so confusing to him that he never requested to participate again.

As far as Chuck could tell, they did kill several Japanese. But like all of our operations, the number was difficult to determine. That was the first skirmish we had with the Japanese out of our base in Namon. By then it was obvious that they were retreating under pressure from the allies in the north and the west. Apparently, the order had been given for them to get out of the country.

I sent McCargar and his company to the east, where he set up a block at a fork in the road and encountered a much larger force of Japanese moving south. We determined later that most of them were actually quartermaster troops, not regular infantry. Nevertheless, they performed admirably. One thing about the Japanese, they were disciplined and knew what to do. When they came up against B Company, it was pitch black dark. They got to the fork and stopped. Those in the lead gathered together in a bunch, trying to decide which way to go. Someone in their group turned on a flashlight, and they all stood around looking at the map. At that moment, McCargar and his outfit opened fire and killed several men at once. The Japanese immediately fell back. Then they began firing flares.

Our base at Namon was just a few miles away, and we could hear the shots and see the flares. One flare went up, I believe it was red, and then another flare, and as I remember, it was green. Or maybe the first one was green. Obviously, each stood for something for them to do. According to McCargar, at the first one, the Japanese reorganized themselves and came back at the Kachins with a banzai assault right straight down the trail. That turned out to be a diversion because the main body of men went around through the jungle and fired the second flare. The group that had attacked stopped shooting, pulled back, and followed the others. So in spite of being chopped up pretty bad at first, most of them got past the road block. The Japanese were well trained. They were good soldiers. I've always said, next time there's a war, I hope they're on our side.

I came over to where the action had taken place while it was still dark. When the sun began to come up, we found the bodies. McCargar's company had killed something over twenty Japanese. How many were wounded, we didn't know. The bulk of the force got around us, and there was blood all over the ground, but even with all the confusion, they had left no one except those that were dead.

McCargar didn't lose anybody in that encounter. There had been no elaborate fortifications for his company. They hid behind trees or dug themselves small foxholes, and it was dark. Roberts didn't lose anybody at Nongsing either. In general, we suffered very few casualties compared to the Japanese. Overall, the figures gathered by the authorities indicated that the entire OSS Detachment 101 killed something over 5,000 Japanese and lost 328 Kachins and 20 some-odd Americans. That's the way guerrilla warfare works. You kill them, but when they get to where they can kill you, you leave.

In the daylight, we were able to determine that the group McCarger's folks had ambushed was a quartermaster outfit, supply troops, not combat troops. As I was going through the bodies, I picked up the map case of an officer, a warrant officer. I knew that from a little pasteboard book that I still have, put together by hand, with a color sketch of the symbol for each rank in the Japanese Army. I kept the officer's red epaulettes and a photograph, which I carried with me the rest of the war. The picture was of himself and his family, his wife and I think, three girls and two boys. The older boy was in a uniform, probably for some military school, the youngest was a baby. It made me wonder, what the hell was I doing? A nice family, father, young children, wife and mother, and here we killed the man in the dark, while he was looking at a map, and shoveled him into a ditch to get him off the trail.

Friendly Fire

The Chinese 1st Regiment was a showcase regiment. They had been issued American uniforms, green fatigues. The rest of the Chinese all wore khakis, but the 1st Regiment's equipment was American; they had American-style helmets and M-1 rifles. They looked just like Americans from a distance.

McCargar was still on the roadblock the next day. The Japanese had gone on by, and he'd sent a group in pursuit. He didn't really expect to catch them, but he did send somebody after them. The scouts went close to an area called Kehsi Mansam and then turned around to bring back their report. At McCargar's roadblock, in the middle of the night, some troops appeared, coming down the track the same way as the Japanese had, and a battle started up. The fighting was very heavy, and those troops began mortaring McCargar's position. It sounded like the Battle of the Marne, big stuff. I went down quickly to check out what was going on. Just then, the patrol that Al had sent out came back with a coolie who had escaped from the attackers and run past Al's group through the jungle. The scouts apprehended him and brought him to me. Firing was going on all around us, while I questioned the fellow. We had some Japanese equipment, so I showed him. "Did they wear a little cap with a bill on it, like this?" "No, no, they didn't. They had helmets on." "What did the helmets look like?" "They looked like pots." Then I said, "What kind of rifles?" I had an M1 rifle, so I said to him, "Like this one?" He said, "Yeah, just like that one." Horrified, I arrived at the conclusion that these must be Chinese troops, an advance element coming down the road from Hsipaw, following the Japanese.

Quick as I could, I got Schultz to send the message to headquarters: "It looks like we're in a fight with the Chinese. They came up on us in the middle of the night. Firing began, and it's been going on ever since. You'd better check with the Chinese headquarters and get this thing stopped." After some maneuvering, headquarters finally got the word to the Chinese, who then withdrew. It's hard to stop a battle like that once it gets started. Getting word to infantry men scattered out in the bushes is difficult. If one of them keeps shooting, why then, others keep shooting, too.

After it was finally over, I had to go talk to the Chinese colonel who was in command. He was really one mad sucker since some of his men had been killed, but ultimately, everybody realized that it was just a bad mistake, a case of friendly fire. I reckon it happens in almost every war. McCarger's men claimed that the Chinese shot first, but who knows. Ironically, it was really the last big battle we fought.

Namon

Namon means warm water, and there was a hot spring there at the village. When the water came out of the ground, it was almost boiling, so the folks there had rigged up split bamboo poles and made a conduit that ran about two hundred or three hundred feet. In that distance, the water cooled off enough to where you could get under it. I had not really had a hot bath in three years, so the first day I was there, I just went over and sat under that darn pipe. It felt great, but I always wondered if that activity brought on a recurrence of my malaria. I had a number of recurrences, but this was a bad one. I was sick as a dog, although I was still able to get around. When malaria strikes you, you get chills and fever, and you lose all your cookies, but you get over it, and you're all right for a while, until it hits you again.

We had been at Namon about two weeks, and I was on the mend, when we got notice that we were to terminate operations. It was the tail end of the war. The Burmese Army had officially switched sides when it was evident we would win. They joined us on March the 27th, 1945. Peers himself came down by plane in May, landing in a paddy field, and told us that we had accomplished what they wanted; the Japanese were in full retreat. The plan now was to move the Chinese Army out of Burma because things were picking up in mainland China. The only thing left for the army to do was to chase the Japanese as they were trying to get out through Taunggyi. Newer battalions were being organized for that purpose. My friend Oliver Trechter was involved in that operation, from about April until July.

On July the 15th, 1945, Peers officially disbanded the entire Detachment 101, but our outfit was disbanded in May. At that time, we were about twelve hundred men. The army did take some of the old soldiers in our outfit who were willing, especially those with previous honest-to-goodness military training, to join the new battalions. I guess about a hundred fell into that category. They took some of the mules, too, but most of us turned around and headed back north.

PART V

THE ROAD BACK

May 1945–August 1945

Celebration

Our orders were to proceed to Namtu, which had long been free of Japanese by then. From there, headquarters left it up to us where and what ceremony we conducted when we disbanded. We lined up and got a picture of everybody, then we marched to Namtu. Walking back up the road, we were all in good spirits. We reached town and made camp around the old British golf clubhouse, right where the Japanese had stayed. Then we held a big celebration on the old tennis courts, with a parade and final formations. It was quite a festival, a *padong manao*, which means a victory dance or victory celebration. The whole thing lasted about three days and nights. Thousands of Kachins came down out of the hills, including women and children. They brought food with them and *lao hku*, a type of alcoholic beverage. People were up all night, every night carousing.

There was a lot of shooting, too. A medic named McLeod happened to be in the midst of all of it. Some Kachins were firing a BAR "boom, boom, boom, boom, boom," full automatic, up into the air. It doesn't take long for that thing to get hot. McLeod said, "Let me shoot that thing," and he reached up and grabbed it by the barrel, and, man, it just fried his hand. The whole palm of his hand, fingers and all. Fortunately, he had some first aid equipment there and treated himself.

The celebration went on late into the night each night, with dances, and not just the joint dance, the *manao*, but individual dancing. There were sword dances, one I remember well where two men performed a kind of a mock fight, dancing and whirling around each other. Hbau Yam Gam composed an epic poem about our exploits and recited it aloud, like Homer. I got him to write it down for me. Nhkum Zau Seng had a typewriter and gave me a copy of the whole thing typewritten. It is 294 lines, 8 pages long.

At one point in the festivities, while I was trying to get some sleep, some soldiers came and grabbed a hold of me, "*Duwa, duwa, elwan sarai. Elwan sarai.* Get up. Get up quick." So I struggled out of bed—not really a bed, I was just lying on the porch of a building—and I went running down toward a large crowd. Everybody there was half drunk and they were ready to kill about four or five men. In a few minutes, the situation became clear to me. We had just paid everyone. We paid in paper money at that point, and immediately afterwards, all these games began. I never could figure out exactly what they were playing, but a lot of cash changed hands, and just like on the ship on the way over, a few folks ended up with all the money. Tubu Gam, the former British pipe major, was in trouble. They had him trussed up and were planning to kill him along with three or four other old soldiers who had won. A huge angry mob of soldiers were all gathered around, carousing and firing up in the air.

I quickly got my three stalwarts Nhkum Zau Seng, Dashi Yaw, and Hbau Yam Gam to help. Then I stood up and said, "Now, everybody just calm down. I'm gathering all the money that was on Tubu Gam and the rest of them, and at daylight tomorrow, we're going to redistribute it." That ended the dispute. They let go of the men and disbursed. The next day we set up a big table, declared those games null and void, and redistributed the money as accurately as we could. It seemed to satisfy everyone since it had really happened on account of too much alcohol.

At Namtu, several banquets were given in our honor. We found a tin container amongst the Japanese supplies, about an eighteen-inch cube. It was soldered shut, completely sealed. Somebody told us that it contained flour. It didn't have any markings on the outside, but it had a handle on it, actually, just a tab to rip the top off. Sure enough, that thing was full of good flour. We found an Indian baker in town to bake it for us and keep half for his trouble. We hadn't eaten any bread for years, literally, and I'll tell you, that was some of the best bread I ever tasted in my whole life. He did a crackerjack job. We feasted upon bread for several days. One banquet dinner in Namtu was given by Ying Siang and his wife. I met her there for the first time. She was a beautiful woman; she had eleven children and still looked just fresh as a daisy. She was the principal cook for the meal at their house, and they went all out. Namtu had been isolated by the war, but they somehow came up with a delicious meal. Another feast was given by a Karen who had been with us, a pharmacist named Saw Judson. His wife, Ma Mi Gee, was a nurse. Their dinner was also a grand affair. Many of the Karens were Baptists, but that night they had plenty to drink. I've got a picture of my good friend Ting Bawm, who was also a Baptist. In the picture, he's passed out, head down, lying across the table. He had just overindulged. *Lao hku* was the beverage, milky rice beer with a lot of bubbles and rice still floating around in it. The Kachins who came down out of the hills for the celebration had brought bamboo tubes, each about as big around as a salad plate and about two feet long, full of that rice beer. And folks drank plenty.

Final Mission

At Namtu, we put the narrow-gauge railroad back in operation for a while and ran a daily service to Bawdwin and back. In the past, we had mined that very track with explosives and weren't exactly sure where, so we put two or three flat cars in front of the locomotive to be on the safe side. Running the railroad for us was just a lark, but the townspeople appreciated it greatly, and we practically had a full train every day.

At an air strip north of Hsipaw, they had us load all of our military equipment, rifles, everything aside from what we needed for bare protection. That's where I lost my hat. I was in the back end of this C-47 helping load rifles, machine guns, and mortars. To this good day I wish we would have left those arms with the Kachins. They might have had a chance in negotiating with the Burmese later. But that's what the British Civil Affairs people wanted. They didn't want an army in the area to interfere with the peace. Anyhow, while I was loading stuff in the plane, I took my hat off and threw it in the back. As soon as the plane left, I realized I'd left my hat in it, the campaign hat that I'd worn almost the whole war. It was like losing an old friend.

When I finally left Namtu and headed back toward Myitkyina, a few men went with me, Chuck Roberts and some others. My main duty on the trip out was to pay the families of those who had been killed, and owners of horses that had been lost. The compensation amounted to three hundred rupees, horse or man, the same price. For about two or three weeks, a few of us wandered from village to village, and I noticed that, in almost every village, folks had removed the thatch from the roofs of their houses. You can see that in the pictures. I think they did it late in the war to fool the American Air Corps into thinking they had already been bombed out.

We only went to the places we had encountered since Pangnang Bum, not to my first stomping ground in the Hukawng Valley, although I wish we could have gone back there. We tried to retrace our steps as best we could, finding and compensating the families of the soldiers of the 7th Battalion and agents who had been killed or severely wounded, and paying for the mules and horses killed or lost. We also had another duty. Headquarters didn't want any weapons left around that had been damaged in drops or were otherwise malfunctioning, so they instructed us to destroy them. We collected quite a few that had been damaged when a parachute didn't open or somebody had gotten mud in the barrel, things like that. We gathered piles of rifles, stocks and all, and set them on fire.

I figured I must have walked, from beginning to end, somewhere around four thousand miles across northern Burma. In all those miles, I had never developed any blisters until I got on the dadgum road walking out. On a paved road where it's flat and hard, your foot hits the same way every time, and it wears blisters on your feet, whereas walking on a good old trail does not.

The Road Back

In June of 1945, I made it to Myitkyina by a combination of boat and truck transport from Bhamo. I had to wait there for an airplane back to India. After that, I didn't know whether I was going to be sent back to the United States or ordered somewhere else. Some Americans were being reassigned to China, especially those who hadn't been in Burma very long. I remember sitting at the airport—it was really nothing but a dirt strip—where they were evacuating Chinese soldiers over the Hump to Kunming. One plane right after another was taking off loaded with Chinese troops. While I was wasting time, I watched one plane come down the runway with the engines revved up, really roaring. Right there in front of me, instead of taking off, it just settled belly down and hit the ground. I never did find out exactly what happened; it seemed like the pilot might have pulled up the wheels before it got off the ground. As it hit the runway, sparks flew every which way, and the plane started spinning and skidding. And I thought, oh, my God.

I hurried toward the plane. As it spun around, I watched a bunch of Chinese troops jumping out the door, tumbling all over the runway. By the time it finally stopped, the plane was burning furiously, with towering flames and smoke. I thought for sure that the crew were dead, since I hadn't seen them get out. But when I got about halfway there, I ran into the pilot, the copilot, and the whole American crew. How the devil they got out, I do not know. Maybe they came out the hatch in the front. Anyhow, they seemed to be all right, so I ran on past them. The Chinese were picking themselves up all along the way. By the time I got there, all had escaped. Some had been hurt pretty bad hitting the runway, and I tried to help. While it burned itself out, the plane blocked the runway and stopped air traffic. So I ended up having to wait around for another day or two before I got out of Myitkyina.

Finally, I caught a C-47 to one of the big airfields in Assam. From there, I got a ride down to Nazira. Colonel Peers was there, and some other folks I knew, including the nine nurses who had originally been with Seagrave. Naomi was not there, but Than Shwe was. I hung around for a few days and met up with some interesting characters from 101. One was a fellow named Phil Weld. Phil had been with Merrill's Marauders. I had first met him when we provided the young guide for the Marauders to get to Walawbum.

I got to talking to Phil, and we decided that since we had some time to kill, we'd take a trip to Imphal. We borrowed a jeep and drove to the B & A railroad near Tinsukia. We got on a freight train with the jeep and rode twelve hours down to Lumding, about two hundred miles to the south. The Bengal and Assam Railway was operated by Americans. A battalion had been put together with employees of the Pennsylvania Railroad. Engineers, firemen, brakemen, everybody from the Pennsylvania Railroad. They had shipped a slew of steam locomotives from America. It would have been late '43 before they really got going. It was all American rolling stock, specially built, and you could hear those whistles blow. The British whistles on their trains just go "beep, beep," but the American whistles have that musical pipe sound. You could hear that sound for miles. It reminded me of home.

We rode the train to Lumding, the farthest point that the Japanese had managed to reach when they invaded India. Of course, they had long since been driven out, but it had been the high-water mark of their conquests. We got off the train and drove the jeep to Kohima. A tremendous battle had taken place there, probably the defining battle of the whole Burma campaign. The Japanese had surrounded Kohima, the only road open to supply the forces in Imphal. The fight lasted months, a grinding, pounding battle, like something out of World War I. The Gurkhas, the Punjabi troops, and British troops all fought. There was no vegetation left on the top of that mountain, even when we were there. Everything had been pounded into powder, the trees were just stalks standing up. The devastation made us appreciate what a hard-fought battle it had been. There's a famous monument there now with the epitaph, ". . . for your tomorrow, we gave our today."

After that, we went on down to Imphal, onto the plain. We ran into J. R. Wilson, who had been assigned there sometime after we had left the Hukawng valley, and we had a good visit with him. He took us to meet General Slim, whose headquarters was in that neck of the woods. He was an interesting fellow, a real self-made soldier who had come up through the ranks in the British Army.

From there, we went to Silchar, I forget how we got there, to tell the truth. Silchar is down on the India side. We ended up eating in the mess hall there. Completely by accident, I ran into a fellow named Pat Robertson, a classmate of mine from Mississippi State. He was one of the few people I saw over there that I had known before the war. Billy Baird of buffalo fame was another. Both were pilots. Then there was another pilot and good friend of mine over there, a high school classmate, but he got killed before I got together with him. My mother informed me that he was with the Air Corps and I should try and find him. But he died before I could. As a matter of fact, his plane apparently just disappeared; nobody knew what happened to him.

Our trip took maybe ten days. Then we returned to Nazira and got together with a bunch of OSS 101 folks. Tom Chamales is probably the most well-known. He had been over on the China border with a battalion, but I only got acquainted with him at Nazira. Interesting man. He later wrote a successful novel called *Never So Few*. I also met a fellow in charge of what we called the "Dirty Tricks Establishment." His group was responsible for making all sorts of things like lumps of coal and cabbages that blew up. They also printed up false messages. The tricksters used paper that was actually made in Japan, and they had Nisei Japanese there who wrote the messages. If we got a hold of a courier, we'd give them a bunch of money or opium to make sure the Japanese got the fake message.

Another fellow at Nazira was Dean Brelis, Constantinos Brelis was his real name. He ended up working for *Time* magazine and writing novels, too. All those folks had been connected with 101 but had been on more or less separate endeavors. Weld and Chamales had both been with Merrill's Marauders, and when the Marauders dissolved, they volunteered to go into OSS 101 in the fall of '44. Phil, was the main one I kept in touch with after the war. I spent some time with him in Boston while I was going to school. Late in his life, he wrote a book called *Moxie* about his sailing adventures. All of our group—Weld, Chamales, Brelis, me, and several more—were sent down to Calcutta.

Calcutta

Our motley crew arrived in Calcutta without incident and stayed for a while. We got to see all the sites, colossal monuments, the biggest banyan tree in the world which covered something like thirty-five acres, one tree, growing like columns. Calcutta was a colorful place, lots of temples, packed streetcars with people hanging all over them. There were rickshaws with huge wheels about five feet high. The fellows that pulled them were barefooted. It was amazing to watch them. They'd run, and when they'd get going, they'd just pick their feet off the ground and ride, balancing up in the air.

We were there in late June, and it was hot. We stayed in an old brick jute mill and slept on rope beds with no mattresses. I still used my same old mattress cover for a sleeping bag. The temperature in the daytime would get well over a hundred degrees, and at night it didn't seem to cool off at all. We'd move those rope cots outdoors to try to get a little air, but it didn't much matter; there was no wind, it was just still and hot. We'd lie there sweltering all night long, and mosquitoes ate us alive. By that time, they had given us bug repellant. I used to pour it into my hair and rub it all over my head and neck, and it helped some. Our living conditions were pretty tough, but downtown, the garrison that had been stationed there all during the war, those folks were practically living in hotels, very fancy ones.

There was an officers' club, mostly local staff, the armchair soldiers who spent the war eating in a dining hall with bearers right behind them, waiting on them. The bearers would have their clothes laid out in the morning. Those folks had it so good, we couldn't believe it. One night a bunch of us went to the club. We were hanging around, trying to guess when the troopship was going to come take us back to the States, and we organized a pool to see who could guess closest to the date of the ship's arrival. We noticed an army type sitting across from us who had on bedroom slippers. Apparently, he lived in the building, one of the lucky ones. He just sat there watching us.

The next day I got, hand-delivered, a message from the provost marshal commanding me to appear in his office at such-and-such a time for violation of security. We were still at war, you understand. VE day, they'd had that, but the whole thing was now centered on Japan. Well, I was stunned to get this letter from Colonel So-and-so, provost marshal for Calcutta for the American contingent. So I put on my Class A uniform, which means I put on a tie, and I went to his office. And there with him sat that same man with the bedroom slippers who had been watching us. I found out right quick, I had been accused of violating security in the guessing game. Apparently, I had guessed the actual date, and I was threatened with a court martial. I tried to explain, "Look, it was just a game. We were just trying to guess when the boat might arrive." "You don't understand, Major. You're endangering the lives of thousands of American soldiers," the slipper man lectured me. Here I was just out of the jungle, wounded once, in battle dozens of times, and the man who accused me had been sitting behind a desk in Calcutta, waited on hand and foot, for the whole war! I was so damned mad. I managed to control myself, however, and continued to explain. Finally, the provost excused my accuser, and we were able to talk. He still gave me a lecture. I suppose he felt like he had to, but he said, "I am not going to do anything with this charge." I'm glad he had some sense. Otherwise, I would have been in trouble, maybe spent a month or two waiting for another boat.

Night on the Town

After that, Tom, Phil, and I went out to Firpo's restaurant to get what they called a steak. The Hindus don't eat beef, so there wasn't any good beef around there, but we wanted to go to Firpo's and have steak, so we did. Then we went to some joint for a few drinks. In the nightclub, they had a rinky-dink band that played "champagne" music, like Lawrence Welk, "rumpty, dumpty, dumpty, dump" which seemed way out of place. We had a few drinks and teamed up with three British officers. They had been at Imphal and Meiktila, so we compared stories.

When we left, we hailed one of those big Packard taxies with a Sikh driving it. Many parts of Calcutta were out of bounds, forbidden to American soldiers. No traveling in the "native quarter," they called it, for fear of trouble. Somehow or another, in our effort to distribute everybody back to where they belonged, we got over the border into the forbidden zone and were stopped by Indian policemen. The taxi driver was forced to follow them, and we were deposited at the police station. There was still a blackout in Calcutta. The war was not over with Japan, so it was dark as pitch everywhere, no streetlights at all. We were put in the lineup outside the station. It was a long line of mostly Indians, but a few other Brits and Americans. Here we were, almost ready to go home, and lo and behold, we were in the hands of the feared police. I seemed to have a knack for ending up in jail whenever I made it to civilization.

The police went down the line one by one, talking to each person, getting his name, serial number, outfit, and so forth. Tom and Phil and I were standing way down at the end of the line, and we got to muttering to each other. On the spur of the moment we decided, by God, let's run for it. I was the ranking man, so I said, "Wait until they're looking the other way. When I give the go ahead, run like hell." So, at my signal, the three of us took off and left our British buddies standing there. I've never run so fast in my whole life. It was completely dark everywhere. We didn't know where we were going; we just ran. It was terrifying. But we got away and managed to find Chowringhee Street, the biggest street in the whole town. Then we knew where we were, so we got another cab and made our way back to our old jute mill home. I felt bad we left those Brits, but it was a spur of the moment decision.

Transport Ship

Finally, the day came. We got on the transport ship, the *William F. Hase*, and sailed out of Calcutta. There were sixteen of us in one compartment, all officers, including Weld, Chamales, me, a Baptist chaplain, a Mormon who was married to a Christian Scientist, some other fellow who was a Roman Catholic. Phil was from Boston, and Tom was from Illinois. There was some crooked politics going on in both places, not to mention Mississippi. We had a lot of interesting religious and political conversations over the month or so it took us to get back home. On our journey, we stopped in Trincomalee, Ceylon. Trincomalee had been bombed during the war. Although things were getting close to the end, Okinawa was still under way, so we had blackouts until we got to the Suez Canal. From that point on, it was lights on.

Naturally, there were some memorable events. I remember someone dared a fellow to drink a whole fifth of whiskey in one big chug. He did it amongst a crowd egging him on, and he collapsed and ended up in bad shape. Also, there was a nurse on the ship who had mental problems. Two medics were assigned to be with her at all times. While walking on a narrow deck below the lifeboats, she took a hold of the rail and vaulted over into the sea. They tried to grab her, but she fell all the way into the ocean. They sounded the alarm, the crew threw the ship in reverse and circled the spot for several hours trying to find her, but there was no trace. It spread around the ship like wildfire that she'd gone overboard, so we all looked, but the only thing we saw were sharks' fins sticking out of the water. She might have hit the screws or something on the way down. It was tragic.

Most days, it was hot as blazes and everybody was up on deck. I went up there once and fell sleep. When I woke up, somebody had picked my pocket and left my wallet there beside me. I had no money in it except the twenty-dollar gold piece that I had carried ever since I was in high school. Some SOB had probably seen my wallet sticking out of my pocket, pulled it out, and took that gold piece, and that was the end of that. Otherwise, we had a good time on the ship, swapping stories and debating. I wish I'd had a tape recorder. It was quite a contrast from the first time I had crossed the Atlantic. We were on a real naval vessel this time, and surprisingly, the food was good. When we stopped in Trincomalee, they picked up lettuce and other fresh stuff. We ate like kings on that ship. If the navy ate that way all the way through the war, they had a good deal.

I remember so well the day we were in that mess hall, when somebody turned on a radio and the first transmission from mainland America came through, at least the first I heard. The radio blared out the old Pepsi Cola jingle. A howl went up from the crowd. I mean, it was kind of a mixed howl. Some thought, "Hooray!" others "Oh, my God, is everything still like that?"

Not too long after that, we put in at Hampton Roads where I had been early on, and we unloaded there. As the ranking officer, I was in charge of the OSS 101 people all the way back. I've still got the list somewhere of the men on the ship with me. I counted them when we got off and made sure that they all got onto the train to Washington, DC. We spent a few days in Washington, during which time they gave me the first psychological test I ever had. I guess they wanted to find out if we'd all gone crazy over there in the jungle. I also got another medal, the Legion of Merit. They pinned it on me at a brief ceremony on the steps of the OSS office at Navy Hill. Then they gave us orders to travel, which we used to get our tickets home. We didn't have to pay; we just showed them our orders, and they gave us tickets. I didn't call anybody. After those couple of days in Washington, I just got on the Southern Railroad and headed home.

Coming Home

The train left early one morning and arrived in Jackson early the next morning. I caught a cab to Whitworth Street. I'd never been to that house before; my folks had moved there while I was gone. I paid the cabby and walked up the front steps. It was about 6:00 a.m. when I rang the doorbell. They were there, my mother and father, and my brother Wes. My brother Donald was on duty in the navy. Wes was also in the navy, but he was on leave. Anyhow, there was great excitement and hugging and whooping and hollering.

It was on a Saturday morning when I arrived, right before they dropped the first atom bomb. As I remember, my father took me to the Rotary Club meeting that Monday. We went to his office first, then we walked down the street to the Heidelberg Hotel. A court reporter by the name of Ralph Godwin was a member, and he would usually walk by the *Jackson Daily News* office on the way and get the latest news since big news was coming through often in those days. This time, he tore off an announcement straight from the machine at the press, and as soon as they rang the bell to start the meeting, he got up and read it to the group. The announcement stated that they had dropped a bomb on Hiroshima, the equivalent of twenty thousand tons of TNT. It had destroyed the whole city; the death toll was estimated at near one hundred thousand. The news caused an uproar in the room.

When things settled down, since I was the only fellow in uniform, they asked me what I thought. That was the first I'd ever heard about a bomb like that. I was on the spot, so I finally said something like, "I was up against the Japanese for most of the war, and from what I have seen, they are brave and tenacious but can be beaten. I can't say that it's a good thing to drop such a bomb. Maybe it will end the war sooner, but so many civilians must have died." I guess I still feel that way. Yamashita was hanged because his men killed civilians, and with this bomb, we killed maybe a hundred thousand civilians, men, women, children, all at once. Of course, I don't know how much of this is hindsight, but I still wonder about the long-term consequences of dropping the atom bomb. On the other hand, many thousands of men were killed late in the war in the Pacific. A friend who was on a destroyer told me, "Man, those planes were boring in at us. If just one of them got through, we were done." There are certainly many strong opinions, and lots of books written about this, so I won't delve into it further. But that Rotary Club experience always sticks in my mind when I think of the end of the war.

The tapes end here February 10, 2007.

> *But now, discharged, I fall away*
> *To do with little things again. . . .*
> *Gawd, 'oo knows all I cannot say . . .*

—from the poem "The Return" by Rudyard Kipling

EPILOGUE

Ka'ang Zhao Lai

The narrative ends somewhat abruptly, but perhaps fittingly, with Pete's thoughts about Hiroshima. His opinions were obviously molded by his personal experience. Unlike many in the military, he was not a member of a crew on a battleship attacked by Kamikazes, didn't charge the beaches of Normandy or participate in airplane dogfights with an enemy whose face he could not see. His war was a saga of characters: Kachin soldiers, Palaung princes, Russian adventurers, British tea planters, Chinese caravaners, Burmese nurses, Indian boat captains, Naga hunters, most of whom he came to know and respect, including the Japanese. He often said that if we had a war in the future, he hoped the Japanese would be on our side. Once, while listening to a story of his, one of his grandchildren became confused and asked, "Grandfather, who were the bad guys?" Without hesitation, he replied, "I guess we were all the bad guys." On the other hand, he once wrote of his band of Kachin comrades that "no greater bunch ever walked on this earth."

For many years after the war, Pete had difficulty communicating with his friends in Burma. Letters were unreliable even before the coup in the 1960s. After that, communication became much more difficult. He was occasionally able to get messages and financial support to folks through missionaries, and once helped Ying Siang get a job in Hong Kong through some connections with a friend who had a business there. But for the most part, his life became centered in the United States. He went to business school on the GI bill, married, and had a family. He did write many letters to the government, even took a trip to Washington to try to help the Kachins, whose contribution during the war was essentially ignored by the US, but he was not able to make any progress. By the time a crack opened in Myanmar's shell in the late eighties, most of his good friends, like Ting Bawm and Mahka La, had died.

At the 1989 reunion of Detachment 101, several folks remarked that Americans owed the Kachins a debt of honor. Since then, the 101 veterans stepped up to the plate. First, with the help of the Institute for the Study of Earth and Man at SMU, they sponsored the translation of the book *Where There Is No Doctor* by David Werner into Jinghpaw and distributed hundreds of copies amongst the Kachins. One group of veterans helped establish and provide funds for schools, and another group, of which Pete was a member, started a crop exchange program. In the mid-1990s twelve former members of OSS Detachment 101, including Pete, returned to Myanmar. Around 3,000 Kachins came down from the mountains to Myitkyina to see them, among them some 250 former Jinghpaw Rangers. There were festivities, speeches, and conferences of Kachin and American veterans. The meetings resulted in a consensus to establish the program they called "Project Old Soldier."

In addition to the veterans' own contributions, they were able to obtain funding from the US government, which was interested in encouraging crops other than opium. With the help of Dr. Ed Runge, an agricultural specialist from Texas A&M, the program supplied seeds, some basic equipment, expertise, and training for Kachin farmers to plant crops. A Kachin woman with a degree in agriculture became the manager and supervised a large group of farm agents. The project eventually came to include around five thousand farms. Corn, vegetable crops, even fish farms were introduced. In spite of the great success of Project Old Soldier, our government's financial support was withdrawn in 2007 in the press for cutbacks, so for the next ten years, the veterans maintained funding on their own. The project continued, even in the face of the changing political situation in Myanmar, only ending when the last few involved veterans died. All of their efforts constituted the old 101 soldiers' modest but heartfelt attempt to acknowledge the sacrifices of the people who had helped them during the war.

Pete himself went back to Myanmar several times, from 1990 until 2006, first helping with the book and later working on Project Old Soldier. He still spoke the language well and knew the countryside. On those journeys, Pete visited many of the farms and met a few of the soldiers who had fought alongside him, but most had passed away. He did see some of his old haunts, met soldiers' relatives, and made new friends among the Kachin people. He gave speeches and participated in ceremonies honoring veterans.

Even though it had been difficult for him to keep in touch with his Kachin comrades throughout the years after the war, they always remained with him in spirit. Photographs of the 7th Battalion, Mahka La, and Ting Bawm held prominent places in his office and at home. A Kachin sword hung over the mantle, and the old tiger skin on the wall in a back room. In his library were many books about Burma, Kachin dictionaries, a Kachin Bible, and his scrap-book of photos. The Jinghpaw ideals, skills and customs were a part of him. He spent a great deal of time out-of-doors with the Boy Scouts, and every time his troop took a hike, he would bend down, take a leaf off a tree, and make a small sacrifice to the spirits of the countryside. His scouts built Kachin shelters on their forays into the wilderness, ate Kachin stew by the campfire, learned Kachin proverbs.

Pete believed it was important to pass down the lessons of the war, even the painful ones, the march of the refugees out of Burma, the villages destroyed, soldiers and civilians who lost their lives. By the same token, he wanted us to know of the kindness that shone in the face of such chaos, the bravery of countless people that helped him, welcomed him into their houses, fed him, fought alongside him, took care of him when sick or wounded. He kept up with the traditions and spirit of the Kachins and told his stories until the end.

—ERL April 2022

GLOSSARY

Abbreviations and English terms and names used at the time

AVG—the First American Volunteer Group of the Republic of China
  Air Force started in 1941 Nicknamed the Flying Tigers

BAR—Browning automatic rifle

Burma—Myanmar

Ceylon—Sri Lanka

Garo—Tibeto-Burman ethnic group in the Khasi Hills, Assam and
  Nagaland, India

Kachins—ethnic group of northern Myanmar, who call themselves the
  Jinghpaw people

Karens—ethnolinguistic group of people living chiefly in Myanmar and
  Thailand

Lisu—Tibeto-Burman ethnic group in the mountains of Myanmar,
  southwest China, and Thailand

Nagas—ethnic people of mountainous northeast India and northwest
  Myanmar

NCAC—Northern Combat Area Command, subcommand of the Allied
  South East Asia Command controlling operations in northern Burma
  under General Stillwell

OSS—Office of Strategic Services, intelligence service of the military in
  World War II

Palaungs—Buddhist ethnic minority in Shan State of Myanmar and nearby
  China

RAF—Royal Air Force, the British air force

ROTC—Reserve Officers Training Corps, a college/university program to
  train officers in the United States

Shans—largest ethnic minority in Myanmar, mostly in Shan State, but also
  in other states, as well as China, Thailand, and other areas

Territorials—volunteer group in the British Army. In Burma, chiefly made
    up of people already in the area such as tea planters
V Force—British intelligence and guerrilla outfit of the Burma Campaign
    in WWII

Kachin and other non-English words
(using Pete's own spelling, pronunciations, and definitions)

basha—a hut usually made of bamboo and grass
bum—(pronounced "boom")—mountain, as in Pangnang *Bum*, meaning
    Pangnang Mountain
duwa—(pronounced "doowah")—Kachin term for a chief or leader
ga—in combination with a name, meaning a village such as Tagap *ga*
    (the village of Tagap)
gampura—Naga headman
hka—water or river, as the Tarung *hka*- Tarung River
hku—headwaters, Tarung *hku*
jaiwa—chanter, shaman
Jinghpaw—Kachin people in northern Myanmar's Kachin Hills, used by
    the people themselves, and a term for their language
Ka'ang Zhao Lai—name given to Pete at the *manao* on Pangnang bum
    meaning "He who has been through it all from beginning to end"
kunkuman—naked or carrying nothing extra
laoban—term used by the Chinese in the area to mean headman of a village
lao hku—a fermented beverage made from rice
manao—a special celebration with feasting and dancing
myrhtoi—a Kachin who serves as shaman, priest, prophet, or magician
nats—animist deities; there are thirty-seven principle *nats* and many others,
    spirits of locations or objects
salang ni—group of elders, counselors
sawbwa—a ruler in the Shan states
tung—customs, laws, or code of conduct of the Kachin people

ACKNOWLEDGMENTS

Our family hopes that the book itself stands as a tribute to those who helped Pete during the war —the Kachins, Nagas and other people of northern Burma to whom he owed so much, his comrades in the Jinghpaw Rangers, the Coast Artillery, V Force, and OSS Detachment 101, the pilots who brought supplies, the nurses of Seagrave's hospital, and the list goes on.

Pete also had many to thank for their efforts long after the war, in repaying the "debt of honor" he and the other veterans of OSS 101 owed to the Kachins. We have done our best to include those who were key contributors. Lahpai Nem Ra with much support from Hkawn Ra translated the book *Where There Is No Doctor*, by David Werner into the Kachin language. Dr. Fred Wendorf and Dr. Ben Wallace were instrumental in facilitating the book's publication through SMU's Institute for the Study of Earth and Man. Robert Saltzstein, an OSS veteran traveled with Pete early on to solidify plans for the veterans to start programs based in Myanmar. Mendel Kaliff, Oliver Trechter, and Stuart Power, all OSS veterans and great friends to Pete over many years, worked tirelessly in support of Project Old Soldier, the crop exchange program whose chief consultant, Dr. Ed Runge from Texas A&M devoted much of his time and expertise to the project including visiting the operations in Myanmar with Pete. The program was run in Myanmar by the extremely talented, efficient, hardworking Nangja Lahpai with help from many enthusiastic Kachin staff members. Others that gave of their time and energy stateside included John Lyle and Blake Tate.

As to the book, over the years, a great number of people helped in making it a reality, too many to name, but here are some we recall. Dr. Abdul Halim Banday, Pete's longtime friend, encouraged him and shared stories of his own wartime experiences with the V Force. Ray Chesley, Martin "Killer" Thrailkill, and Bill Cummings helped fill out details of adventures in which they were involved. Troy Sacquety, the official OSS 101 historian, gave much helpful encouragement and advice, as did David Hale Smith, and Rena Pederson always had time for Pete's stories. Thanks to Brenda Keyes, who spent many hours with Pete typing his text revisions and helping with the chronology of the narrative, and to Paula Burns who typed the original, daunting transcripts of the tapes. The editor Lisa McMurtray and all of the University Press of Mississippi staff were extremely helpful, also the copyeditor Camille Hale. Within the family, special thanks to David who had the inspiration to make the recordings and spent many hours with Pete and the tape machine, to Tom who worked with the cartographers to produce the maps, and to Peter who selected photos from the hundreds in the scrapbook and wrote captions. We also owe a great deal to Louis J. Lyell, the man who, in the end, pushed us to make it happen.

Finally, to Ruth Lutken, the unshakable support behind Pete and all of our family, there aren't enough words to express our gratitude.

—E.R. Lutken August 2022

ABOUT THE AUTHOR

Peter K. Lutken, Jr. (1920–2014) was born and raised in Mississippi. He graduated from Mississippi State College (now Mississippi State University) and then
went into the army and served in World War II in Burma, where he attained
the rank of major. After the war, he attended Harvard Business School and
received his MBA and then worked as a businessman in Mississippi and later
in Texas. He spent much of his life in the outdoors, with his family, as a scout
leader, hunter, fisherman, and master campfire storyteller.

ABOUT THE EDITOR

E. R. Lutken, a family physician, worked on the Navajo Nation for many
years. After early retirement, she taught middle and high school science and
math in rural Colorado for a few more years. Now she spends much of her
time writing poetry and sometimes fishing in the swamps of Louisiana and
mountain streams of New Mexico. Her poems have appeared in journals and
anthologies, and she has a poetry collection, *Manifold: poetry of mathematics*
(3: A Taos Press, 2021).